Created Freedom under the Sign of the Cross

Created Freedom under the Sign of the Cross

A Catholic Public Theology for the United States

DAVID E. DeCOSSE

☙PICKWICK *Publications* · Eugene, Oregon

CREATED FREEDOM UNDER THE SIGN OF THE CROSS
A Catholic Public Theology for the United States

Copyright © 2022 David E. DeCosse. All rights reserved. Except for brief quotations in critical publications or reviews, no part of this book may be reproduced in any manner without prior written permission from the publisher. Write: Permissions, Wipf and Stock Publishers, 199 W. 8th Ave., Suite 3, Eugene, OR 97401.

Pickwick Publications
An Imprint of Wipf and Stock Publishers
199 W. 8th Ave., Suite 3
Eugene, OR 97401

www.wipfandstock.com

PAPERBACK ISBN: 978-1-6667-1110-3
HARDCOVER ISBN: 978-1-6667-1111-0
EBOOK ISBN: 978-1-6667-1112-7

Cataloguing-in-Publication data:

Names: DeCosse, David E.

Title: Created freedom under the sign of the cross : a Catholic public theology for the United States / David E. DeCosse.

Description: Eugene, OR: Pickwick Publications, 2022 | Series: if applicable | Includes bibliographical references and index.

Identifiers: ISBN 978-1-6667-1110-3 (paperback) | ISBN 978-1-6667-1111-0 (hardcover) | ISBN 978-1-6667-1112-7 (ebook)

Subjects: LCSH: Liberty—Religious aspects—Catholic Church | Public theology—United States.

Classification: BT83.63 D436 2022 (paperback) | BT83.63 (ebook)

06/06/22

I would like to dedicate this book to my mother,
Sheila Flynn DeCosse, whose faith has been our anchor.

It is not just a question of fighting wretched conditions, though this is an urgent and necessary task. It involves building a human community where [persons] can live truly human lives, free from discrimination on account of race, religion or nationality, free from servitude to other [persons] or to natural forces which they cannot yet control satisfactorily. It involves building a human community where freedom is not an idle word, where the needy Lazarus can sit down with the rich man at the same banquet table.

—Pope Paul VI

The bonded laborer born into semislavery, the subjugated girl child stifled by a repressive society, the helpless landless laborer without substantial means of earning an income are all deprived not only in terms of well-being, but also in terms of ability to lead responsible lives, which are contingent on having certain basic freedoms. Responsibility *requires* freedom.

—Amartya Sen

Contents

Acknowledgments | ix

Introduction | 1

Chapter One: Catholic Public Theology and the Contemporary American Problematic of Freedom | 16

Chapter Two: Public Theology, Sociology, and the Problem of "Monticello without the Slavery" | 47

Chapter Three: Amartya Sen and Philosophical Complements to Created Freedom | 73

Chapter Four: Karl Rahner and Created Freedom as the Basis for a Catholic Public Theology of Freedom | 104

Chapter Five: A Catholic Public Theology of Freedom for the United States | 129

Conclusion | 158

Bibliography | 161

Author Index | 169

Subject Index | 173

Acknowledgments

I WOULD LIKE TO thank those friends and colleagues who especially conveyed, in large and small ways, their belief in my work as a theologian: Michael Castori, SJ; Gaetano Marangelli; Curt Paulsen; Manuel Prado; Kristin Heyer; the late Paul Crowley, SJ; David Hollenbach, SJ; Lisa Cahill; Stephen Pope; James Keenan, SJ; Andrea Vicini, SJ; Tom Massaro, SJ; Roger Haight, SJ; Bill O'Neill, SJ; Lisa Fullam; Kirk Hanson; Judy Nadler; Miriam Schulman; Karen Peterson-Iyer; Don Heider; Denise Carmody; Tim Myers; Don Dodson; Jack Treacy, SJ; Mark Ravizza, SJ; Victoria Burke; Meg; Marion; Paul Lakeland; David Schultenover, SJ; Tom Roberts; Heidi Schlumpf; Sigrid Muller; and Gunter Prüller-Jagenteufel. I would like to thank so many students with whom I have worked in classes or on myriad projects over the years. I would like to thank the members of the Los Angeles Catholic Worker community; all with whom I have had the honor of accompanying at the Hippie Kitchen; and all of whom I have had the privilege of accompanying in their vulnerability and strength and faith in the United States and around the world. And I would like to thank my family near and far who have been a bedrock more than they may even know: my dear Mom and my late father, Jerome DeCosse; Steve, Satomi, Eugene, Carole, Phil, Quinn, Maggie, Jula, Marie, Sarah, Adelaide, and Mathilda; Uncle Cy, Paula, and Aunt Barbara; and the whole extended DeCosse and Flynn clans.

Introduction

THIS BOOK IS A work of Roman Catholic theological ethics that examines freedom in the contemporary American social and political context. On the one hand, I argue against an overly individualistic notion of freedom associated with the triumph of neo-liberal ideas in American life, especially since the 1970s. On the other hand, I argue in favor of an understanding of freedom that is liberal; oriented to the good and to God; embodied and relational; sensitive to culture and history; and contextual but universal in its reach. As a matter of fundamental theology, Karl Rahner's idea of "created freedom" provides the key term that carries the argument.

The theoretical problem that prompted this book—what in general terms I would call the abstraction of freedom from context and conditions—first presented itself to me in an immediate and concrete way. In particular, I have written this book for the men and women I met working in poor neighborhoods of West Baltimore; accompanying Santa Clara University students on alternative spring break trips to places ranging from the Lower Ninth Ward in New Orleans to the Navajo Nation; serving at the Catholic Worker Soup Kitchen on Skid Row in Los Angeles; and more. I do not assume that I know these men and women well—though I have conversed with many of them and listened carefully to their stories. In any case, at every turn my experience with them confirmed something hiding in plain sight in the increasingly libertarian culture of American society: their exercise of freedom for the sake of important goods was almost always far more difficult than the broader culture acknowledged. It was as if there was not only rich and poor, but there were also competing ideas of freedom—one abstract, belonging to the better off and presuming an effortless self-assertion (short only of government interference), and the other concrete, the purview of the poor, and prizing freedom no less while presuming many more obstacles to its exercise. These observations raised questions.

Is it possible for Catholic theological ethics to have a more adequate concept of freedom—or related concepts like opportunity—that can be applied across such social divides? Or, similarly, is it possible to have a notion of freedom that can be said to be equal, not in the sense of assuring equal outcomes but in the sense of a common theoretical starting place shared by rich and poor alike? What might the theological anthropology of such a starting place be? And what difference might such a starting place make for how Catholic public theology speaks about ethical concerns related to social and political equality?

I found confirmation for such concerns in thinkers across the American spectrum. Political scientist Robert Putnam writes of the loss of a common fate in which one is even aware of the way children on the other side of the tracks are part of one's moral universe—are "our kids," to use Putnam's phrasing that serves as the title of his powerful book.[1] He says: "We are today so far from equality of opportunity, even for talented and energetic kids . . . that there is little danger that we might apply the principle too stringently."[2] From a more conservative perspective, American Enterprise Institute President Arthur C. Brooks argues that "opportunity inequality"—not income inequality—"is the crisis we face today."[3] Furthermore, moral philosopher Elizabeth Anderson has said that in the American context it is not as important to focus on whether freedom results in various unequal distributions of goods as it is to consider how the oppressive nature of unequal relationships results in the distribution of deeply unequal freedoms.[4]

THE SECOND CONCRETE MATTER that gave rise to the focus of this book on the abstraction of freedom was less personal and more encompassing: the stark and increasing inequality throughout American society. Matthew Stewart has argued that we are in the "third wave of American inequality."[5] (The first two were the time of slavery followed by the Civil War, and the Gilded Age of the 1920s followed by the Great Depression.) This inequality now encompasses economic, political, and cultural fault lines. Thomas Piketty has argued that income inequality in the United States today is "probably higher than in any other society at any time in the past, anywhere in the world, including societies in which skill disparities were extremely large."[6]

1. Putnam, *Our Kids*, 260–61.
2. Putnam, *Our Kids*, 242.
3. Brooks, "Confessions of a Catholic Convert."
4. Anderson, "What Is the Point of Equality?," 312.
5. Stewart, "9.9 Percent."
6. Piketty, *Capital in the Twenty-First Century*, 265.

If facile meritocratic assumptions justify excessive pay at the top (i.e., I was paid the huge salary and therefore deserved it),[7] the failure of social mobility locks in falling pay at the bottom.[8] To be sure, the excessive income and wealth at the top of the scale has sought to entrench itself by converting such resources into plutocratic political power.[9] But the challenge of political inequality has also been intensified by demographic changes. Political theorist Danielle Allen has argued that the increasing strains on American democracy are not so much evidence of old problems too long unaddressed. Instead, the strains point to a new challenge staring Americans in the faces of their many multicultural identities: How, for the first time in history, to form a democracy in which no one ethnicity or gender constitutes a majority.[10] Moreover, the pandemic that has ravaged the United States since March 2020 has laid bare devastating inequalities that were always hiding in plain sight for anyone who wished to see.[11]

Such inequalities of material resources and power obviously raise many significant issues of social ethics. But I am especially interested in the way that an abstract, neoliberal notion of an equality of freedom has served often as a primary justification for such unequal distributions. George Monbiot aptly summarized the mindset that allows such an understanding of freedom to sanction inequalities and stifle efforts toward equality: "Inequality is recast as virtuous: a reward for utility and a generator of wealth, which trickles down to enrich everyone. Efforts to create a more equal society are both counterproductive and morally corrosive. The market ensures that everyone gets what they deserve."[12] This book is dedicated to identifying deficiencies in this understanding of freedom and to making a case for a better, more contextual understanding. But for now it is helpful to note how the abstraction of freedom is correlated with hardened inequalities. The sociologist Charles Tilly has identified different modes of the analysis of inequality—some favoring a focus on personal attributes and some favoring a focus on structural and cultural forces. As he puts it, analyses of inequalities too often assume that individuals should be understood as units of clear, purposive thinking detached from internal, confounding complications like powerful passions. Likewise, such analyses also often assume that these abstracted individuals are immune to the power of external forces imposed by

---

7. Piketty, *Capital in the Twenty-First Century*, 334.
8. Stewart, "9.9 Percent."
9. Stewart, "9.9 Percent."
10. Allen, "Charlottesville."
11. Long et al., "COVID-19 Recession."
12. Monbiot, "Neoliberalism."

living in a social and uncontrollable world of relationships. To the contrary, Tilly argues, persistent unequal distributions are the result of complex interactions between contingent, vulnerable individuals oriented from the start to a web of relations and institutions. Only by seeing persons in such a light, he says, can the hardened shape of inequality come into view.[13]

So how did we arrive at this particular point of abstraction in the history of freedom in the United States? There are competing explanations. Patrick J. Deneen's *Why Liberalism Failed* offers one that is insightful but finally insufficient. Deneen argues that modern liberalism, driven by its subjectivist notion of freedom, engendered a vicious, self-defeating cycle. Individuals turned to state and market to liberate themselves from given conditions of constraint. Some such constraints were, in fact, oppressive. But other conditions—for instance, the connection between freedom and moral duties or freedom and community—were often perceived as oppressive when seen through the lens of a subjectivist freedom. In any case, neither state nor market was concerned with such distinctions between reality and perception; the imperative was to remove the conditions, whatever they were. In the course of this process, Deneen argues, power accumulated in state and markets. Correspondingly, the power of individuals declined as the process stripped away the moral and communal conditions that in fact oriented or enabled the exercise of freedom. The individual alone—free but bereft of the purpose or possibility of actually acting freely—was left to face the tutelary power of state and the pervasiveness of the market.[14] Deneen is a harsh critic of what he considers the inherent flaws in the liberal notion of freedom: chiefly, its celebration of subjectivism, self-making, and unfettered choice.[15] He laments the sharp break between this fatally flawed modern notion of freedom and its medieval predecessor, in which a world of obligation, virtue, and self-discipline enframed freedom. In that era, Deneen notes approvingly, freedom was understood to require moral self-rule on the part of individuals and the political community.[16]

But there are problems with this account, beginning with the way that Deneen deploys the word "liberalism" both as a highly unified philosophical perspective on the world and as an almost personified agent of historical change. There's little acknowledgment of different traditions within liberalism indicated, for instance, by the nineteenth-century struggle between the

13. Tilly, *Durable Inequality*, 17–25.
14. Deneen, *Why Liberalism Failed*, 11.
15. Deneen, *Why Liberalism Failed*, 9, 31, 154–56.
16. Deneen, *Why Liberalism Failed*, 23–27.

classic liberal commitment to free labor and the rise of an industrial owner class who re-invented liberalism to favor the interests of capital.[17] Moreover, throughout the book, the disembodied abstraction of liberalism is frequently doing this or that—for example, Deneen says that liberalism seeks to transform all of human life and the world[18] and he also says that liberalism undermines education by replacing the definition of liberty as self-restraint with the definition of liberty as autonomy.[19] But this imputation of agency to an abstraction in fact undermines the significance of freedom understood on its own terms. "Liberalism" seems to bring about changes, not real human beings making concrete choices in specific circumstances. Moreover, freedom in the book is either oriented to self-restraint or subjectivism. But there is little sense for why modern freedom has had such a powerful and emancipatory appeal in the face of constraints of structure and culture. And there is little sense in turn of the modern, liberal appeal of freedom for its own sake, neither understood primarily in terms of self-rule or subjectivism but in terms of what Jesuit theologian John Courtney Murray described as "the primordial demand of . . . dignity . . . that [a person] acts by his own counsel and purpose, using and enjoying his freedom, moved, not by external coercion, but internally by the risk of his whole existence."[20]

Daniel Rodgers in *Age of Fracture* offers a more compelling account of the current American predicament around freedom. Rodgers eschews a grand centuries-long narrative and focuses instead on the dramatic change in the construal of freedom over the last fifty years in the United States. By doing so, he specifies more clearly the causes and changes that characterize the current situation. He also more deftly evokes the interplay between ideas and convictions and structure and culture. A personified force called liberalism doesn't affect all this change. But liberal ideas in a wide variety of hues clash with practices, institutions, and events and out of this churn emerges Rodgers's fractured, American world. One key mark of this world—our world—is that freedom has become "individualized and privatized, released of its larger burdens . . . cut loose from the burdens and responsibilities that had once so closely accompanied it."[21] Another key mark is how much

---

17. See Anderson, "Great Reversal," 206–9. In the essay, Anderson argues that since the 1970s a neoliberal ideology that favors capital over labor has sought to claim the mantle of classical liberalism which, Anderson argues, in fact far more strongly favored the claims of labor than neoliberal thought allows.

18. Deneen, *Why Liberalism Failed*, 37.

19. Deneen, *Why Liberalism Failed*, 111.

20. Murray, "Arguments," 8.

21. Rodgers, *Age of Fracture*, 40.

this stripped-down understanding of freedom represents a change from the recent past. Rodgers notes:

> Conceptions of human nature that in the post-World War II era had been thick with context, social circumstance, institutions, and history gave way to conceptions of human nature that stressed choice, agency, performance, and desire. Strong metaphors of society were supplanted by weaker ones. Imagined collectivities shrank; notions of structure and power thinned out. Viewed by its acts of mind, the last quarter of the [twentieth] century was an era of disaggregation, a great age of fracture.[22]

Rodgers traces this fracturing in economic, political, and cultural spheres. But his analysis puts special weight on economics: the real-world and theoretical developments in the last fifty years that have had a preeminent causal power on the rest of society. It is important to note that for Rodgers it is not simply economics per se that has played this causal role. Instead, it is a highly abstract view of microeconomics and markets that has cast a powerful spell. This way of thinking draws heavily on finance capitalism and downplays market imperfections. And these abstractions have been applied both to markets in themselves and to society more generally. Rodgers says of this strain of economic thought: "It stood for a way of thinking about society with a myriad of self-generated actions for its engine and optimization as its natural and spontaneous outcome. It was . . . a disaggregation of society and its troubling collective presence and demands into an array of consenting, voluntarily acting individual pieces."[23] The effects of such individualized and ideal market theory on the meaning of freedom were profound. "To imagine the market now," Rodgers notes, "was to imagine a socially detached array of economic actors, free to choose and optimize, unconstrained by power or inequalities, governed not by their common deliberative action but only by the impersonal laws of the market."[24]

An emphasis on the possibility and normative importance of unconstrained choice—what Rodgers calls "the most contagious of the age's metaphors"—carried with it as well a problematic approach to equality.[25] Indeed, one of the signs of the times was the dismissal of concerns about equality at all—whether equality of result or equality of opportunity. Another was the libertarian conception of an equal liberty in which the liberty in question was detached from community, institutions, and power. And still another

---

22. Rodgers, *Age of Fracture*, 3.
23. Rodgers, *Age of Fracture*, 41.
24. Rodgers, *Age of Fracture*, 76.
25. Rodgers, *Age of Fracture*, 190.

was the detachment of such a sense of liberty from the past. Here, in fact, lies one of the key paradoxes of our time about the meaning of freedom. On the one hand, there exists a widespread commitment to a libertarian sense of freedom that is considered "historical," insofar as any distributions in society that follow from the exercise of such freedom should be considered just primarily because the distributions are the result of such exercises of freedom (and, in that sense, are "historical"). On the other hand, this libertarian conception of liberty is detached from the past and from a full historical accounting of what might shape the exercise of freedom today. Rodgers notes: "Like the models of perfect markets, the libertarian vision of society was radically timeless. . . . In its 'historical' understanding of justice as a transmission chain of free, voluntary transactions, actual history trailed away in footnotes and silences and vanished."[26] In the end, after the last decades of the twentieth century and the first decade of the twenty-first, we are left with an American scene prizing an abstract freedom detached from what Rodgers calls "webs of dependence and connection": history, structures, institutions, society, equality, race, class, and responsibility commensurate with such contexts.[27]

AMERICAN SOCIETY, THEN, IS going through a convulsion, its long-standing assumptions about freedom and equality under pressure from increasingly assertive libertarian philosophies (which have in any case often played a significant role in American culture) and increasingly evident social inequalities. What can Catholic theological ethics offer to clarify and correct the confounding issues at stake in this convulsion? Important recent work has been done in this regard. I think, among other publications, of Meghan J. Clark's *The Vision of Catholic Social Thought: The Virtue of Solidarity and the Praxis of Human Rights*, Christine Firer Hinze's *Glass Ceilings and Dirt Floors: Women, Work, and the Global Economy*, and Matthew T. Eggemeier and Peter Joseph Fritz's *Send Lazarus: Catholicism and the Crises of Neoliberalism*. Much of this work has rightly criticized common views of autonomy and freedom for the way their abstract, individualistic character provides intellectual cover for unjust social inequalities. Correspondingly, this work has sought to correct such views by arguing that freedom must be understood in light of its inherent connection to relationship and its inalienable immersion in context. I agree with the thrust of such arguments—both critical and corrective—but wish to turn the focus even more to the concept of freedom in itself.

26. Rodgers, *Age of Fracture*, 191.
27. Rodgers, *Age of Fracture*, 271.

Catholic social thought has had an ambivalent relation to the concept of freedom, accepting it in principle but either subordinating it to the demands of the hierarchical social order as in the writing of Leo XIII;[28] or, more recently, seeing it as little more than an empty proceduralism ineffectual in the face of vast social inequalities;[29] or fearing freedom as the leading edge of an unwelcome sexual and reproductive revolution set on remaking nature itself; or subordinating freedom to truth in a way that makes the former feckless and empty apart from its controlling direction by the latter.[30] But important recent sociological, philosophical, and theological work has been done to recover a richer sense of freedom by, among others, Orlando Patterson, Amartya Sen, Elizabeth Anderson, Walter Kasper, Shawn Copeland, Peter Joseph Fritz, and David Hollenbach. The work of these scholars recovers a sense of the importance of freedom for its own sake and for the sake of important goods. But their work also embeds freedom in a world of sharp constraint and empowering possibility. In any case, it is imperative that Catholic theological ethics turn specifically to the logic and language of freedom when addressing a liberal society like the United States. At the Second Vatican Council, the Catholic Church committed itself to the free society.[31] Leading Catholic social theorist Cardinal Reinhard Marx of Germany has argued that freedom is the preeminent principle of Catholic social doctrine.[32] For the sake of self-consistency, the Church must speak the language of freedom. For the sake of having the gospel heard in liberal society, it must do so as well. Catholic public theology should not cede the space of freedom to its contemporary libertarian usurpers.

By "freedom," I am referring to an inherent, uncoerced, and spiritual dimension of human beings—a dimension intimately associated with reason and an awareness of personal responsibility. In philosophical terms, I think of freedom as especially reflecting the "feature of . . . being the ultimate source, or originator, of one's choices. . . . For human beings or any created persons who owe their existence to factors outside themselves, the only way their acts of will could find their ultimate origin in themselves is for such acts not to be determined by their character or circumstances."[33] Freedom and responsibility are expressions of an inalienable human dignity and natural,

---

28. Rosen, *Dignity*, 48–54.
29. Christiansen, "On Relative Equality," 653.
30. John Paul II, *Evangelium vitae*, §69.
31. Second Vatican Council, *Dignitatis humanae*, §7.
32. Marx, "Contribution of Christian Values."
33. O'Connor and Franklin, "Free Will."

given properties of persons. Freedom and truth are mutually implicated as a matter of the given sociality of human persons: "To respect one's own and every other person's freedom—to respect the natural law of persons—is, therefore, an implication of every person's rational obligation to respect and recognize the truth."[34] Of course, such given, natural aspects of freedom are the most encompassing philosophical category. And such natural notions of freedom become specified in many different contexts. For instance, the word "liberty" applies especially to the "legal status of a member of an organized group or society."[35] For this work of social ethics, I consider another specification of freedom—the word "autonomy"—to mean "a second-order capacity of persons to reflect critically upon their first-order preferences, desires, wishes, and so forth, and the capacity to accept or attempt to change these in light of higher-order preferences."[36] In this book, I intend to focus on "freedom" precisely because of its encompassing nature. To reflect on freedom allows us to reimagine terms like *liberty* and *autonomy*, and to consider anew the many different dimensions of freedom in the American social and political context. Moreover, freedom has ultimate significance in the Catholic theological understanding of human destiny. As theologian Karl Rahner put it, freedom is the "presupposition, created by God, to make it possible for God to give God's self to human beings in love."[37]

This is a work of public theology, and I am especially interested in the manifestation of elemental notions of freedom in an American social and political context. To that end, several remarks are in order. First, by calling this a work of "public theology" I wish to bring the theological wisdom of the Catholic tradition to bear on the public conversation about American society. By appealing ultimately to theology (though with plenty of sociology and philosophy along the way), I believe a more coherent and communal notion of freedom can and should become part of this public conversation.[38] Also, my argument is oriented to the "post-secular" time in which I think we are living. Thus I do not think that public theology today must primarily combat a relentless secularism. Nor do I accept the "secularization thesis" that holds that religion will inevitably fade away under the force of modernity. Instead, I accept as fact the fragmentation of grand narratives and the awareness of diverse moral traditions. In the post-secular world, the forces of religion and secularism both remain, but in a new tension. In a personal

34. Dun, "Freedom."
35. Dun, "Freedom."
36. Dworkin, "Autonomy," 444.
37. Rahner, "On the Origins of Freedom," 120.
38. Himes and Himes, *Fullness of Faith*, 4–7.

sense, to believe at all is conditioned by the awareness that one may choose not to believe.[39] Moreover, religion has recovered a vital public presence—but this recovery has occurred alongside the declining purchase of religious institutions. "What characterizes post-secularity is," said Elaine Graham, "its very paradoxical and unprecedented nature. The emergence globally and nationally of revitalized religious activism as a decisive force, alongside the continuing trajectory of institutional religious decline accompanied by robust intellectual defence of secularism in Western societies, takes us into new territory, empirically and theoretically."[40] As a theological response to the post-secular, I argue in this book in terms of "fragments" that find a final unity in the Catholic theological tradition.[41] Thus I appeal to sociology and philosophy for analogues to theological claims. And thus I reject an overarching, exclusively theological argument, even if I am ultimately arguing on behalf of an understanding that I call "created freedom under the sign of the cross." Theological reasons undergird my argument throughout. But sociology and philosophy help shed significant light on the meaning of the vulnerable, hopeful idea of freedom that is the focus of the book.

The central theological concept in this book is what Rahner calls "created freedom." In Catholic theology in the last decades, this concept has often been invoked as a restraint on an otherwise outsized Promethean freedom disdainful of moral truth. "Freedom is not determined by its opposite but by the fundamental relationship between freedom and truth, that is, between the gift of created freedom and its divine Giver . . . *genuine freedom denotes the truthful enactment of created existence*," said Reinhard Hutter, commenting on John Paul II's *Veritatis Splendor*.[42] I accept how the created status of freedom signals its orientation toward truth. But the prevailing formulations of created freedom in the last years in Catholic thought are too essentialist and unaffected by the world. In such formulations, "createdness" signals a dependence on truth made especially evident by norms of sexual ethics derived from unchanging biological laws of the human body. But the notion of dependence at work in this essentialist notion of created freedom sidesteps an abiding sense of a vulnerable, embodied person living in history, affected far and wide by relationships, and disposed toward divine love—not at the expense of such vulnerability but through it. Thus I will be turning primarily to Rahner's account of created freedom, which embeds this orientation toward truth in an embodied, relational, and historical

---

39. Taylor, *Secular Age*, 2–14.
40. Graham, *Between a Rock and a Hard Place*, 34.
41. Graham, *Between a Rock and a Hard Place*, 101.
42. Hutter, "(Re-)Forming Freedom," 119.

context.⁴³ Rahner, I believe, vividly evokes the way that freedom is always dependent—on a body, on history, in a world of mediated and conflictual particularity, and oriented toward the good and God. Against the misplaced abstractness of an excessively rational theology, Rahner offers a concrete antidote. And against a misplaced concreteness of an excessively narrative theology, Rahner offers a transcendent ground. His account of freedom provides a coherent and fundamental way by which to critique the individualism and abstractness bedeviling the idea of freedom in American public life. His account also invites a consideration of analogous accounts of freedom in sociology and philosophy. One of the advantages of appealing to "created freedom" is that the concept is fundamental and generative. It signals a fundamental theological stance about freedom that can then be spelled out in a more specific social ethic.⁴⁴ And it also provides a way of thinking about different manifestations of freedom in, for instance, cultural or economic or political spheres. Indeed, I accept the distinction in kinds of freedom in these spheres spelled out by Rahner and by philosophers like Amartya Sen, who speaks of the "inescapably plural idea of freedom."⁴⁵ But in this book I take special aim at what is a deeply mistaken idea associated with economic freedom that has seeped in to and taken over notions of freedom in cultural and political spheres. The idea has its origins in interpretations of libertarian and liberal capitalist thought meshed with reductionist interpretations of American self-reliance. The dependence at the heart of created freedom stands in contrast to the illusory independence of this idea of freedom.

I WILL PROCEED IN the following way. In the first chapter, I will engage four distinct but related contemporary ways of thinking about freedom that stand in the neoliberal tradition or are, in the case of populism, a reaction to it. The four ways of thinking are libertarian, the thought of Ayn Rand, democratic capitalism inspired by Michael Novak, and the populist

---

43. I am aware of the criticism that Rahner's notion of a subject seems to stand outside of history. I will be appealing primarily to Rahner's later work, where he responds constructively to this criticism. In any case, I think the balance in Rahner's thought between the transcendent and the historical makes his account of freedom persuasive in its own right and powerful as an antidote to sectarian and relativist forces today. I will address the criticisms of Rahner later in the book. For now, it is important to note Declan Marmion's observation: "Rather than claiming that Rahner *exclusively* pursues a transcendental method, which then leads to an insensitivity to social problems, it would be more accurate to claim he follows a two-fold theological method, or rather, a method that incorporates both transcendental and historical reflection." Marmion, "Rahner and His Critics," 4.

44. Himes and Himes, *Fullness of Faith*, 22.

45. Sen, *Idea of Justice*, 303.

nationalism associated with Steve Bannon. Here I am especially seeking to identify the Catholic engagement with such ideas—and to critique that engagement. In the first chapter, I also resituate the discussion of freedom in an American social and political context by, among other things, discussing freedom more specifically in terms of race and gender. Finally, I turn to the thought of moral philosopher Charles Taylor to show more specifically the limits of a libertarian freedom. In all, the first chapter sets the empirical and philosophical context of the problem.

In the second chapter, I will begin to turn in a critical and constructive direction. In Rahner's telling, created freedom is embodied, historical, relational, and oriented to the good and to God. Consistent with this, in the second and third chapters I will turn to accounts of freedom in sociology and philosophy that manifest key aspects of Rahner's account. By doing so, I proceed in a spirit of correlation and confirmation. Rahner's notion of a vulnerable freedom finds confirmation to the degree it correlates with work in other disciplines (and vice versa). Moreover, the abstractions of neoliberal freedom are so pervasive in American culture that it is important to show at length accounts of freedom that tell an entirely different story. We are not fated to keep repeating the neoliberal mistake. Thus, in the second chapter, I will consider freedom in light of the structural and cultural categories of sociology. In many neoliberal accounts of freedom, structural issues pertain almost entirely to concerns about government restrictions. Where cultural concerns play a role, they usually have to do with culture understood especially as a bearer of the Judeo-Christian moral values on which the success of capitalism is thought to depend. But a consideration of two sociologies of freedom tells a different story. Orlando Patterson argues that at the root of the Western commitment to freedom is in fact a prior Western commitment to slavery. Patterson has written extensively on the historical sociology of slavery. His work draws on such knowledge to provide a cultural account of freedom that is relational, embodied, and historical—and that challenges the easy certainties around structure and culture animating many neoliberal accounts. The work of Evelyn Nakano Glenn challenges such easy certainties in a different way. Glenn also engages freedom as a complex structural reality. She sees behind, for instance, classic American republican claims to individualism and independence to find a world of unequal freedom inhabited often by persons of color and women. Thus she shows how a focus on adequately considered structural concerns reveals a more complex world of burdens and opportunities. If we are really going to think about equalizing freedom, then we have to consider carefully the cultural and structural worlds of freedom and constraint portrayed by Patterson and Glenn, which are still present today in analogous ways. And we need a public theology of freedom commensurate with such concerns.

In the third chapter, I turn to the moral philosophy of Amartya Sen for its critique of neoliberal notions of freedom and for its philosophical account of freedom with affinities with the requirements of created freedom. Neoliberal accounts make freedom the central focus of their worldview; this centrality is one of their most powerful substantive and rhetorical modes of appeal. But Sen's moral philosophy also makes freedom the central focus—and in doing so operates on the basis of a very different conception of liberal freedom. Sen incisively dissects the philosophical limitations of libertarian thought and argues himself on behalf of a view of freedom that accounts for embodiment, relationality, and history. His thought is liberal and has a universal appeal even if he eschews that he is arguing in terms of any particular theory of the good. Sen, then, adds important elements to a critique of neoliberalism and offers a compelling liberal philosophy of freedom consonant with key aspects of a theology of created freedom. As with Patterson and Glenn, I consider Sen's work to be a "fragment" that confirms and specifies fundamental theological claims.

In the fourth chapter, I will engage more extensively Rahner's theology of created freedom. At a general level, this theology evokes dependence in three ways: on God the Creator, on the world, and on the redeeming grace of the cross. In a more specific way, I will also focus on what I believe are the key takeaways from Rahner relevant to the challenge of neoliberal liberal freedom in the Age of Fracture: that freedom is embodied, immersed in history and unable to be understood apart from history, relational, and oriented to the good and to God in a manner consistent with liberal assumptions about the human right to religious freedom. I think Rahner's notion of freedom is captured well by the term "constitutive polarity" used by theologian Maureen Junker-Kenny:[46] Rahner's theology of freedom combines the concrete and the transcendental. We are not left in a world of relations without a transcendent reference point. Nor are we left in a world of detached, abstract freedom disconnected from the concrete. Rahner's deft integration of the concrete and transcendent provides a foundational theology remarkably well-suited to finding a way through the postmodern immanence and detached transcendence of the Age of Fracture.

The fifth and final chapter is the culmination of the argument: a theological account of created freedom under the sign of the cross for the United States. This chapter builds on the earlier ones. Rahner's theology provides the background framework and the demand for a theology of freedom

---

46. Junker-Kenny, *Approaches to Theological Ethics*, 210.

integrated with the body, history, relationship, and an orientation to the good and to God consistent with the human right to religious freedom. The sociological work of Patterson and Glenn lays down the requirement that a theology of freedom must engage with race and gender. The exhaustive, contextual philosophy of freedom of Sen points toward the possibility and need for a relational theology of freedom. Accordingly, in this chapter, I offer a constructive public theology of freedom consisting of three key parts or "fragments." First, there is the work of African American Catholic theologian M. Shawn Copeland that draws on narratives of enslaved African American women to make its case for the moral imperative of an "enfleshed freedom": a freedom that refuses to stay in the deceptive world of abstraction but becomes embodied in terms of what the oppressed are freed from and in terms of what the liberated can do. Copeland argues that it is past time to dispense with the myth of the individual freedom of the self-reliant, Euro-American male. If we really want to understand the meaning of freedom, we should heed the directive of the preferential option for the poor and see what freedom means today to the racialized and gendered world of poor women of color. Second, I turn to the American moral philosopher Elizabeth Anderson in order to draw on her subtle account of freedom and relation. Anderson powerfully evokes how oppressive relationships create manifold structural constraints on freedom. She also articulates a persuasive liberal account of what we owe each other in a democracy: what she calls the social conditions of freedom. Copeland and Anderson make clear that we cannot coherently detach freedom from what is often a radical world of constraint. In doing so, they powerfully evoke what Anderson calls the harsh world of freedoms that are the prelude to responsibility. Such a world is an inescapable part of a Catholic public theology of freedom. Finally in the chapter, I turn to the work of American Jesuit theologian David Hollenbach for a coherent and thorough way of integrating the work of Copeland and Anderson with a liberal theory of freedom consistent with a Catholic vision for the good. Hollenbach grounds freedom in a historical and social understanding of human dignity. He reimagines liberalism in terms of human relationality. He articulates a way by which the Catholic in a liberal regime is free to pursue a vision of the common good commensurate with love and justice and confident in the eschatological victory of the city of God. Hollenbach has argued for what he calls a "social ethics under the sign of the Cross."[47] I draw on this idea, in the end, to advance what I call a public theology of freedom under the sign of the cross. By this I mean a public theology that is honest about the radical constraints of freedom in American

---

47. Hollenbach, "Social Ethics."

society; that confirms the possibility of choice represented by the cross; that looks to the cross for the model of Christian love; and that sees in solidarity with the oppressed—with those who struggle with the freedoms that are the prelude to responsibility—the hope of the cross for the transformation of the world.

CHAPTER ONE

Catholic Public Theology and the Contemporary American Problematic of Freedom

WHAT IS THE PROBLEMATIC of freedom in the social and political context of the United States to which Catholic public theology should respond? In the introduction, I appealed to the work of Daniel Rodgers in *Age of Fracture* to argue that the key contemporary questions about freedom arise from the pervasive influence since the 1970s of an understanding of economic freedom associated with an abstract version of microeconomics. In this chapter, I will expand on this argument. First, I will turn to the work of sociologist Daniel Bell to confirm the accuracy of Rodgers' analysis. Next I will consider a group of prominent Catholics in the last decades who have sought to combine Catholic convictions with neoliberal versions of freedom. Then I will consider several alternative views of freedom derived from concerns about economic inequality, race, and gender. These views of freedom highlight the limits of neoliberalism and require the attention of Catholic public theology. In the penultimate discussion of the chapter, I will draw on the moral philosophy of Charles Taylor to show that what Taylor calls "atomist" freedom (akin to libertarian or neoliberal versions of freedom) is self-contradictory; such a view of freedom only emerged in modernity amid cultures and structures that atomist freedom now seeks to deny. Finally, in the conclusion, I will turn to the work of historian John

McGreevy to help specify the challenge that freedom in American social and political life poses to Catholic thought.

DANIEL BELL, HUMAN CAPITAL, AND EQUAL OPPORTUNITY

What Daniel Rodgers saw as an historian looking back in time, Daniel Bell predicted as a sociologist looking into the future. In 1973, at the beginning of what Rodgers came to call the "age of fracture," Bell accurately predicted major aspects of the problematic of freedom in the world we now inhabit. In his book *The Coming of Post-Industrial Society*, Bell argued that the primary intellectual problem of social value in the coming world—the world we now live in—would be the definition of human equality. The problem would arise, Bell argued, because of an increasing disagreement about the meaning of the principle of equal opportunity. During the modern and industrial era, the principle was understood to be the necessary condition for the justness of the merit accorded to individual achievement. All persons having an equal opportunity or an equal freedom, it was considered fair that some, by their own good effort, succeeded and that some did not. In any case, these inequalities of achievement did not last long. A constant equalizing movement up and down the social ladder eventually displaced those who had succeeded with their successors in merit. In the post-modern and post-industrial era, however, the principle of equal opportunity would come to be seen less as a fair means by which anyone could succeed and more as a deceptive justification by which the already advantaged—especially those advantaged in having technical knowledge—repeatedly confirmed their fixed place at the top of a social hierarchy.[1]

Bell insightfully drew attention to the role that "human capital" would play in the formation of present-day inequalities.[2] To be clear, it was not human capital in itself to which he objected. The emphasis on the qualities of a person (intellect, insight, technical education, technical skill, etc.) that correspond with human capital was, he thought, necessary for economic advancement. Such an emphasis was also right. Against what he feared would be increasing suspicion of concepts like equal opportunity and meritocracy, Bell strongly affirmed that such classic ways of thinking about justice were in accord with the achievements of human capital. But he also provided a far-sighted account of how human capital could go wrong. The problem would occur, he said, when productive capacities were overestimated and

1. Bell, *Coming of Post-Industrial Society*, 424–27, 487–89.
2. Bell, *Coming of Post-Industrial Society*, ix–xxxvii, 3–14, 424–55, 487–89.

mistaken for the predominant or even whole of the person. Furthermore, this problem of overestimation would be complicated by the penchant of men and women to see in advanced scientific and technical knowledge a possibility for unprecedented control over events and things. This control would constantly push to overstep its bounds. There would be a belief that technical planning could control the course of events and thus negate what would be considered the destructive effects of what Bell called the "indeterminacy" of change. There would be a tendency to see the world as a vast technical society—united electronically if not through concrete, interpersonal interactions. Such standards of calculation would threaten to transform a true meritocracy into a technocracy: a world in which distribution of reward would be judged increasingly in terms of numerical standards like productivity. Given this power over nature, almost everything about persons would come to be seen as changeable. All persons could make themselves or be made to have the same, equal chance as anyone else.

In the post-industrial world, then, freedom would come to be understood in close association with a circumscribed view of human capital. A person as such would be considered free to the extent that they could exercise these rational, productive faculties. In an extreme sense, inherent human freedom would also be identified with sheer power over human and natural limits. But freedom could only come to be understood in this light by sidestepping what were—contrary to post-industrial presumption—constitutive, ineradicable characteristics of human and natural life. These characteristics include the complex and resistant power of the human world and of nature; the ineradicable presence of contingency; the value attached to the particular and limited, especially with regard to human relationships; and what Bell called the "duplex nature of man himself—the murderous aggression, from primal impulse, to tear apart and destroy; and the search for order, in art and life, as the bending of will to harmonious shape. It is this ineradicable tension which defines the social world."[3]

Bell's concerns about human capital, equal opportunity, and inequality—and related implications for the idea of freedom—have, to an important extent, become true. As an empirical matter, Robert Putnam's book *Our Kids: The American Dream in Crisis* provides confirmation for Bell's concerns. In a series of powerful portraits taken from around the United States, Putnam depicts what he calls the national "opportunity gap." He says: "We have seen how in recent decades the challenges and opportunities facing rich and poor kids have grown more disparate."[4] The driving forces in creating this gap are

3. Bell, *Coming of Post-Industrial Society*, 488.
4. Putnam, *Our Kids*, 227.

economic and educational. Men—the fathers of the kids about whom Putnam writes—have especially reflected these divergent fates. Between 1980 and 2012, he notes, the real hourly earnings of male college graduates rose from 20 percent to 56 percent. During the same decades, the real hourly earnings of male high school graduates fell 11 percent, while the real hourly earnings of male high school dropouts fell 22 percent.[5] With such different economic and educational outcomes have also come powerfully diverging effects—for the well-off, salutary; for the poor, destructive—on families, schools, communities, social capital, political participation, and more.[6]

Today, then, the concept of an equal freedom has been brought into question. At a global level, there are unprecedented opportunities created by new economic and social forces, but there is also a profound helplessness in the United States and throughout the world about how to stave off the negative effects of globalization and how to take advantage of these opportunities. At work in all of this is an idea of freedom that is set radically against the embodied, relational, and uncontrollable conditions of human life. One result of this problematic concept of freedom has been unjustly unequal distributions of goods and opportunities. Another result has been a suspicion on the part of many on the bottom end of these distributions that they are being ripped off—that the actual relationships and often difficult circumstances of their lives are left out of account in the justification of these distributions. Another consequence has been the erosion of the political, economic, and cultural institutions that had in the past been able to hold in check the excesses of this freedom. And still another result has been the erosion of belief in a universal human equality. Crucial to this world is a winner-take-all, no-excuses culture in which freedom is presumed to be a personal attribute with which you can make yourself rich or leave yourself poor. In such a world, you deserve the exorbitant salary you earn or you deserve your failure; no justification is needed for the former and no excuse is acceptable for the latter. It will be helpful to consider more closely the role of the abstraction of freedom or opportunity in several additional contemporary analyses of inequality.

CATHOLICISM AND NEOLIBERALISM

Among aspects of these changes of special interest to Catholic public theology is the embrace by many American Catholics of the abstract economic freedom foreseen by Daniel Bell and criticized by Daniel Rodgers. I would

5. Putnam, *Our Kids*, 35.
6. Putnam, *Our Kids*, 34–39, 227–42.

like briefly to trace four different approaches to freedom: a libertarian approach; an approach based on the thought of Ayn Rand; another linked to the "cultural capitalism" of Michael Novak and others; and a final approach reflecting a populist reaction to this abstraction of freedom.

Libertarianism

Libertarianism has many varieties, some more rights-based and some more utility-based, some leaning right and some leaning left.[7] But one thing that contemporary libertarianism is not is a simple continuation of classical liberalism's primary concern with finding a way for a pluralist political community to live in peace. The writer Will Wilkinson has noted libertarianism's transformation in the twentieth century into a response to socialism in its communist and Nazi versions. As such, Wilkinson argues, libertarianism often operates now in American society as an anti-collectivist, counter-ideal "fortified against socialism with a theory of rights that morally criminalizes redistribution."[8] The fear of socialism may be anachronistic; the "threat of authoritarian socialism collapsed with the Soviet Union thirty years ago," Wilkinson notes.[9] But while the end of the Cold War freed libertarianism from conflict with its chief ideological foe, the end of the war did not free libertarianism from the absolute positions on property rights and government encroachment that it brought to that epic struggle. American political society is now saddled with the destructive consequences of such absolute positions, as is especially evident in reflexive demands for negative freedom from government coercion, Wilkinson argues.

The influential late-twentieth-century libertarianism of Murray Rothbard offers a window into positions that emerged in the context of the Cold War and that remain as powerful ideals of freedom in current American political society. Like other libertarians, Rothbard bristles at the charge that libertarians are "atomists" or little more than discrete, isolated individuals doing their own thing. Instead, he argues in utilitarian fashion that libertarians believe they must cooperate with others for the sake of survival. Nevertheless, this consequentialist connection to others is a second-order concern behind the first-order claims associated with natural rights. "The point is,"

---

7. van der Vossen, "Libertarianism."

8. Wilkinson, "Libertarian Democracy Skepticism." Wilkinson argues that libertarian concerns about democratic threats to property rights have been a driving force behind voter suppression tactics now common in the United States. For a contrary view, see Somin, "Libertarian Skepticism."

9. Wilkinson, "Libertarian Democracy Skepticism."

Rothbard says, "that each individual makes the final choice of which influences to adopt and which to reject, or of which to adopt first and which afterwards."[10] To this assumption of an invulnerable self—that is, a self in a position to *choose* influences but not so much to suffer them—Rothbard adds a decisive rejection of society understood as a relational reality distinct from but inherently connected to individual persons. Persons may not be atomists but they exist in a wholly voluntary world in which they may opt in or opt out of relationships. In turn, he argues, the assumption that society is an "actually existing entity" and not simply a "label for a set of interacting individuals" is one of the "prime errors in social theory."[11]

Rothbard also closely links freedom to self-ownership and property. The ownership of one's body is especially key: Freedom is especially understood as the absolute right of an embodied being bent on survival not to be coerced by external physical force (a force especially manifest in government action).[12] Thus for Rothbard strong materialist presumptions inform his view of freedom. Freedom is so closely linked to ownership of one's body and property for the sake of survival that theft is most accurately understood not as undue possession of material things but as an invasion of freedom.[13] Moreover, external physical coercion is the great sin in an otherwise almost purely voluntary world. Any rationale for such coercion is almost always presumptively far more morally suspect than the sheer physical fact of such coercion. And any other kinds of constraint—for instance, the limitations imposed by disabilities or illness or poverty—are far less morally significant than the explicit, willed coercion imposed by government.[14] Indeed, for Rothbard there is no distinction between democracy and dictatorship, but the state as such is the "supreme, the eternal, the best organized aggressor against the persons and property of the mass of the public. All States everywhere, whether democratic, dictatorial, or monarchical, whether red, white, blue, or brown."[15]

As a libertarian, Rothbard is a natural rights absolutist. Other libertarians are more pragmatic. In an essay in the Jesuit newsweekly *America*, Stephanie Slade framed an appeal to rights within a larger utilitarian justification of libertarianism while arguing that libertarian thought is compatible

---

10. Rothbard, *For a New Liberty*, 22.
11. Rothbard, *For a New Liberty*, 30.
12. Rothbard, *For a New Liberty*, 23, 33.
13. Rothbard, *For a New Liberty*, 33.
14. See also the discussion of a similar issue in the thought of Milton Friedman in Finn, *Moral Ecology of Markets*, 117–18.
15. Rothbard, *For a New Liberty*, 36.

with Catholic social teaching.[16] Thus she affirms the importance of treating individuals as ends in themselves (for her, such treatment reflects a Catholic commitment to human dignity). This primarily means, she says, that "voluntary, nonviolent human interactions" should be preferred over coercion. As with Rothbard, coercion as a willed, external physical force occupies a privileged place among evils. But in Slade's essay there's no sense of structure or culture slowly and coercively grinding people down in body and spirit (to argue in such a way would allow for a more interdependent, less purely voluntary world than Slade acknowledges). Instead, government—because its "dictates are by nature coercive"—stands as the singular and constant threat of the evil of coercion. Libertarian freedom is almost entirely freedom with respect to the government alone. Even if Slade has a more positive view of government than Rothbard, she still attributes to it—but not to the market—an inalienable propensity to dominate, screw things up, and sap initiative. Coercion, then, violates persons as ends in themselves. But, for Slade, the violation becomes especially clear when we consider more consequentialist grounds. Maximizing freedom by minimizing government coercion allows for more prosperity and a greater degree of human flourishing. Moreover, she argues, the success throughout the world of market economies free from government regulation points to the abiding wisdom of libertarian thought and to possibilities for prosperity essential to a Catholic notion of the common good.

In the course of the book, I intend to address the limitations of a libertarian view of freedom. But I would like to note here several preliminary points of critique bearing especially on the construal of freedom in light of the self's relationality. At a 2014 conference at Catholic University of America called "Erroneous Autonomy: The Catholic Case Against Libertarianism," Bishop Blasé Cupich noted how both Catholic social teaching and libertarianism affirm a notion of human dignity that "anchors their insistence on human freedom"; both also affirm that dignity is "not given by society but by the Creator and therefore freedom, self-determination and all other human rights are inalienable."[17] But, Cupich said, from these shared premises the two traditions move in different directions. In particular, Catholic social teaching affirms an intrinsic connection between dignity and solidarity. Our worth as human beings—and the freedom that is expressive of that worth—is inherently tied for better or for worse to our

16. Slade, "Libertarian Case for the Common Good."

17. Cupich, "Response to Cardinal Oscar Rodriguez Maradiaga." For an account of the conference, see Hennenberger, "Can You Be Catholic and Libertarian?," and Williamson, "Catholics against Capitalism." For a response to Williamson, see Stoker, "Adviser to Pope Francis."

relationships to others near and far. Such relationships may be instrumental and mutually dependent; from insurance markets to the stock market, individual freedom is interdependent with the freedom of others for the sake of prosperity and fundamental well-being. But such relationships may also be of intrinsic value: Our freedom finds fulfillment in the experience of community for the sake of the good of community itself.

Ayn Rand

Libertarianism often strips away complex motive and reduces morality to a matter of force—especially government force. Slade refers to such a reductive vision when she says, "libertarianism is merely a philosophy of government. It tells us about the proper role of the state. . . . It cannot answer the far more numerous and consequential questions about how to 'live well' in the private sphere."[18] The work of Ayn Rand shares many things with libertarian thought: an emphasis on freedom; an intense wariness of government; and immersion in a materialist world charged with the threat of physical force. But Rand affirms such priorities in the context of a narrative vision replete with motive, character, and an entire worldview about how a person ought to live well. In this vision, freedom is the purview of the talented and productive—and the dramatic challenge is the effort by "men of talent" to wrest their freedom back from domineering mystics and grasping collectivists.[19]

For Rand, then, freedom is especially crucial because it allows such "men of talent" to undertake their highest moral purpose—survival. Here it's important to note that Rand, even given her emphasis on life and survival, does not lapse into a Hobbesian world. The good is not that which is desired, objective morality be damned. Instead, the good is deeply connected to survival, but still something given and external and rational to which the heroism of the producer is oriented.[20] Her cardinal virtues of rationality, productivity, and pride have no higher moral purpose than sustaining life itself in the mode of a producer.[21] Rationality reaches its greatest manifestation in the economic logic of self-interest. For Rand, freedom is not so much oriented to a contractarian political structure as to the sociality of market exchange. Indeed, a man recovers his true nature when he becomes a producer and is validated by earning his literal sustenance in economic exchange. This

18. Slade, "Libertarian Case for the Common Good."
19. For a condensed, dramatic account of this struggle for freedom, see John Galt's radio address in Rand, *Atlas Shrugged*, 927–93.
20. Badhwar and Long, "Ayn Rand."
21. Badhwar and Long, "Ayn Rand."

logic of exchange provides the context for establishing the true nature of human sociality in the exalted world of trade. In this world, those in need are economic "zeroes" (Rand uses the word often to describe persons in need or persons without the cardinal virtues of rationality, productivity, and pride) who offer nothing of value but demand sacrifice from those who actually have something worthy of exchange.[22] Moreover, heroic producers work among themselves in a seamless web of conflict-free economic rationality driven by self-interest but free of self-deception and greed.[23]

Former Speaker of the United States House of Representatives Paul Ryan, a Catholic, notably said that he often turned to Rand's thought to evaluate whether a policy choice would advance individualism or collectivism.[24] Indeed, Rand's emphasis on the value of human freedom in the face of the encroachment of the collectivist totalitarian state is shared by Catholic social teaching. Moreover, her connection of freedom to personal responsibility, objective values, and virtue (however abridged her values and virtues are) also connects to Catholic thought on the disposition of freedom toward the good. But there are numerous points of departure between her thought on freedom and fundamental Catholic assumptions. Some such points are obvious. Rand thinks the language of love of God and neighbor promotes a servile dependence on religion and the collective.[25] Similarly, she rejects the notion of original sin as a conniving way by which Christian thought tries to sap the bold, independent will of the producer.[26]

Other points of contrast are subtle. For instance, Rand presumes a host of sharp contrasts beyond the contrast between individualism and collectivism. Reason is set off sharply from the deceptiveness of feeling.[27] A morality of survival is set off against both an insidious morality founded on God and a malevolent morality derived from collectivism.[28] Productivity is sharply contrasted with need, and creators are squared off against moochers.[29] I note these sharp contrasts because of their rhetorical power: Rand's prose thrives on such conflicts. But I also note them because they signal the chief analytical problem in Rand's concept of freedom: her inability to imagine

---

22. Rand, *Atlas Shrugged*, 953, 957–58, 984.

23. Badhwar and Long, "Ayn Rand."

24. See "Paul Ryan and Ayn Rand's Ideas." Ryan also has said he rejects key portions of Rand's thought in Rutenberg, "Paul Ryan." See also, "Paul Ryan Rejects Ayn Rand."

25. Rand, *Atlas Shrugged*, 938.

26. Rand, *Atlas Shrugged*, 951.

27. Rand, *Atlas Shrugged*, 938.

28. Rand, *Atlas Shrugged*, 938.

29. Rand, *Atlas Shrugged*, 957–58.

the things that suggest dependence—feeling, God, the community, need—as anything other than entrapment. In Rand's narrative trajectory, the goal is for the talented and strong to regain their heroic freedom by throwing off such confinement. She accomplishes this by having a "conception of people as agents rather than patients, doers rather than receivers, self-sufficient rather than dependent."[30] And, while Catholic thought affirms a person as an agent and a doer and self-sufficient, it only makes this affirmation in the context of the person as always also passive, receptive, and dependent. Finally, Rand's notion of freedom is oriented to a good bereft of an appropriately full range of values. This is especially evident in her dismissal of the "zero" needy and the "scum of the earth" as unworthy of the logic of exchange and, even more, of care.[31] Rand radically divides the world into creators and moochers. For Rand, freedom finally finds fulfillment in heroic productivity and sees in the needy not simply a negation but a positive threat to such self-realization.

Cultural Capitalists

The libertarian and Randian strains of freedom are often embedded in materialist premises. Freedom is closely linked to survival. The enemy of freedom is the willful use of physical force. The coercive character of government action is the great manifestation of this enemy. In these accounts, the connection between freedom and morality is either limited to questions of force, considered a matter of private concern, or attenuated by its tight link to the primary value of survival. But when we turn to the next group of Catholics who have recently embraced the market logic of the "age of fracture," we see a shift to freedom understood in light of spirit and a vivid sense of morality.

I call this group the "cultural capitalists" because of the importance they place on situating freedom within a notion of culture largely understood as common human morality consistent with a more conservative Catholic interpretation of natural law.[32] In this view, market activity, democratic governance, and human morality are deeply intertwined. For instance, Michael Novak, in *The Spirit of Democratic Capitalism*, argues both that "the virtues

---

30. Badhwar and Long, "Ayn Rand."
31. Rand, *Atlas Shrugged*, 979.
32. For examples of such cultural capitalist writers, see Brooks, "Confessions of a Catholic Convert"; George, *Conscience and Its Enemies*; Lay Commission, *Toward the Future*; Novak, *Spirit of Democratic Capitalism*; Novak, *Catholic Ethic and the Spirit of Capitalism*; Weigel, "Two Ideas of Freedom"; Sirico, *Defending the Free Market*.

inherent in economic rationality are not without significance to the virtues of ... political and moral-cultural life" and that the "moral-cultural system is the *sine qua non* of the political system and the economic system."[33] Writing a generation after Novak and amid the culture wars of the twenty-first century, Robert George argues that supporters of the market economy and opponents of gay marriage have common enemies because they share common principles:

> Respect for the human person, which grounds our commitment to individual liberty and the right to economic freedom and other essential civil liberties; belief in personal responsibility, which is a precondition of individual liberty in any domain ... and recognition of the vital role played by family and by religious institutions that support the character-forming functions of the family in the flourishing of any decent and dynamic society.[34]

For cultural capitalists, freedom may be oriented to the good—but it is also liberal. They reject a confessional state and affirm full religious freedom for all, including nonbelievers (even if they see a role for the state to use law to restrict freedoms related to abortion and gay marriage). Novak offers an especially interesting and persuasive account of pluralism and freedom of conscience in light of the apophatic theological concept of "emptiness": We know divine being more by intuitions of the vastness of what we do not know than by the explicit propositional character of what we think we know. Humble in the face of such an endless intelligibility, we should respect the freedom of all others to plumb this mystery as they seek ultimate meaning in their lives. "No institution, group, or person in the United States is entitled to define for others the content signified by words like 'God,' 'the Almighty,' and 'Creator.' These words are like pointers, which each person must define for himself," Novak says.[35]

Cultural capitalists also emphasize the inherently social nature of freedom; we are not in a libertarian world. Individuals do not come first and then, as a matter of choice alone, belong to this or that group as each person wishes. Instead, we are born into a social world and exercise our freedom amid such opportunities and constraints. "The moral and aesthetic traditions in which our sensibilities and our minds are nourished," Novak argues, "are

---

33. Novak, *Spirit of Democratic Capitalism*, 181, 185.

34. See "Common Principles, Common Foes," in George, *Conscience and Its Enemies*, 12–13.

35. Novak, *Spirit of Democratic Capitalism*, 53–54, 351. See also "Religious Liberty: A Fundamental Human Right," in George, *Conscience and Its Enemies*, 115–25.

first given to us by traditions, institutions, a people, which we did not choose for ourselves. Only later do we come to discern, reflect upon, criticize—and either appropriate or reject—our social inheritance."[36] Novak turns to the Thomistic virtue of *caritas* to provide a logic of love linking the freedom of the person and society. On one hand, he says, *caritas* wills the good of the other as other, and by such love brings community into being. On the other hand, to will the good of the other as other necessarily means to regard a person as free insofar as each person is "an originating source of insight, choice, action, and love."[37] The mediating structures of civil society are best understood as the indispensable social means by which *caritas* is made concrete in the larger play of politics, economy, and culture.[38] Moreover, Novak makes clear that the orientation of freedom to community is not only derived from nature nor only propelled by love. It also reflects by analogy the Trinitarian nature of divine being. "The image of the solitary loner," Novak says, "however noble and heroic, however brave in facing the darkness alone, somehow rings false as a representation of the highest of human experiences. What is most valued among humans is that community within which individuality is not lost. To build such community is to share God's life."[39]

The cultural capitalists, then, offer a public philosophy and public theology of freedom that is compatible in fundamental ways with key aspects of the public theology of freedom advanced in this book: liberal, oriented to the good, and inherently social. Nevertheless, there are important shortcomings to the cultural capitalist understanding of freedom. Chiefly, these have to do with a persistent dualism in which the body is either all-but-absent, a threat to be overcome, an idealized site of the moral law, or outside history. Each of these aspects of dualism allows freedom to be less problematic; a matter of spirit alone; more easily able to surmount the burdens and anxieties associated with the body; less readily affected by power and institutions and relationships. Hannah Arendt, in *The Human Condition*, speaks of freedom in a way that illuminates the problem with the cultural capitalist view. There she notes that a person "cannot be free if he does not know that he is subject to necessity because his freedom is always won in his never wholly successful attempts to liberate himself from necessity."[40] This paradox, she believed, was fast being obscured by the ease with which the modern world had liberated

---

36. Novak, *Spirit of Democratic Capitalism*, 61.

37. Novak, *Spirit of Democratic Capitalism*, 357. For Novak's overall discussion of *caritas* and political economy, see 353–58.

38. Novak, *Spirit of Democratic Capitalism*, 339.

39. Novak, *Spirit of Democratic Capitalism*, 337–38.

40. Arendt, *Human Condition*, 121.

itself from previous futilities in the face of nature. As the mastery of these futilities grew, so, too, she feared, would the failure to recognize the necessities in the face of which freedom would have to be forged—if not as often by cultural capitalists then constantly by wage laborers.[41]

We can see the problem Arendt identified by considering a series of related dualisms that figure prominently in Novak's work. First, there is the dualism of mind and body. "What distinguishes a capitalist society from all previous forms of economic order," Novak says, "is its institutional base in processes of innovation, discovery, invention—or, in a word, in *mind*."[42] In arguing in this fashion, Novak surely was setting his theory of democratic capitalism against materialist assumptions of Marxism that had animated the Soviet economic model. He was also seeking to articulate the rationality driving capitalism. But instead of opting for a more unified view of the person combining mind and body, he draws on the thought of Jacques Maritain to establish some sharper distinctions. Maritain distinguishes between the individual and the person. The former category denotes a biological member of a species and an embodied, material quality that humans share with all animals. The category of personhood, by contrast, is characterized by intellect and will and thus a capacity for insight and choice. In this notion of personhood, Novak finds the basis for liberty in general, and for the liberty of the entrepreneur in particular. Personhood so construed, he says, signals a "self-starting capacity, a seat of responsibility, a being that is responsible for understanding and directing its own activities, independently of any other."[43]

But this understanding of personhood presumes a dualism evidenced by Maritain's statement (which Novak approvingly quotes) that "unlike the concept of the individuality of corporeal things, the concept of personality is related not to matter but to the deepest and highest dimension of being."[44] Novak confirms this sense of dualism when he again quotes Maritain to the effect that "man will be fully a person . . . only in so far as the life of reason and liberty dominates that of the senses and passions . . . otherwise he will remain like the animal, a simple *individual*, the slave of events and circumstances."[45] In this dualistic scheme, it is the fusion of reason and liberty in the act of entrepreneurial creation that manifests the fullest

---

41. Arendt, *Human Condition*, 121.

42. Novak, *Catholic Ethic and the Spirit of Capitalism*, 85.

43. Novak, *Free Persons and the Common Good*, 28. See also Maritain, *Person and the Common Good*, 40–41.

44. Novak, *Free Persons and the Common Good*, 194, quoting Maritain, *Person and the Common Good*, 40–41.

45. Novak, *Free Persons and the Common Good*, 33, quoting Maritain, *Three Reformers*, 24.

achievement of the domination of the order of necessity. Or, as Novak puts it, in this act the "human person gains 'dominion' over every force of mere determinism."[46] Given such language attributing an almost divine power of causality to an entrepreneur, it is not surprising that Novak assumes a close identity between capitalist activity and divine creation. "Economic activism is a direct participation in the work of the Creator himself," says the Novak-authored report issued in 1984 by the Lay Commission on Catholic Social Teaching and the US Economy.[47]

Even if we allow that in his time Novak was engaged in a polemic against Soviet and Marxist materialism, the language here is still strong. Reason and will not only can but should *dominate* the senses and passions. The entrepreneur creates in a way that overcomes *every* aspect of necessity in human life. Such exercises of economic freedom are a *direct* participation in divine being. In such language, we can see the concerns raised by Arendt about a modern move away from limitation, necessity, an integral and abiding role for the body in the ongoing practices of human life. We can also see a twofold problem of justice. On one hand, the whole world of chronic constraint inhabited by the poor and oppressed fades from view; it's either not imagined or unrealistically assumed to be fixable in a fashion akin to overcoming *every* aspect of necessity in human life. On the other hand, so much power is attributed to the act of economic production—which is rendered as all-but an act of creation from nothing—that any notion of desert flows heavily in the direction of the entrepreneur. Such a person merits the far-greater share of returns from any act of economic creation. A preceding distribution that shapes the context of the act of economic creation matters far less. It is instructive to see how carefully John Paul II, in the encyclical *Centesimus Annus*, situates economic freedom within the context of embodiment. He notes the increasing prominence of intellect—akin to Novak's invocation of "mind"—as the decisive factor of production in the contemporary economy. But he notes as well that the prominence of intellect as a factor of production does not obviate the importance of situating economic freedom in the context of the most basic needs. "Economic freedom is only one element of human freedom," he says. "When it becomes autonomous, when man is seen more as a producer or consumer of goods than as a subject who produces or consumes in order to live, then economic freedom loses its necessary relationship to the human person and ends up alienating and oppressing him."[48]

46. Novak, "Creation Theology," 34.
47. Lay Commission, *Toward the Future*, 29.
48. John Paul II, *Centesimus annus*, §39.

Freedom and the Populist Turn

In a biting essay in the summer of 2018, Kevin Gallagher argued that the era of the "cultural capitalists"—or, as he called them, the Catholic "fusionists"— was over.[49] By calling this group "fusionists," Gallagher cast them in a similar light to the American conservative fusionists who approach the public square on a platform that combines free market principles with traditional sexual and cultural morality. The Catholic fusionist gloss was to claim that Catholic moral and social principles provided the ground for this fusion—a ground that also held the promise of making the last decades a "Catholic moment" in American public life.[50] One flaw in this approach, Gallagher argued, was that the Catholic fusionists either wrongly assumed or inaccurately asserted that Catholic social teaching was entirely compatible with their Novak-inspired vision of free market capitalism. Another, related flaw, Gallagher said, was the Catholic fusionists' turn to Enlightenment principles instead of to time-honored repositories of Catholic thought like the work of Thomas Aquinas. These were intellectual failures, Gallagher said. But they were also failures of attention; the Catholic fusionists extolled the virtues of the globalizing free market economy and missed how such economic forces laid waste to once-secure communities in the United States. Gallagher notes how the rhetorical power of the word "freedom" turned fusionist eyes away from this destruction. "Following the neoliberal writer Michael Novak and his book *The Spirit of Democratic Capitalism* (1982)," Gallagher says, "fusionist Catholics emphasize what they portray as the good theological assumptions of liberal capitalism and forgo close analyses of current questions in economic policy. The watchword of freedom is enough to corral them back to the Republican platform and prevent any significant attempts to rethink elements of contemporary political economy."[51]

Gallagher combines this critique with a strong dose of retro-Catholicism. He assumes, for instance, "the patent incongruity of Catholicism and the modern world."[52] He also notes approvingly the contemporary "return to the writings of premodern and medieval theologians and of antimodern popes, and . . . [the] growing sense that the late twentieth century trend of 'aggiornamento' in the Church may have been ill-conceived, or at least badly executed."[53] In all of this, he stands in line with Donald Trump adviser

---

49. Gallagher, "Eclipse of Catholic Fusionism."
50. See Neuhaus, *The Catholic Moment*.
51. Gallagher, "Eclipse of Catholic Fusionism."
52. Gallagher, "Eclipse of Catholic Fusionism."
53. Gallagher, "Eclipse of Catholic Fusionism."

and Catholic Steve Bannon. In a 2014 talk via video at the Vatican, Bannon blended a critique of an unhinged capitalism with an appeal to traditional sexual morality and medieval Catholicism—and all of that in service of American nationalism.[54] He critiqued the crony capitalism that he believed led to the bailout of American banks in the aftermath of the 2008 financial crisis and that, in even more corrupt fashion, drives the economies of China and Russia. And he also critiqued the neoliberal, Ayn Rand-inspired capitalism that "really looks to make people commodities" and that sells itself effectively, especially to the young, under the "rubric of 'personal freedom.'"[55] With this economic critique, Bannon paired an appeal to a traditional, medieval-inflected Catholicism opposed to abortion and gay marriage, and standing tall as a civilizational bulwark against an aggressive secularism and a murderous Islam. His assertion of American populist nationalism rests in part on such economic and cultural critiques.

In the thought of both Gallagher and Bannon, then, we see a powerful criticism of the role of the abstraction of freedom in the formal market logic that has fueled what Rodgers called the "age of fracture" in the United States. We also see—more in Bannon than in Gallagher—a shift in the subject of freedom. In Rodgers' critique, freedom in the age of fracture is not only an attribute of an individual but, even more, of an individual understood as an abstraction, apart from community, contingency, culture, history, and the good. By contrast, in the emerging populist nationalism the focus of freedom shifts to the people or nation reclaiming its freedom from the hegemony of the globalized economy and globalized mandates. Yoram Hazony articulated the logic behind this shift: "Millions of people, especially outside the centers of elite opinion, still hold fast to the old understanding that the independence and self-determination of one's nation hold the key to a life of honor and freedom. These are people who believe that no one ever consulted them about giving up on the freedom of their nation to protect its people, their interests, and their traditions."[56]

In concluding this discussion of populism and freedom, it will be helpful to return to the concrete world—a world where economic change wrought by the global economy left many once-secure white, working class Americans with little more than an impotent, self-accusatory freedom. The empirical work of Anne Case and Angus Deaton sheds light on these destructive changes, and on their broader social consequences. For instance, their work shows old inequalities emerging in new, confounding shapes.

54. Feder, "How Steve Bannon Sees the Entire World."
55. Feder, "How Steve Bannon Sees the Entire World."
56. Hazony, "Nationalism and the Future of Western Freedom."

Between 1999 and 2015 mortality rates for African American men and women ages fifty to fifty-four remained significantly higher than mortality rates for white American men and women in the same age group. But during this time period, the mortality rates for the same overall group of African Americans declined sharply while the rates for the same group of white Americans rose. Moreover, if we take all African Americans and white Americans with a high school education or less between the ages of twenty-five and fifty-four, we can see, first, that African Americans have higher death rates across all ages and, second, that death rates are falling for such groupings of African Americans and rising for similar groupings of white Americans.[57] Indeed, Case and Deaton especially note the dramatic rise in the twenty-first century of mortality rates among white Americans from fifty to fifty-four with a high school education or less. This rise, they argue, has especially been driven by "deaths of despair" (for example, suicide, opioid overdoses, and alcohol-related liver disease).[58] The key explanation, they say, is not so much slow wage growth over recent years. Instead, it is a generational issue in which "*cumulative disadvantage* from one birth cohort to the next—in the labor market, in marriage and child outcomes, and in health—is triggered by progressively worsening labor market opportunities at the time of entry for whites with low levels of education."[59] The lives of grandparents and parents held the promise of higher earnings and a more stable family life within traditional structures of meaning. But the cumulative disadvantage of the last years has left this cohort with little more than stripped-down autonomy, with "less structure when they came to choose their careers, their religion, and the nature of their family lives. When such choices succeed, they are liberating; when they fail, the individual can only hold himself or herself responsible."[60] Moreover, on top of a generational sense of losing ground is also the unsettled sense that one is losing ground relative to African Americans and other ethnic groups who had been economically worse off but whose prospects are improving. "If you've always been privileged," historian Carol Anderson said of contemporary white Americans, "equality begins to look like oppression."[61]

In the *Age of Fracture*, Rodgers identifies the appeal to a "distinctly abstract concept" of microeconomic markets as one of the driving intellectual

57. Case and Deaton, "Mortality and Morbidity," 402–5.
58. Case and Deaton, "Mortality and Morbidity," 402–18.
59. Case and Deaton, "Mortality and Morbidity," 397.
60. Case and Deaton, "Mortality and Morbidity," 430.
61. Case and Deaton, "Mortality and Morbidity," 429. Case and Deaton quote Anderson from an interview that appears in Glasser and Thrush, "What's Going on with America's White People?"

forces in the last decades moving American society away from considerations of institutions and power and toward the valuation of freedom and spontaneity.[62] In the preceding discussion, I have reviewed how during this same period of time prominent American Catholics themselves appropriated an abstract, market-based language of freedom in libertarian, Randian, and cultural capitalist terms. Drawing on the work of Case and Deaton, I have also implicated such an abstract concept of autonomy in the creation of the despondent wreckage left behind in American industrial communities by the globalized economy. I would like to conclude this section of the chapter by addressing one final concern: Does economics require such an abstract concept of freedom, whether or not such a concept is consistent with the requirements of Catholic public theology? The work of Catholic theologian and economist Daniel Finn says no; the neoliberal versions of freedom affirmed by Catholic writers are neither economically necessary nor theologically accurate.[63] Finn argues on behalf of three points especially relevant to the discussion here. First, he distinguishes between "disembedded markets"—akin to the abstract microeconomic markets identified in the *Age of Fracture*—and embedded markets. In the former kind of market, the language of preferences and the logic of economic efficiency have reduced restrictions on individuals. In the latter kind of market, moral traditions and moral commitments have more seats at the table in limiting autonomous choices. Second, Finn teases out the distorted ideas of freedom that emerge from disembedded markets. For instance, he argues that the logic of disembedded markets carries with it the assumption that such markets are both scenes of spontaneous choices and also of structures created by spontaneous choices. By contrast, he says, spontaneous choice does indeed prevail internally within markets. But markets themselves are always structured by a context that includes law, regulation, norms, distributions of power, and more (Finn uses the word "ecology" as a way of speaking about such a context).[64] The mistake of libertarian appeals to freedom is to deny or radically diminish the shaping role of such a context. Thus such appeals may speak of individuals within markets as "wholly voluntary" or "completely

---

62. Rodgers, *Age of Fracture*, 41.

63. Finn, *Moral Ecology of Markets*, 103–25. Theologian Vincent Miller argues similarly. He notes the turn to an abstract freedom in the neoliberal ideas of the last decades. And he also notes the place of markets in Catholic social doctrine: "The Catholic Church accepts the good that markets can bring in strict economic terms (production and distribution) and in the specific sorts of freedom they can facilitate. But papal social teaching has consistently stressed that markets are limited and imperfect tools with potentially destructive aspects." Miller, "What Does Catholic Social Teaching Say about the Economy?"

64. Finn, *Moral Ecology of Markets*, 113.

free." But this way of putting things either works as a rhetorical sleight-of-hand that neglects the existence of laws against force or fraud—laws whose existence in themselves signals that a market cannot be a scene of the "wholly voluntary—or radically limits the range of things that could even be considered as unjust constraints on freedom. A forceful action of government stopping me from what I want to do would amount to such an unjust constraint. But other modes of constraint—for instance, ones created by cultural factors or social forces—would less clearly qualify. Moreover, bodily impairments like disability or advanced age would also not be considered constraints on freedom to be ameliorated so much as misfortunes to be endured.[65] Finally, Finn argues that the proponents of disembedded markets traffic often in false and anachronistic binaries: the free economy vs. centralized government; capitalism vs. socialism; free markets vs. a Soviet-style command economy. By contrast, Finn appeals to the metaphor of fences. Every market has fences placed here or there that restrict certain freedoms: "the issue is the extent of freedom that will be allowed to individuals and firms within those markets."[66]

FREEDOM AND ECONOMIC INEQUALITY, RACE, GENDER

We have seen the limits of the neoliberal view of freedom: Too abstract, too individualistic, too disembodied. It will next be important to make more concrete the implications of such criticism. Beyond its conceptual failings, what does neoliberal freedom (and I will use that term interchangeably with words and terms for similarly abstract renderings of freedom like atomism, libertarianism, and extreme autonomy) miss when it is assumed to be the only lens by which to assess the state of freedom in the American social and political context? Earlier in the chapter, we took note of Case and Deaton's description of the "deaths of despair" in once-thriving areas of the United States laid low by a culture of extreme autonomy and the globalized economy. In this section of the chapter, I'd like to consider more specifically the limits of such a view of freedom in light of economic inequality, race, and gender.

---

65. Finn, *Moral Ecology of Markets*, 117–19.
66. Finn, *Moral Ecology of Markets*, 125.

Thomas Piketty, Economic Inequality, and the Freedom of the Supermanager

In *Capital in the Twenty-First Century*, his monumental account of contemporary economic inequality, Thomas Piketty says of contemporary American economic distributions, "What primarily characterizes the United States at the moment is a record level of inequality of income from labor (probably higher than in any other society at any time in the past, anywhere in the world, including societies in which skill disparities were extremely large)."[67] In the United States, the top 1 percent of income earners in the 1970s held 9 percent of national income. Between 2000 and 2010, the share of the top 1 percent rose to 20 percent.[68] Between 2000 and 2010, income inequality in the United States was higher than in India or South Africa during the same period.[69] Piketty does not at length engage the issue of freedom or opportunity. But it is possible to read his work as a cautionary tale on the way that the abstraction of freedom in the context of inequality obscures the actual structures and processes by which such inequalities are created and sustained.

At the heart of Piketty's account of American income inequality derived from work is what he calls the "pure ideological construct" of a "supermanager."[70] In this construct, marginal productivity theory is called on to justify exorbitant pay to top executives on the assumption that such pay reflects the actual value—in Daniel Bell's terms, the value of the "human capital"—the supermanager has added to his or her company.[71] Here such executives assume a seamless blending of their liberty and a system of economic efficiency. Or, as a critic said of libertarian theory, "'Liberty' is all but cognate with a system that efficiently compensates the superstar."[72] To be sure, Piketty notes, a consideration of marginal productivity theory is a crucial aspect of thinking about the problem of economic inequality. At a broad, societal level, the best way over the long run to reduce such inequality is to

---

67. Piketty, *Capital in the Twenty-First Century*, 265.
68. Piketty, *Capital in the Twenty-First Century*, 294.
69. Piketty, *Capital in the Twenty-First Century*, 330. Piketty also notes: "The fact that income inequality in the United States in 2000–2010 attained a higher level than that observed in poor and emerging countries at various times in the past . . . also casts doubt on any explanation based solely on objective inequalities of productivity. Is it really the case that inequality of individual skills and productivities is greater in the United States today than in the half-illiterate India of the recent past (or even today) or in apartheid (or postapartheid) South Africa?" Piketty, *Capital and the Twenty-First Century*, 330.
70. Piketty, *Capital in the Twenty-First Century*, 330.
71. Piketty, *Capital in the Twenty-First Century*, 334.
72. Metcalf, "Robert Nozick."

invest in education (and thus in skills that will enhance productivity) in an egalitarian fashion.[73] But applied to the construct of the supermanager, the theory of marginal productivity obscures more than it reveals. Specifically, Piketty argues, the theory is put in service of a "meritocratic extremism"[74] constructed out of a mix of cultural and structural conditions: For instance, cultural assumptions about the meaning of "winners"; post-1980s changes in tax law highly favorable to outsized executive compensation; the insufficient conflict-of-interest safeguards on compensation committees that set executive salaries; the persistent phenomenon of "pay for luck" (i.e., the company may have done well—but it was for happenstance reasons unrelated to efforts of the supermanager); and the near impossibility anyhow in a complex system of production of specifying the value of a particular executive's contribution.[75]

Piketty emphasizes throughout the book: We get the inequalities we have by the way we make such cultural and structural choices. Moreover, at the heart of such choices are assumptions about freedom abstracted from its constitutive conditions. Thus the mythic, meritorious supermanager has a disembodied quality: His or her reward is determined in a world of pure quantification detached from contingency. Moreover, the supermanager is a lone ranger whose insight and achievement is neither dependent on others nor affected by structural factors: Everything is a function of his own freedom and responsibility. Still more, the freedom of the supermanager accords seamlessly with justice: What his freedom is believed to accomplish in the company is not only commensurate with an exorbitant salary but also with a notion of desert. The fallibility of the pursuit of the good—and the distinction of justice from market outcomes—is lost in the self-deceiving light of abstraction.

Michelle Alexander, the Voluntary, and the New Jim Crow

Michelle Alexander's book *The New Jim Crow* can be read as an effort to unmask how an abstract concept of freedom is used to create and sustain a system of enduring inequality. The work is a powerful indictment of the racially biased system of mass incarceration in the United States. Alexander details the shocking numbers: "In less than thirty years, the US penal population exploded from around 300,000 to more than 2 million, with

---

73. Piketty, *Capital in the Twenty-First Century*, 306–7.
74. Piketty, *Capital in the Twenty-First Century*, 334.
75. Piketty, *Capital in the Twenty-First Century*, 304, 308, 334.

drug convictions accounting for the majority of the increase," she notes.[76] Given the size of the penal population, the United States has behind bars a higher rate of its overall population than any other country in the world. But it is not only the size of the population that matters; it is also the racial composition of those behind bars. Alexander notes: "No other country in the world imprisons so many of its racial or ethnic minorities. The United States imprisons a larger percentage of its black population than South Africa did at the height of apartheid."[77] The chief structural factors here, Alexander persuasively argues, are the laws, policies, and discretionary practices of the War on Drugs, launched in the 1980s at a time when drug crime was in fact declining. "Studies show that people of all colors *use and sell* illegal drugs at remarkably similar rates," Alexander says.[78] But the enforcement and adjudication of laws meant to combat such use fall in grossly disproportionate fashion on African Americans. "In some states," she points out, "black men have been admitted to prison on drug charges at rates twenty to fifty times greater than those of white men."[79] One overarching and fateful abstraction keeps the system in place: That "mass incarceration is officially colorblind."[80] But another, closely related abstraction works in tandem with this first one: That the system is entirely the result of individual freedom and responsibility. "The genius of the current caste system [Alexander argues that racialized mass incarceration is a new caste system like slavery], and what most distinguishes it from its predecessors, is that it appears voluntary. People choose to commit crimes, and that's why they are locked up or locked out, we are told."[81]

But a consideration of the conditions of freedom allows one to see the highly abstracted character of the voluntariness that serves as an ideological justification for the New Jim Crow. The issue for Alexander is not whether there is freedom. Nor is it the link of freedom and responsibility. And nor is it a connection between freedom and the good. Alexander affirms all of these notions and says, "None of this is to suggest that those who break the law bear no responsibility for their conduct or exist merely as 'products of their environment.' To deny the individual agency of those caught up in the system—their capacity to overcome seemingly impossible odds—would be to deny an essential element of their humanity. . . . We have a higher self,

---

76. Alexander, *New Jim Crow*, 6.
77. Alexander, *New Jim Crow*, 6.
78. Alexander, *New Jim Crow*, 7.
79. Alexander, *New Jim Crow*, 7.
80. Alexander, *New Jim Crow*, 183.
81. Alexander, *New Jim Crow*, 215.

a capacity for transcendence."[82] But to say this, she adds, does not make "the conditions of our life irrelevant."[83] In an overarching sense, Iris Marion Young's metaphor of a birdcage stands as an image of the reality of freedom-embedded-within-conditions to which Alexander refers. The structural racism is not represented by one wire alone but by the many wires of the cage, each of which represents some different dimension of constriction.[84]

For Alexander, then, there is no inconsistency in affirming an inalienable capacity for self-transcendence and in acknowledging a world of internal and external conditions that radically constrain the possibility of choice for the sake of such transcendence. In her telling, these conditions include the whole structure of laws and arbitrary enforcement practices that funnel people of color toward incarceration and that sap the spirit of self-transcendence along the way. These assumptions inform the view of voluntariness that rhetorically undergirds the system. And indeed Alexander's view of freedom includes all of these assumptions. For instance, she embeds such assumptions about freedom, responsibility, and the good within an embodied, social, and historical context. Thus her book can be considered a reflection on the embodied aspects of freedom. Thinking of mass, racialized incarceration exclusively in terms of moral failure has the effect of minimizing the moral implications of experiencing the sheer, physical loss of freedom at the hands of the coercive power of the state. Her book can also be considered a reflection on the way that freedom must be considered in terms of relation. For instance, she illuminates what happens after a person is released from prison and moves into a second-class status of shame, contempt, and exclusion. How one appears before others constitutes the heart of the relationship at issue here: Shame and contempt are directed by others on the ex-convict and constitute decisive cultural impairments to freedom—and especially to freedom understood as freedom-experienced-in-community.

Freedom, Women, and Care Work

I would like to note an additional way in which problematic assumptions about freedom factor into the justification of enduring social and political inequalities. Here the chief recipients of injustice are women, especially those involved in paid and unpaid care work. Catholic theologian Christine Firer Hinze has argued that powerful but unexamined cultural assumptions about the body, dirt, and freedom interact with notions of gender or

82. Alexander, *New Jim Crow*, 176.
83. Alexander, *New Jim Crow*, 176.
84. Alexander, *New Jim Crow*, 184.

ethnicity to provide ideological support for enduring inequalities.[85] Hinze's arguments also show that any accurate rendering of the meaning of an equal freedom in social life should be guided by what she calls an "incarnational principle" rooted in inescapably embodied, moral, and spiritual concerns.[86]

We live in a time, she notes, where there is a great separation between the "embodied and face-to-face aspects of economic and social relations and the more abstracted and disembodied dynamics of modern life . . . between those whom currently existing globalized markets massively reward and the many whom it under-remunerates, marginalizes, or excludes."[87] One consequence of this separation is a persistent cultural naivete about abuses of power. A world run on the assumption that everyone is a rationally self-interested maximizer of consumer preferences—and not much more—has little room for understanding the way that the already-advantaged may seek unjustly to preserve the status quo. Here Hinze in particular notes how a potent ideological mix of purity codes and dualist dreams interacts with assumptions about gender to obscure to the public the women who do paid and unpaid care work. Hinze's analysis is not in itself about the abstraction of freedom. But her work sheds significant light on the topic.

For instance, the body plays an especially important role in her critique. Thus she describes how cultural stigmas about bodily fluids or smells inherent to care work consign the women doing such labor into impure, hidden places deemed all-but inaccessible to claims of justice. Powerful if implicit purity codes push these women out of sight, obscuring to others the difficult nature of such jobs; denigrating those involved in such work; and denying to these women the measure of freedom commensurate with appearing in public on equal footing with everyone else.[88] But cultural stigmas are one of the ways affecting how we see their freedom and equality. Another factor is what Hinze calls the enduring cultural power in American society of the "ancient dualist dream of fleeing the body and attaining a state of freedom unencumbered by material limitations."[89] In fact, what has been an ancient dream has found new imaginative material in the repeatedly disembodied practices of the contemporary global economy. Hinze says: "The world's elites now communicate, invent, and trade instantaneously across the globe in a disembodied virtual world. . . . Technological society, swiftly

---

85. Hinze, "Dirt and Economic Inequality," 45; Hinze, *Glass Ceilings and Dirt Floors*, 76.
86. Hinze, *Glass Ceilings and Dirt Floors*, 39.
87. Hinze, *Glass Ceilings and Dirt Floors*, 19.
88. Hinze, "Dirt and Economic Inequality," 47–52.
89. Hinze, "Dirt and Economic Inequality," 53.

moving from a toil-based to a 'knowledge-based' economy, appears to hold out the promise of a world wherein not only dirt but also bodies that produce dirt no longer need to hold anyone down or back from freedom and fulfillment."[90] In such a world, the dominant notion of freedom belongs to the global elite habituated to the assumption that material limitations really can be left behind. In the meantime, the experience of freedom of those who do the body-related toil of care work is hidden inside gated communities or banished to the edges of public consciousness.

Another condition of freedom of special relevance to Hinze's analysis is relationality. The obfuscation brought about by purity codes and dualist dreams not only hides women doing care work. It also obscures the relationality and the accompanying dependencies that characterize human life itself; the personal lives of women doing care work (as mothers or wives or as part of extended families); and the very nature of care work. The consequences of such obfuscation for an understanding of freedom are profound. Hinze, for instance, points out along with other feminist ethicists that the prized "autonomy values" of modern Western culture "can be actuated only in social circumstances arranged to continuously acknowledge and address (through the provision of care work) human neediness 'and the inevitable human dependencies and interdependencies too often ignored in theories that begin with adult moral agents pursuing their own conception of the good.'"[91] Moreover, only by seeing freedom in light of relationality can we see more clearly, as Hinze points out, the vulnerability of care workers to exploitation and the possibility of care work for genuine intimacy.[92]

Hinze's powerful cultural criticism finds resonance in theoretical reflections on feminism and freedom by theologian Margaret Farley. On the one hand, consistent with feminist concerns, Farley cautions against a view of autonomy that is individualistic; linked to a solely self-generated sense of personhood; and abstracted from social histories and concrete bonds. In order to be imagined and even conceived, this view of autonomy has frequently required the devaluation of the Other as the social condition of its own creation.[93] By contrast, Farley argues on behalf of a situated freedom: "If we are free, if we are autonomous, it is not in spite of our world but because we are capable of interaction with our world. In hearing and receiving, knowing and loving, speaking and doing, surrendering and resisting,

---

90. Hinze, "Dirt and Economic Inequality," 53.
91. Hinze, *Glass Ceilings and Dirt Floors*, 45.
92. Hinze, "Dirt and Economic Inequality," 49.
93. Farley, "Feminist Version," 184, 194.

we become ourselves—able (always more or less) to understand our desires, express our intentions, organize our plans, and reveal our loves."[94]

For too much of the world today, the meaning of freedom is determined by a global elite chasing a dualist dream. The freedom in question is disembodied, exclusively rational, and shorn of dependencies. The effort to equalize such an abstract freedom confirms Daniel Bell's fears: Equality is seen as a partner to a deceptive self-transcendence. The abstractness is deployed like a rhetorical gloss. By contrast, the work of Piketty, Alexander, and Hinze all convincingly debunk this abstract dream of freedom. They show how it is not possible to speak accurately about freedom apart from a keen awareness of contingency, embodiment, and relationality, among other conditions. It will next be helpful to consider a specific philosophical critique of neoliberal freedom.

CHARLES TAYLOR AND THE PHILOSOPHICAL CRITIQUE OF NEOLIBERAL FREEDOM

In an influential essay, the moral philosopher Charles Taylor provides an especially helpful analysis of the origin and shortcomings of neoliberal freedom (especially as it relates to the concept of an equality of freedom).[95] Taylor groups such neoliberal approaches in a category he calls "atomism." According to such a category, each person presumes as a starting place a solitary, atomistic state of nature or some similar condition of resolutely discrete human existence. This atomistic starting point precedes entrance into society and provides the basis for determining what if any claims may be placed on an individual. In such a state of nature, an individual has no inherent relation to others outside a small, intimate circle (usually the family). Most fundamentally—in Taylor's analysis—an individual has no inherent relation to society at large and its structures (by "society" and "structures" Taylor means the political, economic, and cultural associations within which one lives). Moreover, the atomist individual assumes that he or she has amassed skills, capacities for effort and insight, and property entirely on his or her own (or with the assistance of family). There is little to no indebtedness to society and structures for having an integral role in the acquisition or development of such attributes. Lastly—and this may vary somewhat with different atomist theories—the individual in the solitude of the state of nature has already arrived fully at his or her understanding of the good. It is the assumption of being able to develop a notion of the good

---

94. Farley, "Feminist Version," 195.
95. Taylor, "Distributive Justice."

in such solitude that in part provides what is often the libertarian's easily pricked sense of moral desert at the perceived slight of society intruding on this private moral domain and presuming to make a claim on him.[96]

This, then, is the starting place: the wholly constituted individual possessing a notion of the good or property or willpower or insight who, after such full formation, chooses to enter society. With such an individual in mind, we can also see the roles of liberty and equal liberty in Taylor's analysis of atomism. For all such individuals entering society, "liberty" functions as protection and represents a zone of non-interference in which the individual is free from any arbitrary intrusion by society and its structures. The value of society to the individual derives in part from the provision of the protection of such liberty; life in society for the individual ought to be safer and more secure than life in the state of nature. Society also provides productive advantages to the individual. More can be produced through the networks of society than can be produced in an atomist existence in the state of nature. But the value of society is contingent, not essential. Generally speaking, an individual is safer and more productive in society but it may be possible, too, to find such safety and productivity in a life of pure independence.[97]

Given these claims about liberty, we can now see more clearly Taylor's critique of a neoliberal understanding of an equality of liberty. First, the governing assumption is of individuals who are formed outside of society and who then freely decide to join society. Second, the liberty in question can be understood as non-interference in the property, capacities, or morality of an individual. Each individual has the same degree of non-interference and thus is allowed equally to choose for one's self how they will make use of these attributes. Moreover, in terms of equality, what is crucial is that each individual shares equally in the expectation that he or she will be fulfilled in their pursuits by their entrance into society. There is no sense of an inherent relation to society. But there is a sense of an instrumental relation—society, generally speaking, provides a better contingent opportunity for fulfillment of aspirations than life outside of society.[98] It is important to tease out several implications of such views. One is that, in an atomist equal liberty, an expectation of explicit individual consent for any intrusions on liberty has powerful appeal. Another is that fairness requires that nothing more is to be asked or demanded of one individual than of another. Everyone is in an equal starting place, no matter how much property or capacity he

---

96. Taylor, "Distributive Justice," 288–93.
97. Taylor, "Distributive Justice," 292.
98. Taylor, "Distributive Justice," 293.

or she may have. Finally, justice demands that whatever the individual is thought to bring to society—however unequal such property or capacities are—should be protected and allowed to accumulate. Thus a libertarian notion of equal liberty is highly compatible with great inequalities and with the normative objection to challenging them.

But Taylor's penetrating critique of the problem of an atomist equal liberty goes further. First, he notes a self-deceptive phenomenon at the heart of bold neoliberal assertions of the heroically individualist self. Such an assertion presumes a self shaped entirely outside of society. In turn, for the libertarian, the rule of law and democratic institutions are intended primarily to protect this whole and heroic self. But, Taylor argues, such assumptions fail to see how even the idea of a libertarian self was only made possible amid the decidedly social context of the structures, practices, and values of modern democratic politics. Thus the libertarian notion of the self did not so much need democratic institutions to protect it as much as it needed such institutions—and related democratic practices of common deliberation—to be conceived as a self at all. "It took a long development of certain institutions and practices, of the rule of law, of rules of equal respect, of habits of common deliberation, of common association, of cultural self-development, and so on, to produce the modern individual," Taylor notes.[99] Moreover, he adds, what was true of the emergence of the atomist self and its accompanying ideas of equal liberty remains true today: such a self and such notions of liberty remain dependent for their very conception and value on the existence of democratic structures and practices. As Taylor puts it, without such a social context sustaining a sense of liberty there would be no way to conceive of liberty as protection.

But the problem of libertarian self-deception goes beyond the blindness to the social context on which the idea of the heroic libertarian self depends. The problem also extends to the way such a self and its commitment to impregnable liberty and unimpeachable inequality often lapses into a destructive tension with the mutual indebtedness and reciprocity that sustain communities of common deliberation.[100] Taylor describes this destructive tension in terms of what he calls the "contribution principle," or the conviction that what the atomist self contributes economically to society ought to be compensated fully with few questions asked. "It remains generally true," he says, "that [the contribution principle] is invoked in an obsessive and one-sided way in our societies."[101] On account of such an invocation, society

---

99. Taylor, "Distributive Justice," 309.
100. Taylor, "Distributive Justice," 298.
101. Taylor, "Distributive Justice," 314.

slowly becomes the place of libertarians alone, with the larger normative structures overlooked or overwhelmed in the ever-expanding desire of libertarianism. With these developments, too, the notion of an equality of liberty becomes increasingly detached from its balancing normative framework. Liberty works to protect whatever accrues to the most powerful and any broader sense of the dependence of freedom on broader structures—and on the broader ideas of equality that upholds such structures—falls out of view. Indeed, Taylor retains a place for the contribution principle in a good society. But that is a balanced society, with vital economic and political structures. An atomist equal liberty left to its own devices undermines the possibility of such a free and equal world.

I have noted often in this discussion Taylor's insistence on freedom's inherent relationality and its orientation to the good. I would like also to call attention to Taylor's discussion of the condition of history. Atomist equal liberty is deeply ahistorical. It presumes an impregnable present: whatever is possessed by the individual is unable to be challenged, other than on the grounds of overt fraud. Thus the history of acquisition, among other things, remains obscure. The atomist insists on liberty in order to protect an accumulation—even a very unequal accumulation relative to others in society—that shall not be questioned in terms of any broader context from which such an accumulation may have been gained. The atomist also insists on a self that is whole and entire and owes little to a past social context outside at most of an immediate family. The implausibility of this atomist account of liberty is clear. Taylor's critique succeeds in showing the incoherence and danger of conceiving of an equal liberty in such fashion.

CONCLUSION

In this chapter, I have identified neoliberal freedom as the problematic of freedom in the American social and political context to which Catholic public theology should respond. "Neoliberal" is a broad term meant to capture a range of views all of which closely associate the meaning of freedom with an imagined agency in idealized microeconomic markets. What is common to these views is a concept of freedom abstracted from notions of embodiment, relationship, history, and the good. Daniel Rodgers identified the turn in American society in the 1970s to this market-based freedom—a turn that has had dominant cultural power to the present day (and a turn predicted in the 1970s by Daniel Bell). One manifestation of such cultural power is the sway of this idea in the last decades among thinkers who sought to combine Catholic thought with such an abstract, market-based freedom. The work of

Daniel Finn has shown that the abstract freedom favored by these thinkers is neither consistent with Catholic assumptions about the contextual nature of freedom nor required by capitalist assumptions about the behavior of markets. In addition to its conceptual shortcomings, I have also aimed in this chapter to show real-world consequences of the American cultural turn to neoliberal freedom. Here the work of Case, Deaton, and Piketty traces the role of an abstract autonomy in the destruction wrought by an increasingly unequal and globalized American economy. The writing of Alexander and Hinze shows how the ideal of neoliberal freedom fails as an interpretive key to explain the actual challenges of freedom associated with the experience of race and gender in American society. Finally I turned to the work of Charles Taylor to demonstrate the depth and cogency of a more extensive philosophical critique of neoliberal—or, as Taylor calls it, "atomist"—freedom.

In his book *Catholicism and American Freedom*, John McGreevy traces the complex, ambivalent history of the Catholic Church's engagement with the founding American ideal. Three observations drawn from the book provide a helpful close to this chapter. First, McGreevy frames the fundamental tension between Catholicism and American freedom as one between the Catholic conviction that freedom is always connected to context (even if freedom per se is not determined by such contexts) and the American predilection for a more circumscribed autonomy shorn of context.[102] Second, the existence of this tension provides a lens by which to understand the long-standing Catholic opposition both to an individualistic economic freedom prominent in late-nineteenth-century America and resurgent in the contemporary "Age of Fracture," and to an autonomy understood as pure choice protected by privacy and put in pursuit of lifestyles expressive of identity.[103] Third, McGreevy's book allows a clearer view of the texture of the contemporary tension between Catholicism and American freedom. I am arguing that the chief problematic to be addressed by Catholic public theology is neoliberal freedom—in effect the newest iteration of a long-standing American tendency to associate freedom with economic agency abstracted largely from embodiment, history, relationship, and the good. McGreevy also shows the historical Catholic ambivalence about racial freedom. Catholics by and large in the mid-nineteenth century opposed abolition in part because they understood the freedom sought by slaves to be an unhindered autonomy sure to lead to public disorder.[104] Catholic public theology today must engage more directly the African American history of freedom on the

---

102. McGreevy, *Catholicism and American Freedom*, 265.
103. McGreevy, *Catholicism and American Freedom*, 154, 260.
104. McGreevy, *Catholicism and American Freedom*, 52.

way toward re-imagining a Catholic notion of freedom for the American social and political context. McGreevy as well offers a cautionary note about the contemporary Catholic criticism of the radical autonomy invoked, for instance, in defense of an absolute right to abortion. In itself, such a radical autonomy will always be problematic from a theological perspective insofar as no authority beyond choice is recognized. But, McGreevy notes, a critique of such autonomy should not also occlude far greater attention on the part of Catholic theology to the experience of women as they struggle to be free.[105] Finally, McGreevy argues that Catholicism faces the challenge of convincing American culture that freedom finds its deepest meaning in love disposed especially toward the strangers and outcasts in our midst.[106] My argument in the balance of this book will build on McGreevy's insights to engage neoliberal freedom on its own terms and via attention to categories of race, gender, and the distinctive Catholic understanding of the relationship of freedom and love.

---

105. McGreevy, *Catholicism and American Freedom*, 267.
106. McGreevy, *Catholicism and American Freedom*, 295.

CHAPTER TWO

Public Theology, Sociology, and the Problem of "Monticello without the Slavery"

IN THE SPRING OF 2018, a major dustup between two African American cultural icons pointed to problems in the understanding of freedom to which Catholic public theology must pay attention. Superstar rapper Kanye West mused in an interview on the long African American history of slavery and said: "When you hear about slavery for four hundred years.... For *four hundred* years? That sounds like a choice." He added: "You were there for four hundred years and it's all of y'all. It's like we were mentally imprisoned."[1] Acclaimed writer Ta-Nehisi Coates was having none of West's provocative musings. While praising West's genius as a musician, Coates called out West's statements for their deceptive affirmations of "white freedom," or what Coates described as "freedom without responsibility, without hard memory; a Monticello without slavery, a Confederate freedom, the freedom of John C. Calhoun, not the freedom of Harriet Tubman."[2]

In this chapter, I will begin where the last chapter left off: with freedom in history and with the imperative, as theologian Karl Rahner has said, that freedom cannot be understood in abstract terms alone but must be engaged as a reality of culture and history.[3] The back-and-forth between West and

---

1. CNN, "4 Wild Things Kanye Said This Week."
2. Coates, "I'm Not Black, I'm Kanye."
3. Rahner, "Dignity and Freedom of Man," 237.

Coates points to the importance of this imperative. West's formulations fail to imagine or engage a brutal past and thus easily detach freedom from its connection to such history. He also sharply separates the mental or spiritual elements from the embodied or relational aspects of freedom. For West, centuries of enslavement cannot be sufficiently explained by the oppressive, physical restraint of slavemasters and by an associated vast legal regimen backed by coercive force. Only a failure of will can account for why things lasted so long. Coates calls out West's account for its naïve and insidious detachment of will from the searing experience of all-encompassing oppression; the detachment from reality represented by such thinking is akin to "Monticello without the slavery." Coates also calls out West for affirming a "thin freedom" that self-deceptively appears only in the present. In this "thin freedom," the past is a burden from which freedom can and ought readily to be separated instead of an anchor that grounds the present and provides the basis from which to move into the future. The work of American Nobel Laureate Toni Morrison shows the deeper logic of Coates's argument. She long criticized the American tendency to praise freedom in abstraction from the history and culture of slavery. "Young America . . . understood itself to be . . . pressing toward a future of freedom," she argued, "a kind of human dignity believed unprecedented in the world."[4] But she said of this bold affirmation of the rights of man: "Its history, its origin is permanently allied with another seductive concept: the hierarchy of race . . . the concept of freedom did not emerge in a vacuum. Nothing highlighted freedom—if it did not in fact create it—like slavery."[5] Morrison identified two ways in which this alliance of freedom and slavery was especially manifest in American literature. First, nineteenth-century American writers turned to what Morrison called an "Africanist" presence in their work to account for the "terror of human freedom." Freedom was what these writers "coveted most of all." But the hovering Africanist presence in their work, Morrison argued, represented the always threatening possibilities of freedom for failure and loneliness and destruction.[6] And, second, the American celebration of freedom drew energy from projection: on one hand, the energy of fear drawn from seeing the not-free and not-me among enslaved persons, and, on the other hand, the energy of guilt associated with an awareness of responsibility for this context of bondage.[7]

---

4. Morrison, *Playing in the Dark*, 33.
5. Morrison, *Playing in the Dark*, 38.
6. Morrison, *Playing in the Dark*, 37.
7. Morrison, *Playing in the Dark*, 36–39.

It is important to note: Coates and Morrison are talking about freedom. They do not dismiss it in favor of the determinism of oppression. But they dismiss an idealized and abstract notion of freedom—a freedom that has nothing to do with such contexts. In doing so, they articulate a theme that has both long been present in American history and that Daniel Rodgers has also identified as especially characteristic of the "Age of Fracture": that the exaltation in the last decades of the capacity of freedom to create something new has come at the expense of the connection of freedom to history—to the past and to the concrete, relational, and complex possibilities of the present to make history.[8] Rodgers explains the paradox in the following way. On one hand, over against state-mandated distributive outcomes, libertarian writers in the last decades have underscored the *historical* nature of distributions in a scheme of liberty. In such a scheme, outcomes are not mandated or fixed—and thus shaped or standing outside of history—but follow from the immense flux of individual agency in an open society and in that sense are historical. In the background of this way of putting things is the great twentieth-century struggle between free societies and the historical materialism of the Soviet Union and its satellite nations. "History" in this context is especially understood as sheer human agency in opposition to the necessity of historical materialism. But that epic struggle is no longer the American context for the consideration of the meaning of freedom in history. In the *Age of Fracture*, Rodgers argues, the challenge of finding the meaning of freedom in history is raised by libertarian and market-based versions of freedom in which "actual history [meaning, the past] trails away."[9] In such versions of freedom, Rodgers says, what has come before has been foreshortened and faded out of view as a scene of struggle, misdirection, and failure constituted by "massive, slow, chaotic processes."[10] Correspondingly, the onset of instant communication and formal market exchanges has obscured if not pushed aside the connection of freedom to custom, tradition, and the dynamics of power and resistance that accompany change.[11]

In the remainder of this chapter, I will address the challenge for Catholic public theology in an American context of responding to Rahner's admonition that freedom can only be known in history. The dispute between West and Coates and the reflections of Morrison and Rodgers point toward the particular nature of this challenge in the present day: freedom must be

---

8. Rodgers, *Age of Fracture*, 191.
9. Rodgers, *Age of Fracture*, 191.
10. Rodgers, *Age of Fracture*, 222–23.
11. Rodgers, *Age of Fracture*, 254.

reconnected to the concrete, to the past, and to contexts of constraint from which freedom emerges. To see how this connection can be understood, I will consider the work of two historical sociologists of freedom—Evelyn Nakano Glenn and Orlando Patterson. Glenn, in her work *Unequal Freedom: How Race and Gender Shaped American Citizenship and Labor*, focuses especially on the period between 1870 and 1930 in the United States to show how in American history the struggle to understand freedom has often been a battlefield between the interpretation of legal structures like citizenship and assumptions about freedom seen through the eyes of socially constructed categories like race and gender. Patterson, primarily a sociologist of slavery, takes a longer historical view and more extensively treats freedom per se (and thus his work will be discussed at greater length). He argues that Western culture valued freedom because it uniquely prized slavery—and that this paradoxical valuation of freedom has deeply marked the American experience since the founding of the country. He also shows how the understanding of freedom has always been a contested space between the powerful and the oppressed. In turning to Glenn and Patterson, I wish to respond to Rahner's claim that freedom must be known in history by having theology turn to historical sociology in order to root itself in the concrete and historical.[12] William Everett, for instance, has argued for the turn to sociology to head off the tendency of theology to consider freedom in the spirit of a misplaced idealism that obscures concrete institutional issues.[13] John Coleman has provided helpful guideposts by which theology can assess a potential sociological partner. Pointing to the implications of fundamental theological categories, he argues that a sociology adequate for conversation with theology should allow room for human agency (i.e., not be deterministic); account for limits to freedom (via structural and cultural forces); and have a sense of tragedy and sin to the point of sufficiently identifying a primary evil to which sociology is addressed.[14] The work of Glenn and Patterson meets Coleman's test and provides helpful insight for the development of a Catholic public theology of freedom for the American context.

---

12. See, for instance, Bellah et al., *Habits of the Heart*, 297–307; Coleman, "Every Theology"; and Everett and Bachmeyer, *Disciplines in Transformation*.

13. Everett and Bachmeyer, *Disciplines in Transformation*, 244.

14. Coleman, "Every Theology," 25.

EVELYN NAKANO GLENN: CITIZENSHIP, LABOR, AND UNEQUAL FREEDOM

In *Unequal Freedom*, Evelyn Nakano Glenn argues that, between 1870 and 1930, the American ideals of citizenship and labor were significantly shaped by the socially constructed categories of race and gender. As such, her book is not about freedom alone. But in fact assumptions about freedom—and especially about the value of greater or lesser degrees of freedom as seen through the eyes of race and gender—play an essential role in her argument. The "unequal freedom" to which the book's title refers is in effect a central, painful reality at stake in battles over the meaning of citizenship and labor. Often, she shows, the dominant, prevailing meaning of citizenship or labor in American society has been bought at the bitter price of deploying constructs of race and gender to justify the unequal freedom of women, African Americans, and other persons of color. She writes of the historical period covered in her book, which ranges from Reconstruction through the Progressive Era: "Although I do not, for the most part, explicitly draw parallels between the historical development of race and gender inequality and present-day conditions, I believe that many of the deep tensions within our contemporary society can be traced directly to the period covered in this book."[15] In what follows, I would like to focus on three aspects of Glenn's argument that are especially relevant to the development of a Catholic public theology of freedom for an American context: her focus on structures; on race and gender; and on the dynamism of relationship.

Glenn explores the meaning of freedom through an examination of the structures of citizenship and labor. In part, such structures are constituted by philosophical traditions. For instance, the civic republican tradition drawn from ancient literature provided ideals of independence and property ownership—and assumptions about freedom associated with such ideals—at the heart of American thought about citizenship.[16] Moreover, the onset in the nineteenth century of classic liberal economic ideas fostered a conceptual connection between labor and the property one has in one's person (a property, for instance, in ideas or effort); with that connection came a corresponding shift in assumptions about freedom.[17] But these are intellectual developments, necessary for the understanding of changing meanings of freedom but insufficient to explain the full measure of these changes. Here Glenn complements her consideration of such conceptual

---

15. Glenn, *Unequal Freedom*, 5.
16. Glenn, *Unequal Freedom*, 21.
17. Glenn, *Unequal Freedom*, 65.

strains with attention to the concrete and contested legal regimes of citizenship and labor. Between 1870 and 1930, great legal and political battles were fought over extending full or partial citizenship (i.e., citizenship without the right to vote) to African Americans, immigrants, and women.[18] Meanwhile, the meaning of labor was contested in struggles over such matters as liberty of contract; the prerogative of a corporate owner to control employees; and the enforcement of vagrancy laws meant to compel the allegedly lazy to get to work.[19] In all of this, Glenn sets down several clear markers for how to go about determining the meaning of freedom; intellectual traditions point the way but the attention to legal structures and to social and political struggle are indispensable for a sufficient engagement with the idea.

Glenn does not write of such struggle in general terms but in the keys of race and gender. In her argument, the meaning of citizenship and labor—and of freedom, too—passes through the contested space of such socially constructed categories. Here she turns to poststructuralist assumptions about power and relationality. Chiefly, she does so to show how meaning is best understood in terms of the struggle for dominant power amid the contrastive dynamism of relationships. This process is both cultural and material: the determination of meaning depends on symbols, norms, and practices and on the brute fact of material conditions.[20] It is not necessary to accept all of the poststructuralist assumptions informing Glenn's argument—in particular, a one-dimensional account of power—to accept the fundamental wisdom of what she says. Ideas of freedom are not simply intellectual abstractions but are deeply shaped in history by a complex play of power, relationship, and the constructed realities of race and gender, among other things. It would be inconsistent with the incarnational imperative of Catholic public theology to formulate a concept of freedom that floats above such an inevitable fray.

In American history, Glenn argues, the legal structures of citizenship and labor have from the start been disposed to favor "whiteness" and "masculinity" (and "favored" in the sense of such socially constructed qualities playing a disproportionate role in the allocation of political power and economic resources).[21] Glenn also underscores the relational, interdependent character of social life. There's no place in her account for an autonomous, detached, libertarian self. And the relationality in question is not static or abstract but instead is infused with conflict, contrast, and the social

18. Glenn, *Unequal Freedom*, 24.
19. Glenn, *Unequal Freedom*, 92.
20. Glenn, *Unequal Freedom*, 12–13.
21. Glenn, *Unequal Freedom*, 1.

psychology of projection.[22] We determine our understanding of things in part as an outcome of the energy of such contrasts fueled by concerns over identity. In the period of Glenn's study, the outcome of these struggles has been resolved generally in favor of whiteness and maleness—and also specifically in contrast to the racialized and gendered categories of others.[23] Thus, in terms of citizenship, Glenn shows how in the early years of the United States white masculinity was both strongly correlated with the full value of citizenship and also strongly correlated with freedom understood as independence. The fullness of American citizenship to the point of the flowering of civic virtue was understood in part to require independence from the private sphere of domesticity and from the arduous demands of labor.[24] Here we have a view of what is often celebrated as freedom-as-independence. But Glenn's work makes it impossible to understand the freedom-as-independence concept as a complete and coherent account of freedom. First, she notes a paradox: the prized freedom-as-independence at the heart of citizenship was in fact only made possible by the involuntary labor of non-citizens or lesser citizens.[25] Second, she also notes that citizenship itself is not a stand-alone concept. Instead, the meaning of citizenship in the American context must be understood in terms of relationality, interdependence, and contrast. What "citizenship" came to mean was informed significantly by what "non-citizenship" or "lesser citizenship" meant.[26] And, in turn, this contrastive struggle for meaning turned on the hinges of race and gender and related assumptions about freedom. Whiteness and masculinity may have been accorded a preeminent value closely associated with independence-as-freedom. But any such valuation was also made in contrast to the racialized and gendered attribution of inherent traits of dependence to African Americans and women. On account of such an attribution of dependence, African Americans and women were rendered incapable of the freedom and independence "needed to exercise free choice and the moral and intellectual qualities needed to practice civic virtue."[27] Here we can see how an abstract notion of freedom—in this case, freedom understood as the independence that creates the possibility of civic virtue at the heart of citizenship—became prized at the expense of considerations of freedom emerging from dependence. In turn, the ascription of greater or

22. Glenn, *Unequal Freedom*, 14.
23. Glenn, *Unequal Freedom*, 14.
24. Glenn, *Unequal Freedom*, 21.
25. Glenn, *Unequal Freedom*, 20.
26. Glenn, *Unequal Freedom*, 20.
27. Glenn, *Unequal Freedom*, 24.

lesser degrees of freedom and dependence becomes a crucial basis for determining who may have citizenship at all or who may have the full measure of citizenship.

A similar set of racialized and gendered assumptions about freedom shape the understanding of labor in the historical period of Glenn's study. In particular, she notes how the onset of the large factories and wage labor of industrial capitalism in the mid to late nineteenth century in the United States provoked a struggle over the meaning of labor.[28] Until that time, the notion of "free labor" prevailed in the northern states. In the early years of the country, the free labor logic rested especially on ancient claims about the connection of such labor to the ownership of productive property. As the nineteenth century progressed, the influence of classical liberal political economy shifted the focus of freedom to the property one has in one's own person.[29] In any case, either way of thinking about labor was thrown into crisis by industrial capitalism. How could the meaning of free labor maintain its coherence in the face of the actual, harsh conditions of assembly line work in which increasing numbers of men began to labor? Glenn notes several sociological responses to this crisis of meaning. One was that efforts were made to heighten the contrast between wage labor and the comparably even more "involuntary" character of chattel slavery and indentured servitude. Making the most out of such relative distinctions allowed capitalist owners to make wage labor appear more appealing and legitimate. Doing so allowed men clinging to the socially constructed significance of whiteness and maleness to hold on to a tenuous, fading notion of free labor as indeed being free, productive, and independent.[30] At least such wage labor was less involuntary than the racialized, unfree labor of enslaved persons. Moreover, however far from the free labor ideal a male wage laborer found himself, he was likely still presiding over a household that presumed on the gendered dependence of women.[31]

Glenn's work provides one way in the American context for public theology to meet the challenge of Rahner's claim that freedom can only be known in history. On the one hand, her work is attuned to the complexity of history: to the structures, dynamism of relationships, and struggles for power deeply affected by race and gender that are significant factors in the development of the understanding freedom. On the other hand, her work also makes clear that the struggles over the meaning of citizenship and labor

28. Glenn, *Unequal Freedom*, 29.
29. Glenn, *Unequal Freedom*, 65.
30. Glenn, *Unequal Freedom*, 28–29.
31. Glenn, *Unequal Freedom*, 58–64.

between 1870 and 1930 in the United States hinged around assumptions of freedom—and that these past struggles over meaning surely affect us in the present day. Public theology can take important methodological lessons from her work about how to go about developing an understanding of freedom. But Glenn works primarily in the sociological key of structure. What about culture? I would next like to turn to the historical sociology of Orlando Patterson to engage especially how his writing on culture and freedom can inform a public theology for the American context.

ORLANDO PATTERSON, SLAVERY, AND FREEDOM

Patterson's sociology is especially well-disposed to address these libertarian and populist times. In response to libertarian assumptions, he makes clear his rejection of an abstract definition of freedom, as he describes a common libertarian way of understanding freedom: "The idea of freedom is seen as 'inherent'—so there is nothing to explain. . . . [The idea is that] 'Everybody wants to be free because it is a part of the human condition.' That's nonsense. Freedom as a value, as a cherished part of one's culture, as something to strive for and die for, is *unusual* in human history. You can't just take it for granted. So the question turns into, how did freedom become important? My explanation is that freedom emerged as the antithesis to the social death of slavery."[32] And, in response to the challenge of populism, he offers a sociological version of freedom that accounts for the tensions between classes and identity groups that emerge in populist societies. He offered a brief account of this version in a magazine profile:

> Under slavery, he explains, there were three groups of people: masters, slaves, and non-slaves. "All three come to discover this thing we call *freedom* through their relationships. For the master, freedom is being able to do what you please with another person: freedom as power. For the slave—well, what does a slave yearn for? To be emancipated, to get rid of the social death that is slavery. Masters *encourage* this notion of freedom, too, as the hope of manumission is one of the most powerful ways to get a slave to work. The third group, the non-slaves or freemen, look at the slaves and say, "We are not them. We are born free." Suddenly, being born free becomes important, in a way it never could be for slaves. Freemen have a different status in society, one that does not depend on their socioeconomic class.[33]

---

32. Lambert, "Caribbean Zola," 46.
33. Lambert, "Caribbean Zola," 46.

Drawing on Patterson's historical sociology, several introductory remarks can be made about the contemporary question of the meaning of freedom. The specific terms of the present-day discussion may be different from what has come before. But the fact of a debate at all over the meaning of freedom is not. Nor is the general shape of the contemporary dispute new, involving as it does a clash between the abstract and the concrete. From the start of the fundamental Western conception of freedom, according to Patterson, there has been a constant struggle not over whether there should be freedom but over which meaning of freedom should prevail and which class should control its meaning. On one side of the struggle have been refined philosophical attempts to define freedom in abstract, clean categories—to say, for instance, that freedom is adherence to truth, or to identify it only with legal rights, or to link it only to the exercise of productive faculties. These attempts at definition per se have not been at fault. But the problem, Patterson argues, has been their abstraction of freedom; they are efforts to think about the concept apart from its origins in the concrete, constricted experience of people's lives. The winner of these intellectual battles has been able to translate conceptual victory into social power. Those favoring abstraction have often been those defending unjust inequalities; those clinging to a concrete notion of freedom have often been those affirming a broad if threatened equality. Patterson concludes of the long-running fact and shape of the conflict over the meaning of freedom, which has continued to the present day:

> Almost from the moment freedom first entered into the stream of Western history, a struggle began to redefine it philosophically, to embrace and refine it apart from its vulgar base, and to render it coherent and acceptable to thinking people and their audience. The result has been not one but two interacting histories of freedom. There is the history of freedom as ordinary men and women have understood it—vague, to be sure, yet intensely held, a value learned in struggle, fear, and hope. Paralleling this has been the history of people's efforts to define "true freedom."[34]

In what follows, I will discuss several key aspects of Patterson's sociology of freedom with an eye toward how it can inform Catholic public theology. First, I will explicate Patterson's arguments for understanding freedom in light of structure, culture, and history. Second, I will consider Patterson's central notion of the "chord of freedom" in relation to the concept of an equality of freedom. The rich, diverse concept of the "chord" offers an

---

34. Patterson, *Freedom*, 2.

insightful way for public theology to prioritize and organize what may often appear to be clashing accounts of freedom.

Freedom and Slavery: Structure, Culture, and History

Why should the concept of freedom to be sufficiently understood be integrated in plausible fashion with the concrete or, in other words, with the human experience of embodiment, relationship, and the good? Patterson, one of the world's leading sociologists of slavery, offers two answers. The first is that the idea and value of freedom were in fact constructed out of the radically constricted experience of slavery. He puts it bluntly: "The origins of Western culture and its most cherished ideal, freedom, were founded . . . not upon a rock of human virtue but upon the degraded time fill of man's vilest inhumanity to man."[35] The second answer is that not only did slavery mark freedom from its birth—but it has continued to do so ever since. As Patterson puts it, freedom has "never been divorced from this, its primordial, servile source."[36]

Several crucial inferences can be drawn from the claim that the development of the idea and value of freedom has never been divorced from its servile source. One is that Patterson posits something like a sociological original sin. The history set in motion in the West by the emergence of human freedom from slavery has never escaped the memory and guilt associated with the enslavement of human beings. Thus the idea and value of human freedom properly resist idealization. Instead, freedom should always be understood to exist in a fraught balance poised between a capacity to oppress and a potential for grandeur. The second crucial inference pertains to more specific sociological implications. The context of slavery from which freedom emerged imprinted on all subsequent concepts of freedom a tripartite structure—Patterson calls it the "chord of freedom"—that allows for a general constancy in the idea and value of freedom amid variations of the shape of freedom in any given society (the chord of freedom includes what Patterson calls sovereignal freedom, personal freedom, and civic freedom). The chord of freedom is especially connected with the moral experience of power over oneself and over others (sovereignal freedom); the meaning of embodiment and community (personal freedom); and the value of democratic self-rule (civic freedom). A third inference is that to understand the idea and value of human freedom in a society, we must look first to the experience of men and women under the greatest constraint—if

---

35. Patterson, *Freedom*, 4.
36. Patterson, *Freedom*, 9.

not specifically to the constraint of slavery then to analogous forms of oppression. Whatever value a society may finally put on human freedom, the beginning of such valuation lies in the struggle of the most constrained in such a society to be free and in the response of the rest of the society to such a struggle.

A final crucial inference points to the importance of understanding freedom at different times of history—and in the present day—in light of the specific sociological configurations of constraint prevalent in a given society. Thus Patterson details the emergence of the idea and value of human freedom amid the slave systems of ancient Greece. But, he also notes, the invariant chord of freedom that took shape then sounded varying notes in different historical periods. Thus during the medieval era, he argues, the great contest of freedom pitted the fragile immunities of serfs against the expansive privileges of lords. Hovering at the edges of this contest were slaves, whose abject dishonor and confinement helped serfs to prize that much more the freedoms they had. "For the oppressed," Patterson notes of the hierarchically favored status of medieval serfs over slaves, "the sociological narcissism of small differences is extreme."[37] During the American Revolutionary period, the incoherence of prizing liberty while enslaving millions resulted in a prevailing form of freedom allied closely with property both in oneself and in what—or, in the case of slavery, whom—one owns.[38]

But understanding slavery will make it easier to understand why freedom emerged from slavery and how slavery has perpetually tainted freedom. "Slavery has to exist," he argues, "before people could even conceive of the idea of freedom as value, that is to say, to find it meaningful and useful, an ideal to be striven for."[39] What, then, were the characteristics of slavery from which was conceived the idea of freedom and which as well have indelibly marked the idea and its emergence as lasting value?

In his attempt to specify the nature of slavery, Patterson has tried to arrive at a universal definition from continuities and similarities across times and cultures. But he has attempted to do so by rejecting abstract, universal standards in favor of focusing on the common experiences of bondage as a multifaceted and paradoxical field of domination through which all other factors like race or property must pass. He has also delineated the interaction of the larger society with the institution of slavery—both the former influencing the shape of the latter and the latter pervasively infecting the former. One critic said that Patterson sees slavery "as a social process in

---

37. Patterson, *Freedom*, 351, 353.
38. Patterson, "Freedom," 153.
39. Patterson, "Freedom," 134.

which the acquisition of the slave, his or her experience as a slave, manumission, and subsequent role as a freedman or freedwoman are all integral parts of the definition of slavery and often determinants of the nature of the slave-owning society."[40]

Too much analysis of slavery has considered it in the singular key of, for instance, law or racism or property. These are necessary ways to view it. But, Patterson argues, an accurate picture of slavery requires an emphasis on the experiences of slavery and on the dynamic interaction between inherent human characteristics and oppressive realities, between culture and structure.[41] The key social reality at issue is power understood as a relation of domination. The power that holds a slave in bondage does so by suppressing a man or woman's physical, social, psychological, moral, and spiritual being. By nature, the slave is neither a blank slate nor a solitary individual. Rather, he or she has longings, relationships, and an integral moral and physical constitution that are attacked by a personal, enslaving power.

Patterson defines slavery as the "permanent, violent, and personal domination of natally alienated and generally dishonored persons"[42] It is helpful to think of this definition as emphasizing three aspects of the personal experience of domineering power—the physical, communal, and moral (which, respectively, correspond to personal, civic, and sovereignal freedom). It is also important to note that this is not a static definition with three distinct and entirely separable elements. Rather, it is one meant to encompass a "complex, interactional process with tension and contraction in the dynamics of each constituent element."[43]

There is first, then, the physical aspect of bondage. "Slavery made possible," Patterson argues, "something that had not existed before: the

---

40. Schwartz, "Attempt at Universal Definition," 358.

41. Patterson criticizes the over-simplification of culture as meaning only "values." He also argues that culture should be seen dynamically in its interactions with structure. See Lambert, "Caribbean Zola," 44. In more technical terms, Patterson understands culture as a product of two related processes. The first, he says, is a "dynamically stable process of collectively made, reproduced, and unevenly shared knowledge about the world that is both informational and meaningful." The second is a process grounded in "pragmatic usage" that "ensures change and adaptation to the environment." He rejects the view that culture is an endless process of contested "meaning making." Instead, he argues that "people normally seek to harmonize their relations, to make sense of and confirm their own and others' intentions and sentiments, through mutual adjustments in their 'affectively generated actions.'" Moreover, he notes that "culture always interacts with structural forces in both constraining and enabling human agency, in the process also facilitating structural and cultural changes." See Patterson, "Making Sense of Culture," 5–8.

42. Patterson, *Freedom*, 9.

43. Patterson, *Slavery and Social Death*, 13.

absolute, unprotected, unmediated power of life and death of one person over another."[44] Thus slavery is constituted by the direct social relation of physical power involving the use of violence in control of one person over another. At root, this is a relation of raw force understood as uncontrolled power and authority over the body of another. This physical powerlessness is analogous to death—"analogous" because slavery is often understood as a substitute for what otherwise would be certain death. In this sense, the slave exists in a state of "living death" that is thought by her masters to be a gracious deliverance from death by war or by her own helplessness. This powerlessness also has an irreducibly personalist nature; whatever systemic structures are involved in the process cannot obscure the fact that enslavement is the result of the violence of one person directed at another.[45]

Slavery is also what Patterson called a state of "social death" in which a person is removed from the social order. Thus what Patterson calls "natal alienation" involves a radical separation from all those things that constitute one as a legitimate member of society. The slave is stripped of all claims of family—to ancestors, present family, and future generations. Moreover, one's cultural heritage—the whole realm of thought and action derived from a shared history—is also stripped away. In place of these fruits of natality, the slave is considered a member of society only by attachment to the family, culture, and symbolic world of the slavemaster. In the eyes of the master, this attachment becomes heritable and perpetual. Moreover, the slave's social death is not a function of relationship to the slavemaster alone. The slave is also socially dead in the eyes of the entire community. The master uses the control of politics and culture to convince the community to acquiesce to the enslavement in its midst. In fact, the community derives a great measure of its cohesion from its collective awareness of not-being-enslaved.

But slavery is not just a relation of violent power or social death. It also involves power intertwined with moral authority and moral judgment. The slavemaster, however much in self-deception, acts from a sense of perverse justice which the community shares. Moreover, this sense of moral right is closely associated with the honor perversely but really obtained from wielding power over others. Like it or not, Patterson argues, masters gained honor simply by domination. Conversely, slaves were subject to a general state of dishonor proportionate to their sheer lack of force. With the loss of physical, bodily power—of not being able to act in the most basic ways on behalf of oneself—came a sense of shame. Moreover, the slave's social

---

44. Patterson, "Freedom," 134.

45. This discussion of the three aspects of the definition of slavery is taken from Patterson, *Slavery and Social Death*, 1–13.

death eliminated the web of relationship and cultural resources that are the presupposition of action on behalf of oneself. The slave knows that she is servile; that what power she has to have the necessities of life is received through another; and that she is unable to do anything about this impotence. In the eyes of a slave society, all of this is cause for shame. Without what constitutes an independent social existence, a slave has no public worth and without such a public worth a person lacks a crucial dimension of freedom.

But why did the idea of freedom emerge from the concrete experience of slavery and what is the process by which that happened? Patterson has a complex explanation that moves from reflections on the basis of culture in fundamental human attributes to analyses of manumission and democracy in the slave societies of ancient Greece. Here I will focus on his discussions of the interactions between fundamental human attributes and the physical, social, and moral dimensions of slavery.

Patterson is not, so to speak, a radical constructionist. He does not assume that an idea or value is simply the product of a social environment. Rather, he adheres to a dialectical method by which inherent human characteristics of desire, thought, and action—what Patterson calls "nature"—interact with social structures to yield sociologically significant ideas and values. It is also important to note that, while Patterson affirms a range of natural human qualities, freedom is not one of them. The idea and valuation of freedom, he insists, are "not a part of the human condition, not something we are born with." Rather, they have been "invented" or "constructed"—not "discovered" or "unveiled"—in the course of the interaction between the nature and personhood of the enslaved and the structures of slavery.[46]

Indeed, Patterson's attitude toward what is part of the "human condition" or "natural" is complex. For instance, while he denies that freedom is part of the human condition, he nevertheless affirms that many closely related qualities to freedom are in fact "natural" or part of the "human condition." In explaining why freedom emerged from slavery, Patterson affirms natural human attributes of self-possession, social relation, and dignity.[47] "The quintessence of slavery," he argues, "was its violation of nature, of what is seemingly most natural in the human condition—being a taken-for-granted part of the community in which one is born; owning, being in possession of, one's most intimate carnal, social, and spiritual self."[48] I have noted the

46. Patterson, *Freedom*, xi.

47. It is important to note that Patterson does not have an extensive philosophical anthropology. Rather, his convictions about the nature of the person have more of an assumed sense than an argued one. See Schwartz, "Attempt at Universal Definition," 358.

48. Patterson, "Freedom," 176–77.

three aspects of slavery—its violent domination, social death, and dishonor. Each of these aspects of oppression in inverse fashion wakened in the slave the intensity of natural qualities and the ideas, desires, and emotions attached to them. Thus sheer physical bondage, Patterson argues, stoked a desire at the "most basic and biological level" for the experience of basic negative freedom—for the sheer fact of not being bodily constrained.[49] The social death of natal alienation, he says, was a "natural injustice" and made that much more prized the idea of life in community.[50] And the dishonor of enslavement stirred the pride at the root of physical resistance to oppression. Patterson notes approvingly the judgment of Frederick Douglass that a "man without force is without the essential dignity of humanity."[51] This essential nature demands expression. In time, Patterson says, human beings will react to enduring oppression "for no other reason than the purely moral fact that sooner or later an inherent sense of dignity demands to be released."[52] The experience of slavery engendered these inherent physical, social, and moral reactions to oppression—reactions that were to be the stuff of the social construction of freedom. Before the experiences of these things people simply could not have thought of freedom in its proper sense. Hence Patterson's statement that "slavery had to exist before people could even conceive the idea of freedom as value."[53]

It may have been natural for slaves to react to their oppression in ways that established the context for the creation of freedom. But it is essential to Patterson's understanding of the social construction of freedom that both instinctive reaction and positive action were necessary for the discovery of the value. Freedom, in other words, was decisively known and valued in the exercise of freedom and in reflection on that exercise. Freedom was also a complex action involving all aspects of the person—bodily, emotional, social, and spiritual.

The second stage of Patterson's reflection on the passage from slavery to freedom is concerned with physical, social, and moral characteristics of persons. The first indispensable aspect of the experience of freedom was the physical removal of bodily restraint—of the material, violent force that, literally, kept slaves in chains. Patterson calls this freedom "in its elementary form": the removal of restraint that corresponds to the "desire simply to be

---

49. Patterson, *Freedom*, 16.
50. Patterson, *Slavery and Social Death*, 8, 337.
51. Patterson, *Slavery and Social Death*, 13.
52. Patterson, *Ordeal of Integration*, 108.
53. Patterson, "Freedom," 134.

Public Theology, Sociology, and the Problem of "Monticello without the Slavery" 63

removed from the power of another."[54] Patterson acknowledges the great significance of an inner spiritual core of a person. But he argues that it is nevertheless the case that basic physical or bodily freedom is the building block from which the idea and value of human freedom were first constructed. Freedom had its origins in slavery and, Patterson says, for one who had been a slave "it was impossible not to love simple, physical, negative freedom."[55]

As necessary as this experience of bodily freedom was, it was in itself not enough for the complete construction of freedom. Two more steps were needed: the transition of slaves from social death to social life and the acquisition of the adequate power and corresponding dignity by which slaves could affect their freedom. The transition to social life began at the basic physical level of the removal of violent restraint. But freedom could not remain an abiding value apart from the conviction of the freed if isolated slave that he or she could fend for oneself economically and in the face of hostility.[56] That conviction extended the notion of freedom to include also the assurance of economic survival and basic personal security. This assurance could not be gained on one's own. In order to survive, an ex-slave had to some extent be integrated into the life of the community of non-slaves.[57]

By becoming free, ex-slaves gained a toehold as members—even if shunned—of a community. But their mere capacity to survive and *de jure* membership in the community were not enough to assure them of sociologically meaningful freedom. Instead, for the ex-slaves to achieve actual free status, the community had in some fashion to consent to the freed slaves in its midst. In turn, the idea and value of freedom also required that the emancipated or manumitted themselves have a self-directed communal experience of freed status. This experience depended both on integration of freed slaves into the community and, paradoxically, on the communal realization among the freed slaves and others of not-being-slaves. In other words, the identification of the community as freed depended on its awareness of those who were still slaves (here we see a dimension of the dynamic of contrast and projection at work in populism). The end of social death, then, meant both the confidence of physical survival within a free community and the communal experience of freed status understood as a relatively secure place in the free community. The end of social death also meant the recovery of one's familial, cultural, and historical roots, and of the independence by which to determine these matters apart from the slavemaster. To

54. Patterson, "Freedom," 154.
55. Patterson, *Freedom*, 279.
56. Patterson, *Freedom*, 42.
57. Patterson, *Freedom*, 4, 42.

become socially alive meant at the least to have independent social worth, an assured standing in the community.[58]

But what more specifically constitutes this worth or dignity? I have already noted that for Patterson dignity is an inherent human characteristic—an innate sense of worth that at some point rebels against oppression. But this inchoate instinct for freedom has two critical elements—positive and negative. Its negative quality is a "refusal to accept an inner and outer status quo." But this negation "affirms something positive . . . 'the drive to touch, to build, to transform, to change the physical world as well as man's inner world.'" This is the "affirmation of true dignity."[59] These general concerns set in context the construction of the moral nature of freedom. For this construction, it is necessary to possess the adequate power and corresponding dignity by which to effect one's actions. Freedom, Patterson says, did not emerge as a static, abstract idea. It is not merely the absence of internal or external constraints. Nor is it merely a power or capacity apart from reference to any constraints. Moreover, these constraints are not neutral obstacles; rather, they have the force and movement of opposition. For freedom to make sense requires the idea of its opposite—that is, the idea of "some endangering force, some image of social death which is negated."[60] It requires this contradiction because to think of freedom necessarily is to think of being freed. In other words, the idea and value of freedom emerged from reflection on the experience of liberation from physical bondage and social death into social life. This was not a passive experience. Rather, it required the possession of the effective power and the attraction of a compelling image by which to act over against endangering, active force. The construction of freedom came about through freedom. To contemplate one's freedom is to think of the experience of a release from bondage, a restoration of community, and the exercise of force and consequent dignity that comes with the successful assertion of physical and moral power. In other words, freedom did not come to be known apart from the complex and dignified experience of becoming free—and of becoming free for some purpose.[61]

58. Patterson, *Freedom*, 1–44.
59. Patterson, *Ordeal of Integration*, 109–10.
60. Patterson, "Slavery," 103.
61. Patterson, "Slavery," 87–92. For a moving account of the emergence of freedom from slavery, see Foner, "Meaning of Freedom": "But instead of a predetermined category or static concept, 'freedom' itself became a terrain of conflict, its substance open to different and sometimes contradictory interpretations, its content changing for whites as well as blacks in the aftermath of the Civil War." Foner shows how Southern whites assumed freed slaves were unprepared for the responsibilities of freedom; that former slaves saw freedom "as an end to the separation of families, the abolition of punishment by the lash, and the opportunity to educate their children"; that former slaves also

Equality and the Chord of Freedom

The problem of the meaning of an equality of freedom runs throughout Patterson's writing even if he does not at length specifically address the issue. Indeed, his work can be considered an extended sociological reflection on the tormented fragility of the idea and value. What could represent more completely the contradiction of an equal freedom than one person who enslaves another? Yet, Patterson argues, it was out of the contrastive experience of such torment that the idea and value of freedom emerged. To be sure, Patterson's historical sociology assumes a given set of natural human attributes—a longing for community and an innate awareness of dignity among them—that factor into his assessment of equality. But his sociology—as a study of what actually occurs in the construction of structure and culture—makes clear that the equality of freedom is in great measure an achievement of society. In this section of the chapter, it will be helpful to consider the chord of freedom and its distinct parts. Doing so not only allows us to see more readily the different sociological contexts in which the drama of the equality of freedom is played out. But it also allows us to take note of what is often obscured in pitched political battles: that often there are competing notions of an equality of freedom, one favored by the rich and powerful, and another by those emerging from situations of radical constraint. What Patterson said of ancient Greece surely still applies today: "the [element of] freedom emphasized would . . . largely depend on the social context and on the most important status difference between the interacting parties."[62]

Each of the notes on the chord has a different relation to the equality of freedom. Of all the notes, personal freedom has the most positive and unambiguous relation to such equality. It signals the removal of power that holds one in a fundamental position of inequality. To the degree that equal freedom is constructed, I have noted, the first step in this construction is freedom in its elementary form as the fulfillment of the desire simply to be removed from the power of another—in other words, what Patterson

---

understood freedom in the consistent key of equality or of the 'enjoyment of our rights in common with other men'"; that beneath more particular aspects of freedom former slaves held to a fundamental desire for "independence from white control, for autonomy both as individuals and as members of a community itself being transformed as a result of emancipation"; and that the outrageous violence inflicted in the South on African Americans *after* the end of the Civil War "reflected whites' determination to define in their own way the meaning of freedom and their determined resistance to blacks' efforts to establish their autonomy, whether in matters of family, church, labor, or personal demeanor." Foner, "Meaning of Freedom," 77–78, 120.

62. Patterson, *Freedom*, 136–37.

calls personal freedom.[63] Throughout history, personal freedom has been the special purview of the lower classes—of the "ordinary people" who have intensely held to freedom as a "value learned in struggle, fear, and hope."[64] As the chord was formed in ancient Greece, the note of personal freedom was especially identified as the tenuous possession of ex-slaves and resident aliens.[65] Moreover, Patterson argues that in its emergence as a value personal freedom was in particular associated with the experience of women in ancient Greece who feared either the prospect or past experience of enslavement.[66] He also notes that no sociological trend is more decisively correlated with commitment to the value of freedom than the willingness of men to accept equality with women.[67]

What of civic freedom and its relation to the equality of freedom? On the one hand, civic freedom is an overtly egalitarian note on the chord of freedom. It exists to the extent that one shares equally in political power as a citizen of a community. On the other hand, the equality of civic freedom has often been affirmed over against an unequal "other"—with the "other" being groups of persons whose alien nature and oppressed status are literal and imaginative sources of the civic community's equality and solidarity. So the equality of civic freedom is often gained at the expense of the stifling inequality of whole classes of people. Of course, examples abound of this phenomenon in both past and present. Patterson, for instance, points to the flowering of republican liberty in colonial Virginia. While celebrated as an unprecedented achievement of political and legal equality—and Patterson acknowledges it as such—it was nevertheless an achievement parasitic on the simultaneous existence of Virginian slavery. The commitment of Virginian citizens—both the white ruling class and lower-class whites co-opted by the ruling class—to republican liberty was intensified by their commitment to the enslavement of men and women of African descent. Due to their treatment of slaves, whites had only to look within themselves to see what it could mean to be at the mercy of a tyrant and thus to prize freedom that much more.[68] Of course, the turn to the equality of the civic freedom of a nation or people at the expense of so-called outsider groups—usually minorities—is one of the common features of the populist nationalism now circling the globe.

63. Patterson, "Freedom," 154.
64. Patterson, *Freedom*, 2.
65. Patterson, "Freedom," 137.
66. Patterson, *Freedom*, 78.
67. Patterson, *Freedom*, 395.
68. Patterson, "Unholy Trinity," 548.

Sovereignal freedom is the note of the chord most prone to inequality and favored by the wealthy and powerful. It is oriented toward control. It also assumes from the start an opposing field of force that must be overcome—not a field of force with which to coexist. Thus sovereignal freedom often inclines toward unequal freedom: The person exercising sovereignal freedom—the slavemaster, the medieval lord, the sweatshop factory owner of the present day—uses his or her disproportionate power to constrain the freedom of others. Sovereignal freedom often accomplishes such domination and constraint by the rhetorical ruse of presenting personal freedom as sovereignal freedom: Personal freedom, which is a "capacity to do as one pleases, *insofar as one can*" is passed off as sovereignal freedom, which is "simply the power to act as one pleases regardless of the wishes of others."[69] The Declaration of Independence is a classic instance of this rhetorical sleight of hand. Jefferson's rhetoric of personal freedom posed an obvious contradiction to the sovereignal freedom that at the time was deployed in the enslavement of millions. Nevertheless, the document's stirring words of liberty were used to justify the absolute power of slavemasters over slaves.[70] But as with any note on the chord, sovereignal freedom may be used for evil or for good—for dominating others in service to an oppressive and unequal freedom or for dominating oppressive forces in oneself and in others in service to a love that seeks the equality of freedom.

The chord of freedom, then, provides a helpful way by which to analyze the challenge of an equality of freedom. Because of its tripartite character, the chord suggests that analyses of freedom in a single, exclusive key often miss what as a sociological matter is a more complex field in which varying and even competing notions of an equal freedom are in play. Here the complexity arises because freedom emerges in society in different keys (personal, civic, and sovereignal) and because different keys tend to be associated with different classes. Demanding an equal, sovereign freedom for a powerful business owner should not be understood to exhaust what may be competing claims to an equal personal freedom on the part of factory workers or to an equal civic freedom on the part of the laboring class.

Patterson and Catholic Public Theology

In concluding this discussion of Patterson's historical sociology of freedom, it will be helpful to note several aspects of his work that should inform a Catholic public theology of freedom for an American context. One such

69. Patterson, *Freedom*, 3–4.
70. Patterson, "Unholy Trinity," 573.

aspect is the nature of his turn to culture. For Patterson, culture no longer operates as a stand-in for the word "values," as is usually the case for the cultural capitalists discussed in the first chapter. When culture is reduced to values alone, the values in question are usually highly particular—for instance, a narrow construal of the values of the Judeo-Christian tradition. Or the values in question exist unaffected by or indifferent to structure. By contrast, Patterson affirms culture as, among other things, including a range of values that are distinctly human—and thus not part of a narrow tradition—and that develops and is deeply affected by interaction with structure. For Patterson, values do have a natural transcendence but they are also deeply shaped by history. His notion of culture invites Catholic public theology to step outside a temptation for too much particularity and to articulate an understanding of freedom that is consistent with Catholic universalistic assumptions at the same time as it is affected deeply by history.

Another crucial aspect of Patterson's sociology—and one he shares with Glenn—is his claim that the battle over the meaning of freedom in Western societies is almost always a hotly contested matter pitting different meanings and different classes against each other (the poor favoring a value of freedom linked to the concrete; the rich and powerful preferring a value more abstract and philosophical). Another key factor in the dynamic emergence of freedom in society is the significance of the contrastive experience of bodily constraint broadly considered (for instance, oppressive working conditions, forced migration, hunger, poor health that compromises bodily movement, the color of one's body as the object of racism, the sex of one's body as an object of sexism or sexual violence, etc.). As much of an intellectual and spiritual value as freedom is often understood to be, Patterson is insistent that it is first necessary to grasp the value of freedom in its relation to embodiment. Here public theology should take note to beware of easy abstractions about intellectual or spiritual freedom. And here public theology should also take note of the structures and cultures that shape the meaning of freedom on the part of the poor and working poor, migrants, the sick, women, persons of color, and others facing ongoing constraint. One other factor to consider is the close relationship between having freedom at all and being considered an inalienable member of the moral community. Here the bright line that distinguishes your membership in a community is the recognition that men and women are capable of exercising their freedom, whether at any time they are using such freedom for good or ill. Of course, often people are rendered non-human—as monsters or vermin, in common if horrible language—and their imputed lack of humanity is meant to render them incapable of freedom and thus written out of the moral community. Public theology must police such boundaries, looking for banishment in the outrageous rhetoric and subtle speech that reduce outcasts to beings without the freedom of moral agency.

Patterson's chord of freedom, considered as a whole and in its parts, can also assist Catholic public theology's engagement with the understanding of freedom. On the one hand, the chord of freedom invites public theology to see the interrelated aspects of the challenge of understanding freedom. The way that the poor will experience personal freedom will affect how the working and middle classes will value civic freedom—and all of this may well be in response to how the rich and powerful value sovereignal freedom. Freedom often does not sing with a single note but instead must be analyzed as part of the complex harmonies and dissonances of Western, democratic societies. Or when freedom is sounded in a more singular fashion, the other notes on the chord are also being sounded more quietly and affecting the structure and culture of freedom as a whole.

On the other hand, each of the notes on the chord provides for Catholic public theology a lens by which to analyze the more specific dynamics of freedom at work in society. Thus personal freedom prompts us to consider the embodied experiences of constraint of the poor, women, persons of color, and the working class—from the constraints of living without a home to the confinement caused by chronic untreated illness to poverty level wages and more. All such matters are the scene of freedom—where the idea and value are re-thought and re-appropriated in the course of experience, struggle, social and political action, and success or failure in such action. Patterson's sociological work also invites us to consider that the drive for personal freedom is not fundamentally about choice per se, as if the freedom at stake was simply the power to choose anything at all. Of course, this *could* be the way that personal freedom manifests itself—a manifestation that is hardly rare in these libertarian times in American society. But such a manifestation is a departure from the consistent sociological construct of personal freedom over time. And what is primarily missing from such a choice-centric view of freedom is the close association of personal freedom and the experience of community and culture. At a fundamental level, personal freedom as a sociological matter involves belonging to family and community.

But paying attention to the struggles in society for personal freedom is one dimension of the public theological consideration of freedom. Turning to the note of civic freedom invites us to consider another dimension: the idea and value of the equality of freedom in the political contexts of Western democratic societies. On the one hand, such civic freedom is valued as an equal participation in the political power of the community. On the other hand, the vigor by which the equality of civic freedom is valued is often fueled by a fearful animus toward a group or groups thought to be threatening the precarious state of those recently emerged from constraint. The price of the equality of civic freedom is often the contemptuous restraint of the poor, the different, and the undocumented.

Finally, Catholic public theology should take note of sovereignal freedom, which in its presumptions about moral order harbors the potential for fostering oppressive inequality or for building the beloved community. Patterson demonstrates the endurance over time of sovereignal freedom understood as the power to dominate others: to assert one's own freedom without regard for the freedom of others. Such assertions of domineering freedom may take many forms—from enslavement to rapacious feudal lords to factory owners compelling production in substandard working conditions to refusing to wear a face mask in a pandemic and more. Of course, Patterson notes, such practitioners of sovereignal freedom usually seek to justify such domination with passionate rhetoric and philosophical purity. This pretense stands on shaky ground. Whatever the rhetoric may be, such sovereignal freedom thrives on its capacity to restrict others—and thus on the creation of distinctly unequal freedoms. But, Patterson also shows, the note of sovereignal freedom is not only sounded in an ominous key. In fact, he describes the ways over time in which sovereignal freedom became the way by which the power of freedom was used for the sake of justice and love to transform an unequal society into a more equal one. Here we see the possibilities of sovereignal freedom for establishing an ever-greater equality of freedom commensurate with the equal dignity of all men and women.

In closing this chapter, I would like briefly to note a contemporary theology of freedom for the way it corresponds to the characteristics of freedom drawn from Rahner and for how it correlates with Patterson's sociology of freedom. M. Shawn Copeland's *Enfleshing Freedom: Body, Race, and Being* stands on its own merit as a powerful, creative work of public theology.[71] But I think Copeland's central claim—that the experience of freedom of poor women of color offers to the church and world a decisively new way of thinking about freedom—receives additional confirmation from its correspondence with the work of Patterson.

Against the prevailing American image of freedom derived from the mythical, white, self-reliant man, Copeland offers the image of freedom

---

71. Copeland, *Enfleshing Freedom*. My discussion of Copeland's work primarily focuses on the correlation between her work and Patterson's concept of "personal freedom." For theological work that could be correlated with Patterson's notion of "civic freedom," see the outstanding essay by Hobgood, "White Economic and Erotic Disempowerment." For theological work to be correlated with Patterson's account of "sovereignal freedom," see Gutierrez, "Liberation and Salvation." For a history of the Catholic Church's agonizingly slow grappling with the immorality of slavery, see Noonan, *Church That Can and Cannot Change*, 15–123.

experienced by poor women of color as a template for thinking about the meaning of freedom for all people. Her choice to focus on such particularity is neither arbitrary nor exclusionary. Guided by the Christian commitment to the poor, she notes the shockingly compromised freedom of women of color around the world. Also guided by a Christian presumption of universality, she explores this compromised freedom (compromised by enslavement, discrimination, abandonment, sexual violence, indifference, cultural barriers based on assumptions of limited intelligence, confinement caused by rigidly defined social roles, etc.) to find what everyone might learn about the meaning of freedom from such profound constraint.

Her arguments find confirmation in Patterson's work. She appeals to a contrastive dynamic similar to Patterson's. As she puts it, "the full meaning of human freedom . . . can be clarified only in grappling strenuously with the 'dangerous memory' of slavery."[72] Her turn to the experience of women as a locus for thought about freedom recalls Patterson's observation that the idea and value of personal freedom in the West first emerged out of the experience of enslaved women in ancient Greece. Moreover, Copeland's discussion of freedom corresponds to the note of personal freedom on Patterson's chord of freedom and the note's emphases on embodiment, community, culture, negative and positive freedom, the moral good, and history. Copeland's most powerful writing in the book focuses on the embodied experience of constraint of enslaved African American women. Indeed, she argues that the realization of freedom in society depends not only on attention to oppressive social relations but also on "cultural perceptions and social (political, economic, technological) responses (affirmation or rejection or indifference) to the physical body."[73] By plumbing the narratives of African American women slaves, Copeland evokes the cultural and social matrix of outrageous violation, contemptuous indifference, and sanctimonious disregard directed for centuries at such women's bodies. She also records the ideas and values of freedom that emerged from such oppression. For these women, the prospect of freedom was for long a dream delayed. When it came—in greater or lesser measure—freedom was certainly valued as autonomy: the sheer capacity for choice, free will, and action (prized values associated with negative freedom). But the testimony of former slaves pointed to a valuation beyond autonomy alone. For such women, the value of freedom lay also in the possibilities of literacy, education, and access to resources (land, capital, etc.) to sustain economic survival.[74] Moreover,

---

72. Copeland, *Enfleshing Freedom*, 3.
73. Copeland, *Enfleshing Freedom*, 8.
74. Copeland, *Enfleshing Freedom*, 40, 47.

freedom from enslavement was "freedom for community and solidarity, for being human together."[75] Copeland does not at length address the topic of the equality of freedom, even if the topic is a constant question running through the background of the book. But the import of her argument points clearly toward where we should look as we consider the fundamental meaning of the equality of freedom—a meaning not to be found in lofty abstraction but in the concrete experiences of constriction of Copeland's women of color and of Patterson's "history of freedom as ordinary men and women have understood it—vague, to be sure, yet intensely held, a value learned in struggle, fear, and hope."[76] I will discuss Copeland's theology of freedom more extensively in the final chapter of the book.

---

75. Copeland, *Enfleshing Freedom*, 49.
76. Patterson, *Freedom*, 2.

CHAPTER THREE

Amartya Sen and Philosophical Complements to Created Freedom

AT THE HEIGHT OF efforts to repeal federal health care reform in 2017, the United States Senate considered the Consumer Freedom Amendment.[1] The proposal fit firmly in line with the neoliberal trend of the last decades; the amendment would allow buyers on the federal exchange to opt out of the insurance pool that included people with preexisting conditions. Doing so, the argument went, would allow buyers without preexisting conditions to pay lower health insurance premiums and to find more fitting, lower-cost insurance packages. Doing so, the argument also affirmed, would be consistent with the logic of freedom: the freedom not to have to pay more for health insurance premiums; the freedom to opt out of insurance pools; the freedom to take care of oneself and one's family apart from an explicit if surely misguided directive of government. Not far from such arguments were ones that tilted even farther into the outer reaches of libertarian logic: that preexisting conditions in themselves were the function of failures of freedom and personal responsibility and that it was therefore unjust to include the responsible and irresponsible in the same insurance pool. US Representative Mo Brooks (R-AL) suggested that people with preexisting conditions should pay more in premiums because they had not "done things the right way."[2]

---

1. For background, see Cunningham, "Health 202."
2. Cohen, "On Health and Welfare."

The amendment failed and federal health care reform was not repealed. But the neoliberal arguments behind the Consumer Freedom Amendment—and, indeed, behind the entire, years-long repeal effort—took center stage again as the preeminent moral language in American public discourse. Invoke "freedom" as it's understood in neoliberal terms, this way of thinking goes, and competing moral goods like health and well-being should rightly fall to the wayside. But this does not have to be the case about either the understanding or the moral status of freedom. In the last chapter, we considered the indispensable importance for Catholic public theology in an American context of situating freedom amid history, culture, and structure (especially as these categories pertain to the American experience of slavery). In this chapter, I would like to shift perspective and ask what public theology can learn from philosophy about the critique and construction of a concept of freedom for the American context. In the background, I am guided by the theological commitments that follow from Rahner's notion of created freedom: that any concept of freedom be embodied, historical, relational, oriented to the good and to God, and liberal. More concretely, I am guided by the arguments of Daniel Rodgers in *Age of Fracture*. There Rodgers says that in the last fifty years, under the pressure especially of abstract microeconomic thought, the notion of freedom in the American context has become "individualized and privatized, released of its larger burdens . . . cut loose from the burdens and responsibilities that had once so closely accompanied it."[3] What Rodgers says here about the distortions of freedom in the last decades could be applied directly to the logic of freedom behind the Consumer Freedom Amendment. Opting out of insurance pools reflects an individualized and privatized notion of freedom released of the burden—and overall social benefit—of sharing fate with the sick. In this chapter, I will turn to the work of Amartya Sen to examine a philosophy of freedom far more compatible with the requirements of created freedom. Such a compatibility adds plausibility to my theological arguments, which can be understood as not only grounded finally in revelation but also rooted in more general constructs of human reason. Moreover, the work of Sen provides a coherent, alternative language of freedom in place of the privatized claims of neoliberalism. In what follows, I will return throughout to the normative importance of health as a crucial social and political good in which to reconsider the meaning of freedom. Finally, I will note not only how the work of Sen is compatible with the claims of created freedom but also how his work challenges such claims, too.

---

3. Rodgers, *Age of Fracture*, 40.

SEN, FREEDOM, AND THE "EQUALITY OF WHAT"

Daniel Rodgers argued that the Age of Fracture prized abstract freedom and devalued equality, whether of result or opportunity.[4] One of the most powerful aspects of Sen's philosophy of freedom is his simultaneous recovery of the ethical richness of both terms: freedom and equality. In what follows in the first section of the chapter, I will focus on Sen's discussion of what he calls the "equality of what." By considering this phrase, we can better understand his argument for the priority of freedom as a measure of justice in society. It is helpful at the outset to note that Sen affirms what he calls an "inescapably plural idea of freedom." By this, he signals his openness and appreciation for a wide range of ideas of freedom. It is also helpful to note that he aligns his own philosophy of freedom with what he calls "realization-based theories of justice" attuned practically to the "lives people can actually live."[5] From the perspective of his realization-based theory, Sen offers a sharp and persuasive critique of the sort of libertarian freedom dominant in American culture in the Age of Fracture and at work in things ranging from the opposition to federal health care reform to the refusal to wear masks in the middle of an airborne viral pandemic. I will take up his critique of libertarian thought at the end of this opening section of the chapter. First, however, I would like to review Sen's arguments for the significance of equality as a measure of social ethics and for the preeminence of freedom as a measure of justice.

Equality of What?

Catholic public theology can learn a great deal from Sen's highly detailed and profound discussion of the equality of freedom. It will first be helpful to consider how he understands the normative nature of the concept of equality itself.[6] And crucial to his understanding of this aspect of equality is his insistence on the ways in which equality is not a purely formal concept. In order to make his case for this insistence, he appeals to two crucial empirical facts—that the idea of equality is present in any lasting theory of justice and that human diversity is the fundamental context amid which the concept of equality must be considered. By appealing to these facts, Sen not only

---

4. Rodgers, *Age of Fracture*, 190.
5. Sen, *Idea of Justice*, 18–19, 303.
6. At the root of Sen's normative conception of equality is the basic idea that "equality is judged by comparing some particular aspect of a person . . . with the same aspect of another person." Sen, *Inequality Reexamined*, 2.

underscores the concrete character of equality; he also shows how the value of equality has practical, moral significance.

In the first place, then, Sen sees the normative requirements of equality in light of the de facto role of equality in all successful social and political theories: "Every normative theory of social arrangement that has at all stood the test of time seems to demand equality of *something*—something that is regarded as particularly important in that theory."[7] In each such instance, this normative presence of equality requires an equal concern for all on the basis of a value regarded as preeminently important.[8] That some concept of equality has figured in these successful theories, Sen argues, is not perhaps (and Sen is tentative in this assertion) due to such formal requirements as "logical necessity" or the inherent role of equality in the "discipline of the language of morals."[9] Rather, he links the de facto presence of equality in these social theories to a normative requirement of "ethical plausibility." It is simply the case, Sen says, that the credibility—and, hence, plausibility—of such theories requires an impartial appeal to and an equal concern for each person.[10]

As we shall see later, Sen does have a conception of the person constituted by reason, desire, and an orientation to value.[11] And he affirms that "basic ideas of justice are not alien to human beings" and that the moral appeal to impartiality is "a formalization of an informal—and pervasive—idea that occurs to most of us."[12] There is an implicit appeal to such conceptions of the person and justice in his case for the ethical requirement of equality. But this is only an implicit—not explicit—appeal. And, in any event, these conceptions of the person and justice are not of enough detail to make precisely apparent why impartiality and equality might be required on the basis of inherent human characteristics. More important to Sen than the formality of such an appeal to inherent characteristics is the empirical fact that lasting ethical theories simply have equality as a condition of their success.

---

7. Sen, *Inequality Reexamined*, 12.

8. Sen, *Inequality Reexamined*, xi.

9. Sen, *Inequality Reexamined*, 3, 17. Sen takes issue, for instance, with the arguments of R. M. Hare that strictly formal reasons require equal concern for all in social and political theories. See Hare, *Language of Morals*; Hare, *Freedom and Reason*.

10. Sen, *Inequality Reexamined*, 16–19.

11. See, for instance, Sen, "Well-Being."

12. Sen, *Development as Freedom*, 262. Sen carefully qualifies this appeal to justice and impartiality: "In examining the possible role of values and norms in individual behavior, it is not my intention to argue that most people are moved more by their sense of justice than by their prudential and material concerns. . . . It is a question of having a balance in our behavioral assumptions." Sen, *Development as Freedom*, 180. See DeCosse, Review of *Development as Freedom*.

This brings us to a second key empirical fact: the deep human diversity that is the necessary context for considering the concept of equality. In a sense, for Sen it is more important to draw out the moral implications for equality from the concrete world of people's differences than to derive normative conclusions for equality from the formal realm of what people share in common. In fact, for Sen, it could be said that what people share in common is a constitution profoundly disposed to differences of experience. These differences arise because of the great diversity of each person's internal characteristics and external circumstances. It is these differences that are the central fact that figures in the social assessment of equality. As Sen puts it:

> Investigations of equality—theoretical as well as practical—that proceed with the assumption of antecedent uniformity (including the presumption that "all men are created equal") thus miss out on a major aspect of the problem. Human diversity is no secondary complication (to be ignored, or to be introduced "later on"); it is a fundamental aspect of our interest in equality.[13]

More to the point, Sen argues that the moral consequences of relying on the formal rhetoric of the "equality of man"—insofar as this ignores interpersonal variations—can be "deeply inegalitarian" by hiding the "fact that equal consideration for all may demand very unequal treatment in favor of the disadvantaged."[14]

Equality, then, is not an "empty concept," Sen says. It derives moral power from its link to impartiality. It can only be understood in light of a world of concrete differences. Moreover, it has practical, moral force and can be an "exacting demand" on patterns of social and political distribution.[15] In terms of this practical role of equality amid the play of values of distributive justice, the crucial question to ask is, "equality of what?" This question recognizes the integral and practical role of equality in any successful theory of justice. The question also calls attention to what Sen calls the "base" or "space" or "value"—for instance, freedom, merit, incomes, utilities, etc.—that is to be the object of equal concern in any such theory.[16]

13. Sen, *Inequality Reexamined*, xi.
14. Sen, *Inequality Reexamined*, 1.
15. Sen, *Inequality Reexamined*, 24.
16. In Sen's usage, "base," "space," and "value" are linked but not synonymous. The "base" is the primary value by which a distribution is assessed. In other words, a "basal equality" in terms of income would be a distribution assessed according to a measurement of income. "Space" refers to any chosen value from income to freedom and so forth. In that sense, it is like "base" insofar as it refers to one of these key values. However, "space" does not refer specifically—as does "base"—to the fundamental framework or base of a particular distribution. Often, Sen uses the term "focal variable" as a synonym

Each such space is the "what" that answers the question "equality of what?," and is the "exacting" measure by which a distribution can be assessed.

Sen's Criticisms of Distributive Theories of Equality

Why should Catholic public theology seek to recover the language of freedom in a social ethic for the American context? And how can the language of freedom itself be recovered from the abstraction and hyper-individualism identified by Rodgers in *Age of Fracture*? To help answer these questions, I would next like to review Sen's critiques of distributive theories of equality. In each such critique, his concerns for abstraction mirror concerns articulated by Rodgers and point the way toward a concrete philosophy of freedom far more adequate to the American context (and far more consistent with the commitments that follow from the theological basis of created freedom).

Sen divides theories of justice into "outcome types" and "opportunity types" (or, analogously, "achievement" theories and "freedom" theories).[17] Outcome types are centered on values like income and utility. In these the assessment of justice is based on a measurable—often quantifiable—result or consequence of action. Opportunity types include theories founded on such values as primary goods, resources, rights, and freedom. These theories rest not so much on measurable results of action as on the absence of barriers to action itself and on the role of primary goods or resources in the creation of possibilities for action. I will first focus on outcome types and then on opportunity type theories; the progression from the former to the latter conforms to Sen's assessment of less just to more just theories.

---

for "space." The word "value," for Sen, has a more general reference than either "base" or "space." "Value" refers to income or freedom or utility or the like: in other words, to any norm or measure by which a distribution can be measured. "Value" also, however, has a wider philosophical scope and is often used by Sen to refer to things of inherent importance. A further note: It is important in reading Sen to keep in mind that he writes as both an economist and a moral philosopher (not that he'd very widely separate those tasks himself). Hence, he frequently uses terms that have quantitative meaning—for example, "space" and "set" and "value"—and considers how such terms have philosophical bearing. As we shall see, for Sen the fact that a so-called philosophical space like freedom can yield numerical data by which to assess a distribution is an essential aspect of his approach to both economics and philosophy. See Sen, *Inequality Reexamined*, 1–11.

17. Sen, *Inequality Reexamined*, 73–74.

Income as the Basis of Equality[18]

The widespread use of income as a measure of one's position in a social arrangement, Sen says, makes obviously good sense.[19] Income is the crucial means for determining how well one can live. Moreover, income statistics are more available than many other measurements of social well-being.[20] Still, Sen argues, such statistics are inherently limited. This is apparent, for instance, in assessing the deprivation of women in the developing world. Income data provide a less accurate picture of these women's disadvantage than data on rates of mortality and morbidity. The limits of income data also become clear in comparing the developed and undeveloped world. For instance, the per capita income in the United States far exceeds that of Costa Rica. However, life expectancy in Costa Rica is the same as that in the US.[21] Even within the US, comparisons of income reveal important but limited aspects of questions of justice and equality. Writing in the 1990s, Sen pointed out that African American men between thirty-five and fifty-five had two to three times the mortality rate of white men of the same age. However, only half of this difference can be explained by the lower income of the African Americans.[22] More recently, Angus Deaton and Anne Case have shown a dramatic reversal in mortality data pertaining to middle-aged non-Hispanic white men in the United States—data that draws on income and health and social factors. Deaton and Case in particular note between 1999 and 2013 the singular rise in "deaths by despair" (via suicide, alcoholism, opioids, etc.) among American middle-aged white men with no more than a high school degree. Where in 1999, the mortality rate of this population group was 30 percent lower than a similar population group of African American men, by 2013 the mortality rate of the middle-aged white men was 30 percent higher than that of middle-aged African American men.[23] In such dramatic swings, income surely plays an outsized role. But clearly so does culture, health, family, religion, structural factors, education, and more.

18. The use of income as a focal variable for equality has close links with the use of utilitarianism for the same purpose: Income is often understood in part as a metric of utility. I will distinguish the two by confining the discussion of income to numerical or commodity amounts and utilitarianism to distinctly philosophical norms like desire and satisfaction.

19. Although the focal variables of income and commodities are obviously distinct, they are also closely related. In this discussion of income, I will at times refer to the commodities approach to equality.

20. Sen, *Inequality Reexamined*, 102–14.

21. Sen, *Inequality Reexamined*, 122–25.

22. Sen, *Inequality Reexamined*, 114.

23. Case and Deaton, "Rising Morbidity and Mortality"; Case and Deaton, "Mortality and Morbidity."

Real income theory depends on the concepts of preferences and choice—on the idea that what people share in common is a calculus for choosing bundles of commodities on the basis of preferences derived primarily from monetary value alone. Often, however, little distinction is made between preference and choice; the latter is made a function of the former.[24] Within the scope of this theory, there are few if any other assumptions about common interpersonal traits. As Sen sees it, this wholly instrumental view of preference and choice says little about the actual lives people lead and the choices they have. Also, the notion of preferences is handicapped by its inability to ground substantive interpersonal comparisons amid the reality of human diversity. Common norms like needs or rights cannot be accommodated by the theory.

Moreover, one commodity bundle is assumed improbably to yield the same level of value to a wide range of different persons who are differently situated. Sen notes the following factors of diversity that affect how income contributes to the evaluation of equality. In the first place, there is the extensive range of internal or personal heterogeneities. Those include differences in motive, desire, courage, and other mental or emotional states that affect how a person uses income. They also include the personal differences of age, disability, sickness, gender, and racial or ethnic identity; the physical limits or cultural attitudes or structural arrangements linked to each of these categories influence what each person is able to derive from an income. Moreover, Sen points out, the distribution of income is often measured in terms of distribution within families. And within families, he notes, there are often unequal patterns of distribution tied to attitudes, for instance, about amounts of income needed or deserved by sons or daughters. There are also external conditions that profoundly affect what can be done with an income. These include environmental factors (pollution, rainfall, etc.); social conditions (crime, education, housing, etc.); and circumstances of health (presence of infectious diseases, quality of health care, etc.). Furthermore, the use of income is also contingent on the intangible issue of what amount of money in a particular community is considered enough to buy the commodities understood in that community to be indispensable for the maintenance of self-respect.[25]

For Sen, then, incomes are a necessary but not sufficient aspect of the evaluation of equality. Their accuracy is limited in the specification of poverty and justice. In fact, Sen says, getting outside the income space forces

---

24. See Sen's discussion of this point with regard to the possibility of a Paretian liberal in social choice theory in Sen, "Liberty as Control: An Appraisal," 209.

25. Sen, *Development as Freedom*, 67–72.

one into an inevitable consideration of the wide range of information and values at play in the assessment of justice and equality.[26] Moreover, the limited normative nature of income is made apparent by the fact of profound internal and external human diversity. Who is more disadvantaged, Sen asks, the person with less income and good health or the person with more income but with a serious illness that makes it difficult to put that greater income to use?[27] Attention to such diverse factors is not an afterthought, Sen insists, but rather the starting point of social assessment without which fundamental human equality cannot be determined. Income at best, then, is a derivative value dependent on many personal, social, and natural circumstances. Moreover, the importance of an income depends on a person's actual choices and actions amid these diverse circumstances. Much of Sen's critique of a singular reliance on income as a measure of justice stands in line with Daniel Rodgers's critique of notions of choice and freedom in the formal abstractions of economic thought in the Age of Fracture.

Sen's Criticism of Utilitarian Equality

The classic utilitarian formula, Sen says, requires "judging every choice by the sum total of utilities generated through that choice."[28] There are three key components to this formula. The first component is consequentialism, which requires that all choices be judged by their results. The second component is welfarism or the restriction that assessments of states of affairs must be made in light of the utilities in the respective states of affairs. Thus welfarism bars direct attention to concerns like the fulfillment or violation of rights; these concerns are relevant to assessments of justice and equality only in terms of the utilities they generate. The third component of the utilitarian formula is sum-ranking. According to this component, utilitarian justice requires that all individual utilities be summed up into one aggregate total. In turn, the size of this total indicates the achievement of justice—regardless of how the utilities are distributed. There are also different kinds of utilitarianism. Some, for example, favor the welfarist component over the consequentialist component. Others use different standards of utility itself.

For Sen, income was limited as a metric of equality and justice because it said little about the problem of what people can, in fact, do with an income. Utilitarianism offers a more appealing but still inadequate norm

---

26. Sen, *Development as Freedom*, 110.
27. Sen, *Inequality Reexamined*, 102–5.
28. The discussion in this section is taken from Sen, *Development as Freedom*, 58–63; Sen, "Equality of What?"; Crocker, "Functioning and Capability," 599–602.

of equality. Positively, utilitarianism requires that attention be paid to consequences—a key factor for Sen in the assessment of equality. Utilitarianism also, Sen says appreciatively, insists on the importance of human well-being "rather than looking only at some abstract and alienated characteristics of states of affairs."[29] But utilitarianism's faults as a standard of equality outweigh its merits. With many other critics, Sen criticizes its "distributional indifference": adding and averaging all utilities yields a notion of equal total utility that cannot account for the extent of inequality between the high and low end of a distribution. Sen also, as with others, argues that utilitarianism neglects the intrinsic importance of norms like rights.

But I would like to focus on his analysis of the inadequacy of the norm of utility itself as a measure of equality. Utilitarianism may have called attention to the importance of well-being in ways that other theories of justice have not. But, even so, utilitarianism's standards of well-being have failed to provide the basis for interpersonal comparisons and, hence, for the assessment of equality. In the essay, "Well-Being, Agency, and Freedom," Sen asks in what sense utility can be considered well-being.[30] He examines three ways—choice, happiness, and desire—all of which fail as adequate norms due to neglect of personal and interpersonal realities. Utility understood as choice fails as a measure of well-being because choice per se is an empty notion. Choice is too abstract to serve as a useful basis for interpersonal comparisons. It fails to account for motives beyond choice itself. For example, it does not distinguish between choice on behalf of taste, well-being, obligation, or values. The abstraction of choice is a common feature of the Age of Fracture.

Utility as happiness fails as a definition of well-being because it considers happiness as only a mental state. On the one hand, this focus on a mental state alone involves what Sen calls "physical condition neglect." Due to this neglect, utilitarianism as happiness ignores conditions like starvation as integral to the issue of well-being. Such conditions only enter the category of well-being insofar as they are "indirectly covered by mental attitudes of happiness or desire."[31] Utility as a mental state of happiness also fails as a measure of well-being because of what Sen calls "valuation neglect." There are other mental states than happiness crucial to well-being—chief among them the whole realm of moral values.

Sen's analysis of the inadequacy of assessing well-being in terms of the utility of desire evokes in greater depths the issues raised by the inadequacy of utility as choice or happiness. In the first place, Sen notes, too

---

29. Sen, *Development as Freedom*, 61.
30. The following discussion is taken from Sen, "Well-Being," 186–93.
31. Sen, *Commodities and Capabilities*, 13.

many utilitarian theories ask what one *would* desire in unspecified circumstances. But it is impossible, he adds, to know the nature of desire apart from attention to what is *in fact* desired in particular circumstance. Second, Sen says, desire is only evidential—a second-order piece of information signaling something that is already valued but not indicating the factors that determined the degree of desire in the first place. Third, the comparative intensity of desire fails as an interpersonal metric because such intensities are influenced by many arbitrary and contingent circumstances. Lastly, desires reflect "compromises with reality" and easily adapt to keep in line with one's predicaments. In a moving passage, Sen writes:

> Desires reflect compromises with reality, and reality is harsher to some than to others. The hopeless destitute desiring merely to survive, the landless laborer concentrating his efforts on securing the next meal, the round-the-clock domestic servant seeking a few hours of respite, the subjugated housewife struggling for a little individuality, may all have learned to keep their desires in line with their respective predicaments. Their deprivations are gagged and muffled in the interpersonal metric of desire fulfillment. In some lives small mercies have to count big.[32]

Utilitarianism, then, fails as a metric of equality because of its distributional indifference and its neglect of intrinsic concerns like rights. Moreover, utilitarianism is unable to engage such distributional and intrinsic concerns because it neglects the physical and valuational conditions that are given aspects of human life and that affect persons' desires and their positions in the social structure.

Sen and the Rawlsian Equality of Primary Goods

For Sen, the role of an equality of freedom in John Rawls's moral and political philosophy represents a decisive, if flawed, improvement over the egalitarian possibilities of utilitarianism. At the least, Rawls in his first principle of justice puts equal liberties at the core of his philosophy.[33] Utilitarianism, on the other hand, relegates freedom to secondary status behind the

---

32. Sen, "Well-Being," 190–91.

33. The first principle of justice reads, "Each person has an equal right to a fully adequate scheme of equal basic liberties with a similar scheme of liberties for all." Rawls, *Political Liberalism*, 291. Rawls articulated his two principles of justice—the priority of liberty and the difference principle—in *A Theory of Justice* and the revised the principles in subsequent works. This chapter will draw primarily on the principles as they appear in *Political Liberalism*.

primary claims of a metric of utility. Thus Sen sees Rawls as having moved the discussion of equality in a more fruitful direction—from an "outcome" of utility to an "opportunity" for achievement. However, Sen also sees Rawls as not having moved the discussion far enough. Rawls may put equal liberties at the center of his philosophy. But he does so while also understanding freedom as at best a means—if the preeminent one—but not as an end in itself. And it is this latter substantive view of freedom that for Sen provides the best basis for egalitarian justice.

Sen bases his criticism of Rawls's egalitarian notions on the latter's use of primary goods as means to action. Rawls says primary goods are

> things which it is supposed a rational man wants whatever else he wants. . . . With more of these goods men can generally be assured of greater success in carrying out their intentions and in advancing their ends, whatever these ends may be. The primary social goods, to give them in broad categories, are rights and liberties, opportunities and powers, income and wealth.[34]

Throughout his writing, Rawls held to the "priority of liberty" or to the requirement that the primary goods of the liberties have a pre-eminent value relative to all other primary goods. In other words, the first principle of justice must be fulfilled before the second principle of justice—the difference principle—can be invoked.[35] Thus all persons must have an equal share in the basic political and civil liberties. But primary goods other than these basic liberties—for example, income and wealth—need not be held equally so long as any inequality in such holdings is to the "greatest benefit" of the least advantaged.[36]

---

34. Rawls, *Theory of Justice*, 92.

35. The second principle of justice reads, "Social and economic inequalities are to satisfy two conditions. First, they must be attached to offices and positions open to all under conditions of fair equality of opportunity; and second, they must be to the greatest benefit of the least advantaged members of society." Rawls, *Political Liberalism*, 291.

36. Rawls's account of the priority of liberty has changed in the course of his work. Especially in response to the criticism of H. L. A. Hart, Rawls has more clearly specified the grounds for this priority. See Hart, "Rawls and Liberty." And see Rawls's response to Hart in *Political Liberalism*, 289–324. Rawls also has weakened the condition of liberty as set forth in the first principle of justice. For example, in *Theory of Justice* in 1971, the first principle of justice required the "most extensive total system" of liberty. In *Political Liberalism* in 1993, the phrase "most extensive total system" is replaced by the phrase "a fully adequate scheme of equal basic liberties." See Rawls, *Theory of Justice*, 60, 250, 302; Rawls, *Political Liberalism*, 291; and Sen's discussion of Rawls's later, weaker condition of liberty in Sen, *Inequality Reexamined*, 75.

Sen, a liberal, in fact accepts to some extent Rawls's classically liberal notion of a priority of the political and civil liberties.[37] But Sen disputes the overall adequacy of the notion of primary goods—whether of the primary goods of liberties or of something else. What Sen sees as the flaw in Rawls's idea of liberty—that it is at most a means—is what Sen sees as the flaw in the rest of the primary goods—that they are "fetishist" or at most instrumental means for each person's achievement of the good. This focus on instrumental goods alone, Sen says, would be adequate as a measure of equality if one were to work—as Sen says Rawls does—from a fundamental assumption of human similarity. But one must start the assessment of equality from the assumption of diversity—of people with "very different needs varying with health, longevity, climactic conditions, location, work conditions, temperament, and even body size. . . . So what is involved is not merely ignoring a few hard cases, but overlooking very widespread and real differences. Judging advantage purely in terms of primary goods leads to a partially blind morality."[38]

By beginning with the assumption of diversity, Sen says, it is possible to see the great variety in how people are able to convert or use primary goods in choosing to live a particular life. In fact, he notes, an equality of primary goods can co-exist with and cover up serious inequalities. The thrust of Sen's criticism here is similar to his criticisms of the role of real income theory and utilitarianism in establishing equality. For instance, a person with a disability may have more primary goods—for example, more income—but less possibility than those with less income to live a full life. Moreover, the picture of poverty often cannot be conveyed by an amount of primary goods alone. What is necessary is attention to characteristics like age, disability, and disease-proneness that provide the context for the conversion of primary goods into actual choices on behalf of ends.[39]

For the determination of equality, then, it is not enough to focus on primary goods alone—whether the primary good of liberty or of something else. Rather, Sen says, equality can be determined only in terms of a relation between goods and persons—between goods held and the capacity to use them in pursuit of ends.[40] Rawls's conception of justice is concerned with "inter-end variations." Primary goods provide the common index of instrumental means for pursuing a variety of ends that are irreducible to one

---

37. See Sen, *Development as Freedom*, 63–67. I will discuss this later in the chapter.

38. Sen, "Equality of What?," 215–16. It is important to note that Rawls responds to Sen's criticism here by conjecturing that variables in physical capacities of citizens can be accounted for by legislative action that devises an equitable index of primary goods for the disadvantaged. See Rawls, *Political Liberalism*, 178–87.

39. Sen, *Inequality Reexamined*, 81.

40. Sen, "Equality of What?," 216; Sen, "Justice: Means versus Freedoms," 115.

theory of the good. But, Sen argues, Rawls's theory of justice fails to account for "inter-individual" variations—for the real, textured individuals who in fact use goods to pursue these ends. Equality, then, cannot only pertain to each person's freedom understood as the absence of obstacles in the pursuit of one's ends. Rather, a just distributive measure of equality must account both for the unencumbered pursuit of ends and for the power—whether emotional, physical, political, etc.—to undertake this pursuit.[41]

Sen's criticism of Rawls with regard to inter-end and inter-individual variations of freedom has similarities to Norman Daniels's noted criticism of Rawls's distinction between liberty and the "worth of liberty."[42] In *A Theory of Justice*, Rawls says of liberty: "Therefore I shall simply assume that liberty can always be explained by a reference to three items: the agents who are free, the restrictions or limitations which they are free from, and what it is they are free to do or not to do." He also notes: "Thus persons are at liberty to do something when they are free from certain constraints either to do it or not to do it and when their doing it or not doing it is protected from interference by other persons."[43] This definition, then, provides a basis for Rawls's notion of an equality of the civil and political liberties. This definition of a negative liberty also, however, excludes the notion of an inability to exercise liberty. This notion, Rawls says, is not constitutive of the definition of liberty but is pertinent instead to what he calls liberty's "worth." As he puts it:

> The inability to take advantage of one's rights and opportunities as a result of poverty or ignorance, and a lack of means generally, is sometimes counted among the constraints definitive of liberty. I shall not, however, say this, but rather I shall think of these things as affecting the worth of liberty, the value to individuals of the rights that the first principle defines.[44]

Daniels calls this distinction between liberty and its worth "arbitrary." He says that Rawls's distinction neglects the obvious empirical links between the unequal political power and freedom derived from the unequal possession of wealth and income, which in turn is derived from a condition of legal equal liberty. "Is it useful to be able to say," Daniels asks, "my liberty is equal to

41. Sen, *Inequality Reexamined*, 85.
42. Daniels, "Equal Liberty."
43. For both citations, see Rawls, *Theory of Justice*, 202.
44. Rawls, *Theory of Justice*, 204. In *Political Liberalism*, Rawls describes the worth of liberty as referring to the "usefulness to the persons of their liberties." Rawls also says in this latter work that the distinction between liberty and the worth of liberty is "merely a definition and settles no substantive question." Rawls, *Political Liberalism*, 326.

Rockefeller's, but I cannot exercise 'it' equally?"[45] Daniels's criticism of Rawls is in line with Sen's insofar as it questions sharply the exclusion of the ability to act from the definition of liberty. However, Sen, as we shall see, allows more than does Daniels for freedom itself to be defined by internal emotional and bodily characteristics as well as by a wide range of external forces.

Sen and Libertarian Equality

Libertarian theories of justice (which track closely with neoliberal theories of justice) assume an equality of liberty to be the fundamental distributive norm by which to measure human equality. Sen's misgivings with such notions of equality are evident already in his criticism of Rawlsian equal liberty.[46] Many libertarian notions of liberty are only instrumental and as such have the same liabilities as does Rawlsian liberty—for instance, the failure to account for actual, diverse possibilities of action. But libertarian equality is without the protective range of concerns represented by Rawls's primary goods. Moreover, there is usually little beyond the requirements of efficiency—and certainly nothing like Rawls's difference principle—that exerts some aggregate, equalizing influence on the unequal distributive effects of the libertarian priority of liberty. This singular libertarian focus on liberty is an especially sharp focus of Sen's criticism.

More so than in his discussion of Rawls, Sen in his criticism of libertarianism deals explicitly with the shortcomings of the notion of a purely negative liberty—the notion at the heart of libertarian equal liberty.[47] Sen criticizes negative liberty on several grounds. Two of these grounds—the "rights-based" and "procedural" perspectives—he shares with other critics of libertarianism. Two other critical perspectives are distinctly Sen's; he calls these grounds of criticism the perspectives of "control" and "constraint." All of these terms refer to different aspects of the same problem of negative liberty. All of these aspects, Sen says, are in some problematic way "formal" and

---

45. Daniels, "Equal Liberty," 259. See Rawls's articulation of what he calls the "Fair value" of the political liberties in response to Daniels's criticism in Rawls, *Political Liberalism*, 324–31.

46. The work of Robert Nozick is the principal target of Sen's criticisms of libertarian liberty. See Nozick, *Anarchy*; Nozick, *Examined Life*. Sen's criticism of libertarian theories of equality is just the focus of such essays as "The Moral Standing of the Market"; "Freedom of Choice: Concept and Content"; "Liberty and Social Choice"; "Liberty as Control"; and "Rights and Agency."

47. It is important to recall here that Sen, a liberal, does not reject negative liberty outright.

"idealized." Specifically, each in some fashion fails to account for the nature of power, the role of consequences, and the fact of human interdependence.

I have already noted Sen's general criticism of the concept of negative liberty: that the negative liberty to perform an act is formal or empty if a person is without the power in fact to act. In saying this, he affirms the link between negative and positive freedom.[48] Sen also argues that libertarian notions of exclusively "rights-based" or "procedural" negative liberty correspond to an equality of freedom understood only as clearly demarcated zones of noninterference. Thus more complex questions of power are excluded as issues of moral concern. Moreover, the sole normative focus on negative liberty blocks the consideration of outcomes or consequences. The profound injustice of such a view, Sen says, is made manifest in famines:

> In fact, it is easy to show that, with a system of rights justified independently of consequences, it is possible to have disasters of this kind occurring without anyone violating anyone else's rights at all. The contingency of ownership, as well as influences that determine transfers and terms of trade, can easily lead a particular occupation group into absolute deprivation, destitution, and decimation, without anything illegitimate and perverse having happened from a rights' perspective.[49]

Sen also argues that a pure rights-based view of negative liberty is incoherent due to its neglect of positive freedom and what he calls "multilateral interdependences." The negative view of liberty insists on noninterference and often requires the positive, active defense of this noninterference in the face of the inevitable conflict of rights arising from the fact of human interdependence. But the focus on freedom as only an absence of external constraints does not provide the conceptual justification for the positive freedom required for an active defense of non-interference.[50] Moreover, due to interdependence, it may be the case that the only way to stop the violation of the liberty of one person is by violating the liberty of another. But the justification for doing so requires the consequential trading off of one "bad" action versus another "worse" action. And a sole distributive principle of equal negative liberty does not allow for such a prudential balancing of claims.[51]

---

48. See also Sen, "Freedom of Choice," 272–76.

49. Sen, "Moral Standing of the Market," 6. Sen has written extensively on the economic, political, and social aspects of famines. His chief work on the subject is *Poverty and Famines*. For a more recent treatment by him, see Sen, *Development as Freedom*, 160–84.

50. Sen, "Freedom of Choice," 274.

51. Sen, "Rights and Agency," 6–7.

Sen also criticizes negative liberty in terms of what he has called the idea of liberty as "control."[52] There are three ways to view personal liberty, Sen says: as power, control, and constraints on others. Liberty as "power," he says, refers to the "*power* that the person has over decisions in certain personal spheres." Sen understands this as either the power that one exercises oneself or the power exercised collectively by others on one's behalf. In other words, it is whatever power one has whether one exercises it oneself or not.[53] Liberty as "control" refers to "the extent of the control that [a person] has over decisions in certain specified spheres." This means that one is free only to the extent that one personally exercises levers of power. The "constraint" view of liberty is an offshoot of the control view. It, too, is concerned with power wielded by oneself. But, more specifically, this view refers to the "*constraints* imposed on *others*, stopping them from reducing a person's control." As Sen sees it, libertarian notions of liberty are based on the notion of liberty as control and use the notion of liberty as constraint in order to protect liberty as control.

But there are two problems with this libertarian point of view; both problems signal the excessively formal nature of libertarian freedom. The first problem is the singular identification of liberty with control. In fact, Sen says, the control notion of liberty does not exhaust the scope of freedom. One can have freedom as power without having immediate control and personally exercising that power. The dynamics of modern social structures and interdependence frequently mandate that issues of freedom pertain to matters beyond one's immediate personal power. Thus, for instance, Sen says that it is not possible to control all factors that affect one's morbidity in the face of epidemics. But that impossibility of complete control does not eliminate all issues of freedom at stake in avoiding epidemics. The second problem with this libertarian view is the close link between control and constraint—with the latter understood as constraints on others from reducing a person's control. Thus liberty as control is only violated when another person violates one's own immediate sphere of control. But if liberty is only violated in such cases, then liberty is not violated when one loses control due to either internal factors or external causes not involving another person's violation of one's sphere of control.

---

52. This discussion is taken from Sen, "Liberty as Control," 207–8, 215–18.

53. In later writings, Sen uses the term "effective freedom" instead of "freedom as power." The word "effective," he says, more clearly conveys the sense of freedom as not simply power but power exercised successfully by oneself or others on one's behalf. I will discuss more later the meaning of effective freedom. See Sen, *Inequality Reexamined*, 64–66, especially 65n13.

The "Procedural Priority" of Negative Freedom

It will next be helpful to consider more closely Sen's position on negative freedom beyond his criticism of the libertarian reliance on negative freedom. After all, such an understanding of freedom provides the basis for Sen's identification as a liberal. But such an understanding is also at the basis of the libertarianism that he sharply critiques. How does he distinguish his view of negative freedom from libertarianism? And on what basis, at least in terms of negative freedom, does he call himself a liberal? The key is his connection of negative and positive freedom.

For Sen, positive freedom is freedom in its most comprehensive sense—a sense which includes negative freedom. One critic said of Sen's thought: "Freedom in the comprehensive, positive sense is not merely—as in negative freedom—'the absence of restraints that one may exercise over another (or the state or other institutions may exercise over individuals).' Positive freedom includes the absence of other kinds of restraints, such as poverty and ignorance, and the presence of genuine options."[54] Sen, then, accords conceptual priority to positive freedom—to the fundamental capability to live. He places negative freedom within this fundamental conceptual framework. In doing so, he breaks with the libertarian and Rawlsian positions that see negative liberty as a bulwark against external constraint but not as part of a larger moral context.

But within this framework, negative freedom for Sen has special normative status: "The importance of the *over-all* freedom to achieve cannot eliminate the special significance of *negative* freedom."[55] This significance is derived in part from the importance that Sen gives to the notion of liberty as an inviolable personal domain; such negative liberty is in fact of inherent value and cannot be subsumed entirely by the concept of positive freedom.[56] The inherent value of negative freedom is attached to liberty understood in procedural terms.[57] It is in light of this inherent value that Sen says the "violation of [negative] liberty is a procedural transgression that we have reason to resist as a bad thing in itself."[58]

Indeed, the significance of negative liberty is especially derived from what Sen regards as its preeminent instrumental role in the activation especially of political freedoms which in turn disproportionately affect many

---

54. Crocker, "Functioning and Capability," 596, quoting from Sen, "Individual Freedom as a Social Commitment."

55. Sen, *Inequality Reexamined*, 87.

56. Sen, *Inequality Reexamined*, 87.

57. Sen, *Development as Freedom*, 17.

58. Sen, *Development as Freedom*, 65.

other freedoms. On this basis, Sen argues that there is no basic dichotomy between political freedoms and economic needs. In fact, he says, the "intensity of economic need *adds* to—rather than subtracts from—the urgency of political freedoms."[59] Such freedoms play an indispensable, instrumental role by allowing those in need to press their claims before the public. Moreover, these freedoms serve the constructive purpose of permitting through public argument and political deliberation "the conceptualization of 'needs' (including the understanding of 'economic needs' in a social context)."[60] On the basis, then, of both its inherent and instrumental characteristics, negative liberty has what Sen calls "procedural priority."[61]

Liberty as Control and Effective Freedom

One other aspect of Sen's understanding of negative freedom is important to note: how he situates negative freedom within an inescapable social context. We can see the implications of this in the contrast he draws between "liberty as control" and what he calls "effective freedom."[62] I referred briefly to this distinction in the discussion of the shortcomings of libertarian freedom. Sen argues that the libertarian notion of liberty as control wrongly assumes that freedom is only a function of whether a person herself exercises control over a process of choice. But this notion of liberty fails to account for the issues of freedom at stake in situations over which one does not exercise entire control. These are instances of "effective freedom." In other words, what matters in terms of freedom is not only that an individual pulls levers herself as that levers are also effectively pulled on her behalf. Sen often refers to the "counterfactual" basis of effective freedom. "Being able to live," he says, "as one would value, desire and choose *is* a contribution to one's freedom."[63] Thus living in a situation without a pandemic is an instance of having

---

59. Sen, *Development as Freedom*, 148.
60. Sen, *Development as Freedom*, 147–48.
61. Sen, *Development as Freedom*, 65. In *The Idea of Justice*, Sen says: "Why must any violation of liberty, significant as it is, invariably be judged to be more crucial for a person—or for a society—than suffering from intense hunger, starvation, epidemics and other calamities ... we have to distinguish between giving some priority to liberty ... *and* the 'extremist' demand of placing a *lexicographic* priority on liberty, treating the slightest gain of liberty, no matter how small—as enough reason to make huge sacrifices in other amenities of a good life—no matter how large" (300).
62. Sen, "Well-Being," 209.
63. Sen, *Inequality Reexamined*, 68; for following discussion, see Sen, *Inequality Reexamined*, 64–69; Sen, "Liberty and Social Choice," 18–20; Sen, "Well-Being," 208–12; Sen, "Rights and Agency," 15.

effective freedom. One lives as one would will to live—i.e., without disease—even if one may be radically limited in what one can do oneself to ward off the disease at issue in the epidemic. Thus the success of pandemic prevention does not depend so much on oneself—on the levers one controls—as much as on the actions taken, for instance, by government agencies that aim to block the spread of disease. One has effective freedom from the pandemic because of the successful actions of these government agencies.

The issues involved in this discussion of effective freedom point to Sen's constant concern to link outcomes and freedom. In other words, Sen holds that it is possible to infer the existence of freedom from data on well-being. For instance, strong public health measures to prevent a pandemic enhance well-being by diminishing the presence of disease. And the absence of disease per se indicates some measure of freedom. Thus the libertarian presumption that the value of liberty or rights is consequence-independent fails. A person's overall freedom can in fact be morally assessed by attention to the "realized states" represented by fundamental economic, social, and political indicators. Liberty as control cannot account for the moral importance of such outcomes. Effective freedom can.

It will be helpful to consider the Consumer Freedom Amendment from the 2017 effort to repeal federal health care reform in the United State Senate (and which was discussed at the start of the chapter) in light of Sen's critique of libertarianism. His threefold categories of power, consequences, and interdependence are especially relevant. First, the provision in the amendment that would allow the healthy to opt out of the insurance pool with the sick represents what Sen calls liberty as control. The amendment would return the levers of power to the one opting out; participation in the insurance pools would no longer be compelled by government directive but would be the result of individual choice. But the effective freedom, to use another term of Sen's, would be diminished for the one opting out. The option to buy a bare-bones insurance policy instead of the more complete policy available in the insurance pool would leave the one opting out more vulnerable to the inner contingencies of disease and to the outer mishaps of ill fortune. Moreover, the one opting out would be doing so at the expense of significant potential consequences. By opting out, one increases the likelihood of the insurance pool failing. Such pools rely economically on the shared, pooled risk of the healthy and the sick. Moreover, the person opting out also would do so in effect by taking on the likely possibility of freeloading on the health care system in the event of becoming unexpectedly sick or injured in a way that demands care beyond the coverage available in his or her bare-bones plan. The nearest emergency room, supported not by his or her bare-bones premiums but by community resources, would become the freeloading refuge of the rugged individualist who opts out. And that likely fate would be the fruit of a failed understanding of interdependence manifest especially in a diminished sense of a shared fate. The one opting out wrongly assumes that he or she can be spared the same possibility of poor health that afflicts the sick.

SEN AND THE FRAMEWORK OF FREEDOM

Sen's critiques of contemporary distributive theories of justice show the coherence and plausibility of a philosophy of freedom that is embodied, relational, attuned to culture and history, and liberal. In particular, he dissects the profound conceptual weaknesses of libertarian freedom. In doing so, he provides an account of freedom that in its concreteness contrasts sharply with the abstract theories of freedom chronicled by Daniel Rodgers in *Age of Fracture*. Sen's philosophy of freedom also provides a complement to some of the key theoretical requirements that follow from Rahner's theology of created freedom: that a public theology of freedom be embodied, relational, immersed in history and culture, and liberal. I would like, in the next section of the chapter, to show more specifically how Sen affirms liberal freedom while also affirming an understanding of personhood that nevertheless stops short of being an account of the good. To be sure, Sen's understanding of personhood is not as substantive as, say, Rahner's. But Sen's understanding is nonetheless a significant and persuasive attempt to articulate a theory of freedom that is integrated with fundamental—even radical—human vulnerability; that does not retreat into problematic abstraction in the face of the clash of theories of the good in pluralist society; and that is liberal.

Well-Being: Functioning and Freedom

The concept of well-being is at the heart of Sen's concrete understanding of the concept of freedom and of the related concept of a person. In fact, well-being is for him the sine qua non of freedom—the former providing the concrete basis for the latter. Although to an extent tautological and open-ended—well-being is the "quality or wellness of a person's being"—Sen's definition of the concept has several revealing aspects. In the first place, well-being has to do with "wellness," an adjective modifying a notion of activity. Well-being, then, in some sense involves activity and is not a matter only of the static possession of something like utility or primary goods.[64] In

---

64. "The philosophical basis of this approach," Sen says, "can be traced to Aristotle's

the second place, Sen's definition links the notion of activity to the notion of person. Even given the absence in Sen's writing of a complete theory of the person, this linkage signals a more complex view of personhood. In turn, he adds to this complexity by integrating a notion of activity—or, as Sen often says, of "doing"—with a notion of being. Sen rejects any metaphysical or strictly foundationalist basis for his thought.[65] Still, his use of the concept of being suggests some characteristic of constancy inherent in persons as such. Moreover, his integration of being and activity suggests that his characteristic of constancy is closely related to a notion of action—or, more to the point, of freedom. Sen provides another definition that serves well to summarize the points made in this paragraph. Well-being, he says, is "something"—thus a constant state—"in her"—thus distinctly personal—"that she achieves"—hence integrated with action.[66]

But this is a general characterization of the meaning of well-being. What is Sen's more specific understanding of the concept? What is needed is a concept of well-being that corresponds to what Sen calls "changing personal features"[67]—a concept that, so to speak, objectively reveals the subjective, contingent reality of discrete and vulnerable persons and populations. Here Sen turns to the concept of "functionings" or "what the person succeeds in *doing* with the commodities and characteristics at his or her command."[68] Functionings, he argues, reflect well-being on the basis of the "straightforward fact that how well a person is must be a matter of what

---

writings, which include a penetrating investigation of the 'good of man' in terms of 'life in the sense of activity. . . . Aristotle had gone to examine—both in *Ethics* and *Politics*—the political and social implications of concentrating on well-being in this sense, involving 'human flourishing.'" See Sen, *Inequality Reexamined*, 39n3. It is important to note that Sen's ideas have emerged primarily out of utilitarianism, social and rational choice theory, welfare economics, and Rawlsian moral philosophy. Thus he is not per se an Aristotelian, even if Aristotle's ideas have influenced his thinking. In particular, the Aristotelianism of Martha Nussbaum has been a key influence on Sen. See, for instance, Nussbaum, "Non-Relative Virtues"; Nussbaum, "Nature"; Nussbaum, "Human Functioning and Social Justice," 202–4; Nussbaum, *Women and Human Development*.

65. One critic described Sen's (and Nussbaum's) aim as to construct an "internalist . . . foundationalism that aims to surmount the dichotomy of absolutism and relativism. The former aspires to nonhistorical Truth, and the latter settles for merely local or provincial truths. We start 'digging' from *within* human experience and discourse and engage in an evaluative inquiry about what things we do and should count as intrinsically worthwhile in our human lives. We stop searching when we find, through 'cooperative critical discourse,' what sorts of ethical concepts best interpret these objects of intrinsic value." Crocker, "Functioning and Capability," 588.

66. Sen, "Well-Being," 195.
67. Sen, *Commodities and Capabilities*, 6–7.
68. Sen, *Commodities and Capabilities*, 6.

kind of life he or she is living, and what the person is succeeding in 'doing' or 'being.'"[69] Sen also states that functionings are constitutive of a person's being,[70] and that they are both activities and features of states of existence of a person.[71] Functionings range from "elementary ones, such as being adequately nourished and being free from avoidable disease, to very complex activities or personal states, such as being able to take part in the life of the community and having self-respect."[72]

Several observations pertinent to Sen's concept of concrete freedom can be derived from this discussion of well-being as functionings. When Sen says that well-being is a matter of the "kind of life he or she is living," he is not referring so much to the quality of moral character as to basic aspects of human survival. His list of functionings has been criticized for its brevity and lack of higher-order human concerns, such as regard for others and practical reason.[73] But this lack of breadth serves the purpose, Sen says, of providing the practical possibility of just political agreements on policy matters: it's easier to agree if there's not as much to agree on.[74] But it is not

69. Sen, *Commodities and Capabilities*, 19.
70. Sen, *Inequality Reexamined*, 39.
71. Sen, *Commodities and Capabilities*, 6–11.
72. Sen, *Development as Freedom*, 75.

73. Sen does not offer an exhaustive list of functionings relative to other authors who also use the concept of functionings; he more or less repeats the list I have provided here. Nor does he offer an extended rationale for the list he does choose. With Sen there is a certain commonsensical element at work: He assumes the existence of common functionings more than he goes to length to justify what in particular they are. By contrast, Nussbaum offers an explicit series of functionings and an accompanying justification for same. Moreover, Nussbaum and others emphasize far more than does Sen such basic human qualities as practical reason and an inclination to be other-regarding. See, for instance, Nussbaum, "Human Functioning and Social Justice," and her justification for and list of inherent human functions and capabilities. Her justification involves an extended reflection on the meaning of essentialism and of the Aristotelian conception of human life. Her list explicitly includes hunger, thirst, shelter, sexual desire, mobility, capacity for pleasure and pain, cognitive capacity, early infant development, practical reason, affiliation with other human beings, relatedness to other species and to nature, play, and separateness. Her list also includes such corresponding capabilities as: being able to live to the end of a complete human life; being able to have good health; being able to avoid unnecessary pain; being able to use the five senses; being able to have attachments to things and persons outside ourselves; being able to form a conception of the good; being able to live for and with others; being able to live with concern for world of nature, being able to laugh; and being able to live one's own life and nobody else's, Nussbaum, "Human Functioning and Social Justice," 214–23. For a critical view of Sen's notion of functionings, see Qizilbash, "Capabilities," 146.

74. "The greatest relevance of ideas of justice," Sen says, "lies in the identification of *patent injustice*, on which reasoned agreement is possible, rather than in the derivation of some extant formula for how the world should be precisely run." Sen, *Development as Freedom*, 285–87.

so much the brevity of Sen's list of functionings as his particular focus that is important for my discussion here. He clearly includes as functionings such activities as living in community and self-respect. But his list emphasizes more the most basic aspects of human life—length of life itself, nourishment, shelter, health, etc. His focus on these fundamentals includes his claim that these elemental functionings are of intrinsic value. Moreover, he also evokes the close interrelation among these constitutive, bodily aspects of life; one basic functioning can profoundly affect all others. In short, Sen's account of well-being as functionings powerfully evokes the inherent, embodied contingency of human life.

But for Sen it is not as if well-being is the foundation and freedom nothing more than an overlay upon this basic structure. Instead, he accords freedom an integral role in well-being—a role signaled by the importance Sen gives to the concept of "well-being freedom." I noted above that the concept of well-being as functionings has simultaneous reference both to states of existence and corresponding activities. Thus well-being is not only a matter of having enough food but also of the act of nourishment itself. And it is with reference to such basic human acts that the problem of freedom enters. "The existence of genuine choice," Sen says, "may actually affect the nature and significance of the functionings achieved."[75] Sen also notes: "The achievement of well-being is not independent of the process through which we achieve various functionings and the part that our own decisions play in those choices."[76]

But what more precisely does Sen mean by the concept of well-being freedom or, what is the same thing, the freedom to choose well-being? He does not mean freedom only understood as the increase of choices. This definition—though popular in economics and contemporary moral philosophy—is too abstract. Instead, it is helpful to think of well-being freedom in two key ways. The first is that this kind of freedom is exercised with reference to a cluster of given human inclinations and values; this cluster is represented by the list of functionings. Thus, for instance, Sen says that "living long" is a functioning—in other words, an activity that corresponds to a natural orientation toward life that is valued by all persons. Moreover, Sen adds, living long is also linked to freedom. This correspondence is not because long life is simply one choice alongside other equally compelling ones. Rather, freedom pertains to the value in which life is held—a value obvious

---

75. Sen, "Well-Being," 201; the discussion in this section of the chapter is based on Sen, "Well-Being," 195–203.

76. Sen, *Inequality Reexamined*, 49–50.

because the "option to live longer is typically grabbed by each individual."[77] Well-being freedom, then, is at least activity undertaken within a valued framework of fundamental human functionings.

But well-being freedom is characterized by more than this framework of action. It is also a matter of the possibility of successful action within this framework. Sen puts it: "Acting freely and being able to choose are . . . directly conductive to well-being, not just because more freedom makes more alternatives available."[78] Sen also describes freedom in general as the "real opportunity to accomplish what we value."[79] The distinction between "opportunity" and "burden" is crucial. The former, Sen says, refers to choices that "*can* be made by oneself"; the latter refers to choices that "*have to be* made by oneself."[80] Well-being freedom is the culmination of the movement from living as burden to living as opportunity—opportunity understood as the ability to choose to participate in the most basic aspects of life. These choices are to be guided by reasons that correspond to the values of well-being. Thus Sen clearly affirms well-being freedom as a humanizing activity. And he locates this humanizing quality especially in the increase of freedom over necessity.[81] Sen's account of well-being and well-being freedom stands as a powerful philosophical analogue to the vulnerable, embodied character of created freedom.

Agency Freedom

The concept of well-being, then, pertains to the basic constituents of human life: to functionings and to the freedom to achieve functionings. In normative terms, well-being provides the basis for understanding a person as a beneficiary or in need of justice (and this is the case even given Sen's active notion of well-being).[82] As a matter of fact, Sen notes, well-being and well-being freedom are the areas in which most moral evaluations of inequality take place.[83] As a matter of principle, though, these are also the areas that provide the framework for any normative considerations of inequality. All such considerations—even on the basis of other norms—are undertaken with at least implicit references to the spaces of well-being and well-being freedom.

---

77. Sen, "Freedom of Choice," 280.
78. Sen, *Inequality Reexamined*, 51.
79. Sen, *Inequality Reexamined*, 31–32.
80. Sen, *Inequality Reexamined*, 63.
81. Qizilbash, "Capabilities," 146.
82. Sen, "Well-Being," 208.
83. Sen, *Inequality Reexamined*, 71.

To see why this is so, it is helpful to consider how Sen understands the relationship between well-being and what he calls "agency." Each person, he argues, is constituted by a well-being aspect and an agency aspect. These are linked but distinct parts of a person: The former part is concerned with basic functionings constitutive of life and survival, the latter with the whole range of a person's goals, values, or ends. The agency aspect is broader than and may include the well-being aspect. It refers not solely to the space of functionings and well-being—to a person as a beneficiary. Rather, it pertains to a person's conception of good and, hence, to what a person is free to do or achieve whatever goals or values or ends he or she has (and a person may regard well-being as one such value). Thus agency refers to matters of personal morality and responsibility. And one's agency aspect will include a central role for well-being to the extent that one's theory of the good includes the values of well-being. Thus the well-being and agency aspects may align or diverge. But whether well-being and agency values align or diverge, Sen nevertheless says: "There is no way of reducing this plural-information base [i.e., the plurality of both well-being and agency values] into a monist one without losing something of importance."[84]

Or, in another way of putting it, there is no way of entirely splitting off the agency aspect from the well-being aspect. At one point, Sen asks whether well-being can be assessed entirely from within each person's agency perspective. In other words, it is the most that can be said that each person is a singular judge of the value of well-being and that there are no common, normative standards of well-being that can be affirmed regardless of one's agency aspect? Sen rejects this understanding. The objectivity and value of well-being and well-being freedom, he argues, are not conditional on how much priority one gives to these concepts in one's agency aspect. To see it otherwise would be to assume too polar a view of choice—a view that would deny the broad uniformity of value and desire on which well-being rests.[85] Moreover, the exercise of one's agency is also not detachable from well-being and well-being freedom understood in concrete terms. Sen says:

> The substantive freedoms that we respectively enjoy to exercise our responsibilities are extremely contingent on personal, social, and environmental circumstances. . . . The bonded laborer born into semislavery, the subjugated girl child stifled by a repressive society, the helpless landless laborer without substantial means of earning an income are all deprived not only in terms of well-being, but also in terms of ability to lead responsible lives, which

---

84. Sen, "Well-Being," 203–8; Sen, *Inequality Reexamined*, 61–62.
85. Sen, *Inequality Reexamined*, 69–72.

are contingent on having certain basic freedoms. Responsibility *requires* freedom.[86]

Moreover, the process does not go one way. Agency and responsibility can also profoundly affect well-being. Sen, for instance, says of the contemporary situation of women in the developing world:

Perhaps the most immediate argument for focusing on women's agency may be precisely the role that such an *agency* can play in removing the inequalities that depress the *well-being* of women. Empirical work in recent years has brought out very clearly how the relative respect and regard for women's well-being is strongly influenced by such variables as women's ability to earn an independent income, to find employment outside the home, to have ownership rights and to have literacy and be educated participants in decisions within and outside the family.[87]

Capability

Well-being and well-being freedom constitute, then, the framework of freedom: the concrete context of functioning, circumstance, and value amid which what Sen calls "certain basic freedoms" are exercised. For Sen, "capability" is the primary shape that real freedom takes—meaning the actual opportunity to act whether the action pertains to well-being freedom or to agency freedom. Capability, he notes, is "primarily a reflection of the freedom to achieve valuable functionings."[88] Similarly, he says that it is "a kind of freedom: the substantive freedom to achieve alternative functioning combinations."[89] These are definitions from the perspective of Sen the moral philosopher. But capability is also a technical economic concept and, as such, represents in economic terms the linkage of freedom and achievement. As Sen the economist puts it, capability is

> a set of vectors of functionings, reflecting the person's freedom to lead one type of life or another. Just as the so-called "budget set" in the commodity space represents a person's freedom to buy

---

86. Sen, *Development as Freedom*, 283–84.

87. Sen, *Development as Freedom*, 191.

88. Sen, *Inequality Reexamined*, 49. Sen usually uses capability with reference to well-being and well-being freedom. But capability can also be applied to notions of agency and agency freedom.

89. Sen, *Development as Freedom*, 75.

commodity bundles, the "capability set" in the functioning space reflects the person's freedom to choose from possible livings.[90]

Capability, then, is not only for Sen the primary shape that freedom takes; it is also a fundamentally concrete notion of freedom. Sen affirms this concreteness in a number of ways. Capability is not freedom understood as a means. Rather, it is a substantive notion. One critic notes: "Capabilities add something intrinsically and not merely instrumentally valuable to a human life, namely, positive freedom in the sense of available and worthwhile options."[91] Such freedom, Sen notes, can be of "direct importance for the person's quality of life and well-being."[92] Moreover, the concreteness of capability is underscored by Sen's emphasis on "available" and "worthwhile" options. Capability as freedom is not simply a matter of abstract possibilities. On the one hand, it is linked to the notion of "being able to choose."[93] The exercise of capability depends on personal characteristics and social arrangements.[94] It is also freedom exercised within an already-given field of value. And this is the case even if Sen may be reticent about how this field of value is specifically informed by a theory of the good.[95] Thus Sen's concept of capability is founded on the claim of the humanizing value of choice operative in the most fundamental matters of human well-being. In the movement from life as helpless burden to life as real opportunity is manifest the value of capability and the basis of human equality. Here again Sen provides a philosophical analogue to the embodied and relational emphases of created freedom.

It will be helpful briefly to consider again the American debate over health care in light of Sen's philosophy of freedom. Here I would like to touch on another aspect of federal health care reform in the United States: the extension of Medicaid to millions of low-income adults. And, in particular, I would like to focus on the effort by a number of Republican-controlled state governments to impose work requirements as a condition for receiving Medicaid on the assumption, as Arkansas Governor Asa Hutchinson said, that "responsibility should have to accompany a social benefit such as Medicaid."[96] On one hand, the neoliberalism of the last decades is marked by an increasing turn to policies like work requirements, welfare reform, and reductions in

90. Sen, *Inequality Reexamined*, 40.
91. Crocker, "Functioning and Capability: Part 2," 159.
92. Sen, *Inequality Reexamined*, 51.
93. Sen, *Inequality Reexamined*, 51.
94. Sen, *Development as Freedom*, 282–89.
95. Sen, *Inequality Reexamined*, 83.
96. Pradhan, "Conservative Health Care Experiment."

food stamps for the poor. On the other hand, the turn in the last decades to the emphasis in social policy on individual responsibility marks a return to older tropes. The American philosopher Elizabeth Anderson has noted that contemporary American appeals to work requirements and welfare reform contain all of the elements present in the early-nineteenth-century writing of Thomas Malthus: the emphasis on individual responsibility; the assumption that social benefits induce laziness; the stigma cast on recipients of such benefits; and the assumption that the undeserving poor who receive such benefits are a burden on the deserving middle class who pay taxes to support them.[97]

Like the neoliberals who back such policies, Sen understands the aim of justice to be freedom. But, unlike the neoliberals, Sen is far more attuned to the structural and cultural dimensions of freedom; to the persistence and complexity of deprivation and thus to the sheer difficulty of freedom; and to the moral significance of freedom at every stage of a possible movement from burden to opportunity. In the neoliberal account, the emphasis is solely on the individual's agency, which is understood to be impaired far more by the state's provision of a moral good like health insurance than it is by any preceding structural or cultural factors. By imposing the requirement, the policy presumes that the mandate to work will move a person from dependency to freedom and from being a passive recipient of taxpayer largesse to being an active, responsible agent in society. By contrast, Sen's philosophy of freedom invites the consideration of both the individual's agency *and* related structural and cultural factors. Doing so means that his account of deprivation cuts far deeper and problematizes freedom far more. The focus moves from individual questions of desert, which are almost always in fact impossible to determine (especially in complex social systems), to the possibilities of freedom in a structural and cultural context. Poor health impairs well-being and well-being freedom. Being healthy also enables choice in itself in contrast to the constraint of sickness. Moreover, the maintenance of health across a broad population by the provision of Medicaid is an instance of Sen's concept of effective freedom (a freedom enjoyed by all as a result of social policy). In all, Sen proposes a path from burden to opportunity that passes through fields of personal, structural, and cultural constraint. As he puts it (and as I noted earlier): "Responsibility *requires* freedom."[98]

97. Anderson, "Great Reversal."
98. Sen, *Development as Freedom*, 283–84.

CONCLUSION

Sen, then, turns to a notion of contingent well-being as the key characteristic of the framework of freedom. He appeals to the concept of functionings to evoke the constitutive, valued, and contingent aspects of well-being. He says that there is a range of overall freedoms that correspond to the range of functionings. And he affirms that these freedoms are intrinsically important values. He also affirms the importance of instrumental freedoms. Moreover, Sen insists that ability or power is an integral aspect of a correct concept of freedom. Thus freedom in its comprehensive sense is best understood as positive freedom or capability—two closely related ideas both of which include the notion of power. It is not, then, for him a sufficient definition of freedom to point to the mere negative absence of obstacles. Nor is it sufficient simply to identify freedom with the personal control of the levers of power. The value of freedom—understood as effective freedom—is implicated even when one cannot entirely exercise these levers oneself. In such situations, what ought to be desired and valued in common—represented by well-being functionings—provides the basis for the assessment of real freedom. This brief summary provides a picture of Sen's understanding of the framework of freedom—of the context of embodiment; of positive and negative freedom; of the diversity of gender, age, and culture; of community; and of the world of functionings and well-being into which freedom from the start is integrated. I have noted the affinities between Rahner's key conditions of freedom and Sen's theory of freedom and I believe this chapter has made those affinities even clearer. But it is also helpful to note here that Protestant theologian Harlan Beckley likens Sen's argument for a situated freedom to Calvin's notion of common grace. For both Sen and Calvin, freedom is not autonomous but dependent, activated or inhibited by a world of nature, culture, history, society, and the selves we bring to each choice we make.[99] Beckley has also noted the affinity between Sen's work and the egalitarian implications of Christian love, which considers all person of equal worth and which understands that equal consideration does not require identical treatment but treatment according to the particular needs of a person.[100] Finally, Beckley finds affinities between Christian assumptions of vulnerability and grace and Sen's account of equality of opportunity. In a critique fitting for the thin accounts of equal opportunity common in the Age of Fracture, Sen argues that the actual measure of whether there are equal or unequal opportunities can only be determined by attention to the deep and pervasive diversity of human

---

99. Beckley, "Capability as Opportunity," 124–25.
100. Beckley, "Capability as Opportunity," 118–19.

characteristics and conditions.[101] But attention to these fundamental diversities is precisely what is missing from the libertarian reading of the concept of equal opportunity. Sen says that such a thin concept requires only the "equal availability of some *particular means* . . . [or the] equal applicability (or equal *non*-applicability) or some *specific barriers or constraints*."[102] Sen also criticizes the commonly invoked neoliberal incentive argument, which says that inequalities are justified insofar as they provide incentives for achievement and encourage work. These arguments, Sen notes, rely on assumptions about effort and decision-making: those who work hard and choose better deserve their greater rewards. But these assumptions, Sen says, often fail to account for the role of "antecedent diversities" like gender, age, or class in how effort and available choices are constituted.[103] For Beckley, Sen's probing analysis of antecedent diversities is a complement to Christian notions of grace that undermine easy appeals to merit and that offer possibilities for hope when the disadvantage of antecedent diversities interacts with despair.[104] It is now time to turn to a more specific engagement with the theology of created freedom in the next chapter, with a discussion of the work of Karl Rahner, and in the final chapter with a constructive account of a Catholic public theology of freedom for the United States.[105]

101. Sen, *Inequality Reexamined*, 28.

102. Sen, *Inequality Reexamined*, 7. Sen notes: "It is important to be careful . . . not to define 'opportunity' in the limited way in which it is often defined, e.g., whether the doors of a school are formally open to John (and not whether John can financially afford to go through those doors), or—going further—whether John can afford a certain school (but not whether John has the real opportunity of using the facilities there, given his physical or mental handicap)." Sen, *Commodities and Capabilities*, 4.

103. Sen, *Inequality Reexamined*, 142.

104. Beckley, "Capability as Opportunity," 125, 129.

105. It is important to note that Patterson understands freedom to be a value especially associated with the West while Sen understands freedom to have emerged in a more global context. Thus against authors (Asian and Western) who say that there are no traditions of freedom in Asia, Sen points to isolated but significant strands of freedom in the varied history of Asian cultures. In fact, he notes, these inchoate instances of freedom in the Asian past are comparable to traces of freedom present in the ancient West. In both Asia and the West, he argues, there emerged similar ideas of "*the value of personal freedom*: that personal freedom is important and should be guaranteed for those who 'matter' in a good society." But it is only in the modern West, Sen implies, that this commitment to personal freedom has evolved into the widespread concept of an "*equality of freedom*: [in which] everyone matters and the freedom that is guaranteed for one must be guaranteed for all." This, of course, is a different account of the history of freedom than Patterson supplies. Where Sen sees ancient and comparable traces of freedom in the West and East, Patterson locates the actual, social birth of freedom only in the ancient West. And where Sen sees Western freedom only flourishing in modernity, Patterson argues that the modern West has only taken over an already-abundant

CHAPTER FOUR

Karl Rahner and Created Freedom as the Basis for a Catholic Public Theology of Freedom

IN THIS CHAPTER, I will turn to the work of Karl Rahner to establish the fundamental basis for a Catholic public theology of freedom for the United States. In the next chapter, I will offer a specific elaboration of this public theology by drawing on the work of Shawn Copeland, Elizabeth Anderson, and David Hollenbach. But before beginning the shift in the balance of the book to an exclusively theological discussion, it will be helpful to recall earlier steps in the argument. From the start, I turned to Rahner's rendering of freedom in the context of the doctrine of creation. Then, in the first chapter, I turned to the work of Daniel Rodgers to lay out the problem: For the last fifty years, neoliberal economic thought has emptied the concept of freedom of its connection to circumstance, sociality, and the good. Along the way, this emptying has ushered in a clashing, dissonant era that Rodgers calls the Age of Fracture. In broad terms, Rahner's account of created freedom supplies a concept of freedom that has gone missing in the Age of Fracture: a concept that is embodied and relational; sensitive to culture

---

Western history of the concept. See Sen, *Development as Freedom*, 227–48; also, Sen, "Human Rights and Asian Values." In a footnote in *Development as Freedom*, Sen says of his differences with Patterson: "His arguments do indeed point to the political freedom in Western classical thought (especially in ancient Greece and Rome), but similar components can also be found in Asian classics, to which Patterson does not give much attention" (343n4).

and history; oriented to the good and to God, and also liberal. But those are theological claims and this is a public theology intended for a pluralist American audience. And so in the second chapter I turned to the secular science of sociology to see if there were sources there to respond to Rodger's critique and to provide an analogue that might in effect translate some of the key aspects of created freedom into a secular context. Here I turned to the work of Evelyn Nakano Glenn and Orlando Patterson and their arguments that American ideas of freedom have been deeply influenced by interaction with the structural and cultural legacy of slavery. In the third chapter, I turned to the work of Amartya Sen for a philosophical account of the "normatively human" in which freedom plays a central role in a way that defies the abstractness of neoliberalism. Sen's philosophy of freedom is resolutely liberal, concrete, contextual, and attuned to culture and power—in other words, it possesses key characteristics that make it a philosophical analogue to Rahner's concept of created freedom.

Throughout, I have been proceeding on the basis of two related methodological assumptions. The first is consistent with what theologian Robin Lovin calls "Christian realism," or the conviction that "God's dealings with humanity also provide the framework for ordering and understanding human life." This assumption holds that creation both lies "beyond human experience *and* [is] the framework within which each experience is lived."[1] Putting things in this way justifies both my fundamental appeal to creation as the starting point for thinking about freedom and the role of sociology and philosophy in helping to understand how created freedom is lived. The second key methodological assumption is taken from Maureen Junker-Kenny's contemporary re-appropriation of the classical sources of theological ethics. In the case of this book, Scripture provides the starting points: creation, redemption, and corresponding accounts of human agency. Tradition offers the richness of theology, stories, art, and more in a constant but changing stream of reflection on freedom. Philosophy provides normative accounts of the human. And sciences like sociology likewise fill out the meaning of human agency.[2] By authority, iteration, and analogue, these sources combine to form an objective account of human freedom. But it is now time to turn to the fundamental basis of this account in Rahner's idea of created freedom. I

---

1. Lovin, "Christian Realism," 7–11. See also Lovin, *Reinhold Niebuhr and Christian Realism*, 4–32. I also regard my arguments as corresponding to the work of theologian Don S. Browning and his evocations of the "naturalistic movement" in theologian ethics—a movement that assumes a form and structure to nature that is nevertheless shot through with contingency. See Browning, *Fundamental Practical Theology*, 2–12, 139–207.

2. Junker-Kenny, *Approaches to Theological Ethics*, 9–81.

will first discuss the particular aptness of Rahner's theology of freedom as a response to the challenges of the Age of Fracture. Next, I will engage crucial distinctions between his theology of freedom and truncated liberal ideas common in the Age of Fracture. Then I will discuss the depth and breadth of his theology of created freedom. And, finally, I will conclude with reflections on Rahner and public theology in the American context.

RAHNER AND THE AGE OF FRACTURE

In turning to Rahner's theology of freedom, I do so aware of criticisms of his work raised by figures like Walter Kasper, Johann Baptist Metz, and Hans Urs von Balthasar.[3] Indeed, I think there is relevance to some of these criticisms. The human subject at the heart of Rahner's theology of freedom can seem at times awkwardly historical: a person whose transcendental dimension can seem too far removed from the push and pull of history and whose social dimension can seem too detached from the influence of structural and cultural forces. But I am appealing to Rahner's later work in which he responded to such criticisms by a deeper integration of the transcendental and concrete; by acknowledging the play of structure and culture; and by insisting on the unity—but not the identity—of the love of God and love of neighbor.[4] Even more, I believe the synthesis he achieved in his later work provides a theology of freedom suited especially well for our times. I have noted already how his integration of the transcendental and concrete—what Junker-Kenny calls a "constitutive polarity"[5]—offers a compelling alternative to the neoliberal abstractions of freedom in the Age of Fracture. In such abstractions, freedom is drained of its depth and becomes a lonely, hollow pole detached from connection to the poles of relationship, circumstance, power, and more. But the suitability of Rahner's theology of freedom extends even further as a response to deficiencies in competing worldviews in the American public square. For instance, Junker-Kenny has called attention to a diminished sense of a self in contemporary Catholic appropriations of classical natural law and in feminist theology. In the former case, the imperatives of an objectivist morality overwhelm the complexities of a self inescapably having to interpret moral choices. In the latter case, the insistence on social construction too often leaves out the transcendental dimension of a person

---

3. See, for instance, Kasper, *Jesus the Christ*, 50–51; Metz, *Faith in History and Society*, 40, 49–83, 159–61; Balthasar, *Moment of Christian Witness*.

4. For an insightful account of Rahner's response to his critics, see Marmion, "Rahner and His Critics."

5. Junker-Kenny, *Approaches to Theological Ethics*, 210.

who is constituted by social relations, but also capable of self-reflection and choice in the face of such social relations.[6] What Junker-Kenny says here provides a rationale for turning to Rahner's theology of freedom: "The factor that enables resistance to succumbing to the alleged genesis from intersubjective formation needs to be identified, especially in connection with a power analysis. The duality of the formal, transcendental level of freedom and its concrete realization . . . [is] the basis on which one can distinguish between action and behavior, morality and social adaptation, individuality and collectivity; without it, also the call of God to each human being as well as her response cannot be theoretically anchored."[7] Also, Rahner's emphasis on the transcendental nature of the person provides a firm, unconditioned ground for the protection of religious freedom and for the neutral basis of the liberal state. In turn, his integration of the transcendental nature of the person into history opens the way for Catholicism to appeal to powerful biblical metaphors of hospitality, equality, and solidarity as the Church faces the exclusionary powers of American populism.[8]

What is most important, then, in my discussion of Rahner's theology is how finite human freedom is both oriented toward the absolute and essentially dependent—a dependence that defies the illusory independence ransacking through the Age of Fracture. In order to evoke this dependent nature of freedom, I will appeal to Rahner's fundamental notion of "created freedom." Rahner says that created freedom exists in the mode of a creature whose dependence is made evident by the constraints of power, the mediated nature of freedom, and the awareness that freedom is finite because at the same time it is disposed in a context of infinite being.[9] Thus the dependence of created freedom goes all the way up—even to God. In other words, the concept of created freedom provides a rationale for how freedom retains its character of spontaneity even though it is always dependent on God. The key here, Rahner says, is the nature of causality between spiritual creatures and God in which the higher degree of spiritual being corresponds to the greater degree of dependence on God. God's creative power endows human beings with life, existence, and rationality—all things that human beings did not create and on account of which they are dependent. But God's creative power also endows human beings with the even more radical dependence

---

6. Junker-Kenny, *Approaches to Theological Ethics*, 166–74.

7. Junker-Kenny, *Approaches to Theological Ethics*, 210.

8. I have been influenced here in my reading of Rahner by Junker-Kenny's discussion of the neutrality of the liberal state and its dependence on pre-political factors like the moral resources of religious communities. Junker-Kenny, *Approaches to Theological Ethics*, 224.

9. Rahner et al., "Freedom," 361.

of freedom on grace for the achievement of selfhood and salvation. Thus Rahner describes created freedom as "responsible self-mastery, even in the face of God, because dependence on God—contrary to what takes place in intra-mundane causality—actually means being endowed with free selfhood."[10] He also says the created "existentials" that constitute universal human experience—for instance, embodied, incarnate existence; freedom-and-responsibility; person-and-community; and nature-freedom-and-grace—are the universal presuppositions for the possibility of an encounter with the saving love of Jesus Christ.[11]

In turning to the concept of created freedom, I am also signaling the importance of the doctrine of creation in my overall argument. There is a paradox here. In order to show the historical character of freedom, I am appealing to a concept associated with the doctrine of creation—a doctrine more commonly linked in Catholic theology in the last decades to the subordination of freedom to timeless, natural truths. For instance, Reinhard Hutter has said of John Paul II's arguments in *Veritatis Splendor*: "Freedom is not determined by its opposite but by the fundamental relationship between freedom and truth, that is, between the gift of created freedom and its divine Giver . . . *genuine freedom denotes the truthful enactment of created existence*."[12] In this way of putting things, we can see an objectivist morality certain about the bases of moral truth in nature if deficient in its account of the self in the face of moral choice.[13] But Rahner's historical understanding of creation helps resolve the paradox of the appeal to the doctrine of creation. For him, creation is not alone a one-time event in the past that established the world in being. Rather, it is also the "ongoing and always actual" establishment from outside of time of each existent.

---

10. Rahner argues that even the free, imputable denial of God in fact affirms freedom's createdness. See Rahner et al., "Freedom," 361–62. It is instructive to compare Rahner's emphasis on createdness—and thus, in part, on the givenness of being—with a Whiteheadian approach to created freedom that emphasizes far more how human freedom itself creates being. The Rahnerian approach, I argue, better assures the foundation of moral norms of justice and equality. See, for instance, Ford, "Can Freedom Be Created?"

11. Rahner says: "Thus the theological doctrine of freedom proclaims the grace of God, while the 'natural' freedom of human beings in potency and act is only the presupposition, created by God, to make it possible for God to give God's self to human beings in love." See Rahner, "On the Origins of Freedom," 120. For Rahner on philosophy and theology, see Rahner, *Foundations of Christian Faith*, 24–25. For commentary on Rahner on the same topic, see Dych, "Theology in a New Key," 7; Carr, "Starting with the Human," 17–18. For an account of the existentials, see Rahner, "Dignity and Freedom of Man," 239–40.

12. Hutter, "(Re-)Forming Freedom," 119.

13. Junker-Kenny, *Approaches to Theological Ethics*, 209.

Moreover, this unique relationship with the divine is discovered only from within historical experience and, hence, only from within human freedom.[14] Here Rahner turns from a premodern emphasis on the inevitability of God to a modern emphasis on the possibility of the divine. And, with this shift in emphasis, Rahner also makes clearer God's freedom to create and redeem and the finite human freedom to respond to the divine call. There is nothing inevitable about any of this. Rather, reimagining creation in the key of freedom makes clearer the divine choice to love at the basis of creation.[15] It is also important to note that Rahner's doctrine of creation affirms the stability of created realities while also opening up these realities to the influences of history and the demands of human interpretation. Thus freedom's "createdness" embeds freedom within the abiding if historicized constants of creation such as embodiment, relationality, normativity, rationality, and the spirit. These constants in turn are always interpreted by freedom. Walter Kasper has spoken similarly of human freedom situated in the "theonomy of the order of creation."[16]

RAHNER AND LIBERAL FREEDOM: CRITIQUE AND COMPATIBILITY

From the start with Rahner's theology of freedom, we are far from the abstract neoliberalism animating many of today's concepts of freedom. As a way into a more detailed discussion of his theology of freedom, it will be helpful here to consider his critique of such an abstract neoliberalism and also the compatibility of his conception of freedom with a classic understanding of the liberal political order. Here I will consider related, liberal claims: that freedom is a defined, fixed concept, and that freedom is at most a fact, something whole and entire, as it is that must be protected by government. Here we can also see the relevance of Rahner's claims that freedom cannot be understood apart from history and culture and that freedom is both gift and task.

---

14. Rahner, *Foundations of Christian Faith*, 75–77. Michael Buckley interprets Rahner on creation in the following way: "To be a creature does not refer to one relationship among others, as if it were another instance of the general relationship of dependence. It refers to an absolute and unique relationship of utter dependence, unlike any other in my experience: The total dependence upon Mystery as upon the context of reality which gives direction to the movement of inquiry and establishes the freedom of choice and personal responsibility." Buckley, "Within the Holy Mystery," 45.

15. Junker-Kenny, *Approaches to Theological Ethics*, 140–41.

16. Kasper, *Theology and Church*, 52–53.

Freedom, Culture, History

It is best to begin with how Rahner even knows what freedom is.[17] And here he is clear about the historical nature of the concept. Freedom is not, he says, a fixed or self-evident idea—one that can be defined with clear certainty for all time. Rather, the nature of freedom itself defies all efforts to define it with pinpoint clarity. This follows from an epistemological fact: the understanding of freedom can only be sufficiently derived from the experience of freedom. To be sure, Rahner affirms what he calls "real freedom of choice" as an inalienable capacity of a person not to be compelled from within or without in the essential moral and spiritual matters of one's life.[18] But he also argues that what freedom means is inseparable from how freedom is lived. Thus he says that men and women grasp the fact of their freedom by the awareness that they are "incapable of being turned into an object."[19] What one person understands of freedom at one period of life will change with the passage of time and the use of freedom. The lived experience of consequential social and political realities will deeply affect how freedom is understood. The radical constraints of war and oppression change the way that freedom is conceptualized and valued. Moreover, the success or failure of political and social movements that seek to foster or curtail rights inevitably changes the way that freedom is understood. Here we see the basis of Rahner's claim that to know the meaning of human personhood one cannot appeal to abstract or essentialist categories alone but must turn to culture and history for a sufficient if always finally opaque understanding of the meaning of freedom.[20] To understand this meaning, then, we cannot be satisfied with consulting the abstract libertarian image of numerous, discrete, solitary individuals standing outside history. Instead, we must turn to an image of free persons embedded in communities and in the world.

Freedom as Fact and Task

Thus at the outset it is important to note that it is not a simple issue to say what for Rahner freedom is; the historicity of freedom complicates the matter. Nevertheless, it is possible at this point to note in general terms several

---

17. The following discussion is taken from Rahner, "Theology of Freedom," 178–83. For a related discussion of human dignity as fact and task, see Rahner, "Dignity and Freedom of Man," 235–46.
18. Rahner, "Theology of Freedom," 179.
19. Rahner, "Theology of Freedom," 191.
20. Rahner, "Dignity and Freedom of Man," 237.

things that freedom is not—things that in themselves fall outside the rubric of freedom's created and historical nature. For instance, freedom is not just a given quality—or, as Rahner says, "fact—to be assumed that people possess as something unproblematic and complete and thus to be protected but otherwise treated indifferently. Rather, freedom is always both the fact of a fundamental capacity for non-compulsion and the reality that such a capacity is oriented toward action—or more specifically, in Rahner's terms, a capacity that has an inner impulsion as a "task" or "demand."[21] To assume that freedom is simply something that people have is to miss the truth that freedom is also something that must be achieved—that it is, as Rahner often says, inherently oriented toward being "responsible" and "creative." Not seeing this can lead to the exercise of freedom not being valued for its own sake but only for the results in produces. Similarly, the assumption that freedom is only unproblematic fact means that norms and standards are assessed far more in terms of their achievement but far less in terms of whether they are achieved freely.[22] By contrast, Rahner calls freedom understood as oriented toward exercise a reality of the "highest order" and as meant "for its own sake."[23]

One pitfall in the definition of freedom, then, is the assumption that freedom is only a fact. A closely related pitfall is the assumption that freedom is only a matter of non-coercion: I am free inasmuch as no one stops me from doing what I want (as classic liberal accounts of negative freedom hold). To be sure, Rahner affirms that freedom at the least is non-coercion or choice in the sense that no one can be compelled entirely by internal or external force. He is also clear about the non-coercive or negative aspect when he notes that freedom is in part characterized by the self not losing itself in the other or having its being only from the other.[24] But to hold singularly to such a view of freedom as non-coercion would be to deny to freedom the profound action of self-making and self-understanding inherent in its historical nature. This is the fundamental action that is freedom's "task" and "demand" (or what Rahner calls the "fundamental option").[25] Ultimately,

21. Rahner, "Theology and Freedom," 179.
22. Rahner, "On the Origins of Freedom," 112–21.
23. Rahner, "Dignity and Freedom of Man," 247–48.
24. Rahner, "On the Origins of Freedom," 119.
25. Here it is important to recall Rahner's discussion between what he calls basic freedom (also known as the fundamental option) and categorical freedom. Basic freedom involves the final commitment of freedom made over the course of one's life. However, this lifelong commitment is constituted by if not identical with all of the acts of categorical freedom undertaken in one's life; acts of categorical freedom are those "individual acts . . . which can be localised in space and time and which can be objectified

this task of constituting one's self in interaction with grace is "true" or "real" freedom and as such "creates something final, something irrevocable and eternal."[26] Freedom understood only as non-compulsion is often associated with erroneous views of the neutrality and mutability of the self. In one such view, a person is able easily and often to determine oneself anew by use of freedom as a dilettante power to do this or that. In another erroneous view, freedom's sole character as non-coercion means responsibility is traceable only to discrete and disconnected acts but not to a self who precedes, acts out, and follows such acts. Against such views, Rahner affirms a concept of freedom that is both negative and positive—with the negative, as we shall see, embraced within the positive. Thus Rahner's historical understanding requires that freedom be possession and action, fact and task, created and creative. In this, he provides a profound justification for the significance of the liberal primacy of freedom, which in his view is not meant to protect alone the capacity of free choice but also to defend the possibility of such choice fundamentally constituting one's very self.

CREATED FREEDOM: TRANSCENDENTAL, CONCRETE, CHRISTOLOGICAL

Thus far we have seen how Rahner affirms the primacy of freedom in a manner consistent with liberal concerns, if in ways markedly different from a libertarian approach. It will next be helpful to deepen and broaden this view: to turn more specifically to the way that the concept of "created freedom" provides a persuasive and coherent theological framework for a better understanding of freedom that is both compatible with liberal concerns and essentially dependent. Rahner praised modern philosophy for its turn to the subject—a turn, he argued, that was profoundly Christian in its emphasis on the person as such. But he was also sharply critical of the "un-Christian" tendency of this philosophy to portray the human person as an autonomous subject aloof from the experience of continual dependence "with his origin in and orientation towards God."[27] How this dependence marks freedom—with each mark a sign of freedom's createdness—will be the focus of what follows. I will proceed in three steps, each integrated with the other two. These

---

with regard to their motives." Thus Rahner says that "the concrete freedom of man by which he decides about himself as a whole by effecting his own finality before God, is the unity in difference of the formal '*option fondamentale*' and the free individual acts of man." See Rahner, "Theology of Freedom," 183–86.

26. Rahner, "On the Origins of Freedom," 119.

27. Rahner, "Theology and Anthropology," 38–39.

steps correspond to three aspects of created freedom—as transcendental, mediated, and Christological.[28] In fact, it would be incorrect to think of these three aspects as sharply distinct or successive. Rahner insists on the unity of human freedom alongside his insistence on the unity of all experience. Similarly, he emphasizes the simultaneity of experience.[29] We do not first experience the transcendental and only then become aware of the material. Instead, the experience of both is one and simultaneous. It is an experience only divisible after the fact. And precisely in the course of such a process of divisibility, we are always affirming ourselves as a unified person.[30]

The Transcendental Aspect of Created Freedom

In the essay "Theology of Freedom," Rahner says that freedom's createdness is evident in the fact that "in its transcendental nature this freedom experiences itself first of all as borne and empowered by its absolute horizon, an absolute horizon which it does not form but by which it is formed."[31] This pregnant statement is worthy itself of a book. I can only here evoke several key points that illuminate the concept of created freedom.

For Rahner, the human person is by nature "pure openness for absolutely everything, for being as such."[32] This openness is experienced at what Rahner calls an "original" level of the person. In other words, this openness toward pure being wells up from the origins or depths of the self in lived interaction with the world.[33] But what Rahner calls this "transcendental" human openness or "spirit" must be understood in both an active and dependent sense. As for its active aspect, each person's openness is marked by a dynamism toward being—toward the objective and universal and toward the transcendent reality on which the objective and universal depend. The fundamental, unspoken experience of unity between self-presence and transcendent reality includes the innate striving to issue forth in the spoken,

28. I am deriving this three-fold distinction of created freedom from Rahner's discussion of created freedom in his essay "Theology of Freedom," 193–95. It should be pointed out, however, that Rahner there does not set out this three-fold distinction as any sort of schema. Moreover, elsewhere he refers in different ways to aspects of created freedom. Nevertheless, this three-fold distinction provides a useful way for grasping the central points of Rahner's concept of created freedom.

29. He says, for instance, "freedom always concerns the person as such and as a whole." Rahner, *Foundations of Christian Faith*, 38–41.

30. Rahner, *Foundations of Christian Faith*, 31.

31. Rahner, "Theology of Freedom," 193.

32. Rahner, *Foundations of Christian Faith*, 20.

33. See Dych, "Theology in a New Key," 4.

objective communication of being. In light of this striving, each occasion of what may appear as settled self-knowledge is in fact the occasion for ever deeper questions. The original experience of being is developed and deepened but never finally able to be rendered objective and communicated in a way commensurate with the experience of its truth. This desire or dynamism is, then, "transcendental," in the sense that it continuously "transcends" one rational explanation in search of a better one in the "endlessly intelligible" reality of the transcendent.

This openness to pure being, then, also has the character of dependence—of dependence on the transcendent. In a succinct way of putting it, the drive toward being is "simultaneously and necessarily" a being-given-to-oneself.[34] But it is helpful to characterize the ways in which this being-given-to-oneself occurs. Thus the human spirit is not an aimless rational drive simply for one different answer after another—as if the possibility of difference or newness in itself were what was at stake in the dynamism. Nor is it a drive that generates of itself the pure being toward which it is oriented—as if there were not from the start a given context of reality amid which the dynamism finds itself. Instead, Rahner argues that this inherent human drive is toward coherence, integrity, and love. Moreover, he argues that this drive occurs from the start in the context of the infinity of reality, or infinite being, or being as such, or what he calls the "Mystery" or "horizon"—in other words, of God. A person is a transcendent being, he says, "insofar as all of his knowledge and all of his conscious activity is grounded in a pre-apprehension (*Vorgriff*) of 'being' as such."[35] Theologian Michael Buckley identifies three ways in which this horizon of being is experienced: as context, source, and end. As context, the horizon is "that *within which* I experience anything directly, as the given situation of the real." As source, the horizon "evokes and opens up the possibility of all human transcendence." As end, it is the given reality toward which one "moves spontaneously in all . . . questions and decisions" and from which one receives integrity and coherence. As end, it is also that which draws one "continually to transcend each and every object in search of the explanation of the object." Buckley concludes: "This infinite context, direction and source of human transcendence is what we call God."[36] It is also important to note the way in which God confers integrity and coherence: by directing the person away from the silent, infinite context of reality to "something finite as the object of direct vision."[37]

---

34. Hurd, "Concept of Freedom in Rahner," 143.
35. Rahner, *Foundations of Christian Faith*, 33.
36. Buckley, "Within the Holy Mystery," 39.
37. Rahner, "Theology of Freedom," 180.

It is important here to note the close association in Rahner's theology between a metaphysics of knowledge and a metaphysics of freedom; the latter represents the higher value but the former represents the field of concepts in light of which the latter is often depicted.[38] I would like to call attention to the two ways in which Rahner elaborates their close association. The first way pertains to the spirit's apprehension of the universal. The inherent human drive toward being as such is a drive to know and, as such, aims toward universal, objective knowledge. But the human spirit is only able to attain such universality by becoming able in a positive sense to "return to itself," and in a negative sense to not become submerged with the universal objectivity that it encounters in the world. Because of this capacity, it is possible to say that the experience of knowledge or form or objectivity is also necessarily an experience of freedom. Hurd calls this close linkage of knowledge and the return to self the "emergence of freedom."[39]

But there is also a second, related way in which a metaphysics of knowledge and a metaphysics of freedom are closely related. This way pertains less to the apprehension of the universal per se than to the fact that knowledge itself is caught up in the movement of transcendence. Thus Rahner affirms that knowing is never complete but is always surpassed by the drive toward and the gift of the "endlessly intelligible." And here freedom appears as an indispensable and higher partner to knowledge. It is the very unsettledness of knowledge that accords freedom primacy. In other words, freedom originates in the negative awareness that no universal norms can entirely satisfy the human spirit's drive for self-understanding in the context of the divine Mystery. Moreover, freedom positively fulfills itself as love by accepting and surrendering to this unknowing and to Mystery.

How, then, does created freedom fit into this picture of human and divine transcendence? Here it is first important to note a tension in Rahner's thought. On the one hand, he at times depicts the dependence associated with created freedom in a negative way—as what is not able to be controlled by the power of created freedom. Thus created freedom is evident from the fact that the infinite context of reality "cannot be mastered"[40] and is "uncontrollable."[41] On the other hand, this idealist urge in Rahner is more often tempered by a positive notion of the dependent status of created freedom as integral and fitting to human being. It is in light of this positive

---

38. My thoughts in this paragraph have been influenced by Hurd, "Concept of Freedom in Rahner."

39. Hurd, "Concept of Freedom in Rahner," 144.

40. Rahner, "Theology of Freedom," 180.

41. Rahner, *Foundations of Christian Faith*, 35.

assessment that Rahner uses the concept of created freedom to underscore the fact that freedom is "borne and empowered by its absolute horizon." Or, to put it in similar terms, we could say, following Buckley, that created freedom from the start finds itself in a given context of infinite reality; that freedom experiences its character as transcendence by having its source in this infinite context; and that freedom is drawn toward and uplifted by a graciousness at the heart of this horizon. No doubt it is easy to miss the everyday experiences that signal this indebtedness.[42] But, even so, all of these aspects of freedom's dependence on divine transcendence are characteristic of the primordial experience of createdness:

> To be a creature does not refer immediately to one relationship among others, as if it were another instance of the general relationship of dependence. It refers to an absolute and unique relationship of utter dependence, unlike any other in my experience: The total dependence on Mystery as upon the context of reality which gives direction to the movement of inquiry and establishes the freedom of choice and personal responsibility.[43]

Moreover, Rahner adds that freedom's createdness becomes that much more apparent when it is understood that Mystery empowers freedom not to a distant, abstract goal but to the "absolute *nearness*"[44] of Mystery itself.

How the created dependence of transcendental freedom affects other key normative categories can be seen from a brief reflection on what Rahner calls the "existentials"—or specifically human characteristics—of personhood and responsibility. Each existential captures an aspect of the meaning of freedom, which Rahner calls the "form of transcendental experience as such . . . [insofar as] the subject knows itself to be incapable of being turned into an object and thus knows itself to be free."[45] Each existential also is inescapably marked by freedom's created dependence. For Rahner, the person as such is one who "possesses himself knowingly and in freedom—in other words, is always objectively referred to *himself*."[46] But personhood can never be reduced to a simple objectivity. The person is never just an instance of the universal. Rather, he or she is always dependent on and disposed in the "freedom of being."[47] Thus the reference to self at the heart of personhood is a "conscious and free relationship to the totality of itself"—a totality

42. Hurd, "Concept of Freedom in Rahner," 149–50.
43. Buckley, "Within the Holy Mystery," 45.
44. Rahner, "Theology of Freedom," 193.
45. Rahner, "Theology of Freedom," 191.
46. Rahner, "Dignity and Freedom of Man," 245.
47. Rahner, "Theology of Freedom," 184.

oriented to transcendence.[48] This is the philosophical basis of human dignity—a dignity enhanced by the fact that each person "is called to be the direct partner of God."[49] This experience of transcendental dependence is also at one and the same time an experience of freedom and of responsibility. In fact, responsibility cannot even be understood apart from the dependence of created freedom. Responsibility is anything but the occasion of pure self-reliance of American myth. "For it is only," Rahner says, "in the presence of the infinity of being . . . that an existent is in a position and has a standpoint from out of which he can assume responsibility for himself."[50]

A few preliminary thoughts are in order here about how the transcendental aspect of created freedom affects the meaning of the social ethics. In the first place, Rahner offers a powerful philosophical and theological basis for the significance of liberal claims to things like the right to religious freedom. To be a person, for Rahner, is to be inherently disposed toward the transcendent, divine mystery. Also, for Rahner, human freedom is not in opposition to God but experiences its character as freedom through dependence on divine mystery. The true and good do not constrain freedom, as strains of liberalism hold. Instead, freedom derives its character from a surfeit of intelligibility—from being disposed in the "endlessly intelligible." Liberal freedom does not follow from agnosticism about the good but from the awareness of manifold visions of the good life, the great variety of which is finally grounded in Divine Mystery. Thus the right to religious freedom—and the equal claim to this right by all persons—is grounded in the claim that all persons are oriented to the transcendent reality of God amid a multiplicity of paths and in a cloud of Mystery. Walter Kasper teases out an additional implication for liberal freedom of this created dependence on divine transcendence: human freedom cannot confer complete satisfaction on itself or on its projects, personal, political, and otherwise. Such a view requires that all ideologies and utopias be viewed critically.[51] Thus Rahner grounds human freedom in a fundamental state of dependence on God. This means that created dependence both allows freedom to retain its spontaneity and also to be "borne and empowered" by the divine. The fact of this dependence is what all persons share equally.

---

48. Rahner, *Foundations of Christian Faith*, 30.
49. Rahner, "Dignity and Freedom of Man," 246.
50. Rahner, *Foundations of Christian Faith*, 34.
51. Kasper, *Theology and Church*, 64–66.

Created Freedom: Mediated, Finite, Sinful

If we were to stop with what I have said thus far of Rahner's concept of the transcendental aspect of created freedom, we would be in a quasi-abstract world. Freedom would be transcendental—an expression of the subject as such. And freedom would be associated almost entirely with the rational capacity for transcendence. But Rahner's picture of created freedom meshes such transcendental concerns with the material world. In fact, he argues that the experience of transcendence itself can only occur through the experience of finitude. In a general way of putting it, this means that we only experience God by going out into the world.[52] In more philosophical fashion, this means that infinite being is only disclosed upon the encounter with finite, sensible objects—not before or after but simultaneous with this encounter. Rahner describes the person's intuition of the infinite through the finite in the following way: "Insofar as he experiences himself as conditioned and limited by sense experience, and all too much conditioned and limited, he has nevertheless already transcended this sense experience. He has posited himself as the subject of a pre-apprehension (*Vorgriff*) which has no intrinsic limit."[53] Accordingly, for Rahner, the freedom or self-possession or subjectivity that characterizes personhood as such depends on the mediation of sense objects, with concrete, embodied, other persons holding privileged place in this process. Thus the dependent character of this self-possession comes more clearly into view. Material mediation is the indispensable context for the existence and achievement of personhood.

How does the concept of created freedom fit into this picture of the mediated character of human transcendence? In "Theology of Freedom," Rahner says that the created nature of freedom is also shown by the fact that human freedom is

> necessarily mediated by an environment and intersubjectivity which of themselves are *a posteriori*, uncontrollable and ultimately unplanned. Man always exercises his original freedom towards himself by merely accepting and passing through the history pre-given and imposed on him. Freedom is the free answer of yes or no to necessity and once more experiences in this its created nature.[54]

---

52. Rahner, "Reflections on the Unity of Love," 245–46. Rahner is reflecting in this passage on the scholastic thesis that God can only be known *a posteriori* from the created world.

53. Rahner, *Foundations of Christian Faith*, 20.

54. Rahner, "Theology of Freedom," 193–94.

Elsewhere Rahner states that created freedom exists in the mode of a creature whose finiteness is known in history, due to its bodily nature, and because of the limits imposed by power.⁵⁵ I will first discuss the concepts of body, necessity, and power as key factors in the dependent and "uncontrollable" quality of created freedom (here we see the condition of freedom in relation to the body). I will next discuss created freedom and intersubjectivity (and here we see freedom in light of the condition of relatedness). In the course of these discussions, I will also touch on what Rahner identifies as a key characteristic of the mediated nature of created freedom: the fact that the situations that mediate such freedom are "always and unavoidably co-determined by guilt."⁵⁶

Rahner says that human freedom is "bodily freedom."⁵⁷ The basis for the positive correlation between freedom and embodiment is the doctrine of the unity of body and soul. Among other points, this doctrine holds that body and soul are not two distinct realities subsequently united but are two constituents of one person—an incarnate being. Moreover, the doctrine holds that the body is the external act of the soul.⁵⁸ It follows from these claims that freedom, which in its transcendental aspect pertains to the soul, is nevertheless always connected by its embodied character to some materiality. This is an ontological connection: Material things become intrinsic aspects of acts of freedom themselves. The positive correlation between freedom and the body means that there can be no perfectly interior acts of freedom unaffected by the sensible world. It also means that there can be no perfectly interior

---

55. Rahner, *Sacramentum Mundi*, 361.

56. Rahner, "Theology of Freedom," 194. Rahner says: "Original sin . . . expresses nothing else but the historical origin of the present, universal, and ineradicable situation of our freedom as co-determined by guilt, and this insofar as this situation has a history in which, because of the universal determination of this history by guilt, God's self-communication in grace comes . . . from the God-Man Jesus Christ." Rahner, *Foundations of Christian Faith*, 114. It is helpful to keep in mind two interwoven trajectories in Rahner's argument. One trajectory is more positive in tone and evokes freedom's fitting dependence in a world in which a person is at home in creation and finitude. The other trajectory sounds a negative note and portrays freedom bound by finitude and constrained never to be complete. This trajectory is associated, as we shall see, with the doctrine of sin; it is also the result of Rahner's lingering idealism. Neither trajectory is entirely separable and it would be a mistake to interpret his theology in light of one of these trajectories alone. Moreover, even given his integration of these two aspects of freedom, Rahner at times appears to favor the positive note of creation and at other times the negative note of sin. In any case, because he speaks of the "createdness" of freedom—and thus of a more historical understanding of creation—it is important to understand Rahner's notion of created freedom in terms of the complex mix of good and evil that always marks human existence.

57. Rahner, "On the Origins of Freedom," 122.

58. Rahner, "On the Origins of Freedom," 122–24.

acts of freedom that do not themselves affect the sensible world. And insofar as material situations are always in some way objectifications of personal guilt, the clouded and tragic nature of guilt enters into freedom itself. It is often not possible to determine what has arisen from freedom, what from necessity, and what from guilt.[59] Here Rahner's arguments counter the constant libertarian tendency to abstract freedom from the concrete and from complexity. Rahner, so to speak, anchors freedom in the body and all the material mediation suggested by embodied existence. He makes freedom an inalienable aspect of the most fundamental human drives for nourishment, shelter, health, and more—all those drives that are often the necessary and predominant focus of the lives of the poor. The indignity endured by the poor in not having a roof over their heads derives both from the exposure to the elements and from the inability of their freedom to arrange such shelter for themselves. Rahner also provides the plausible logic by which to understand the vulnerability of freedom: how, for instance, the concrete condition of prolonged unemployment or hunger or homelessness can profoundly affect the capacity of a person to exercise freedom.

In ontological terms, then, acts of freedom cannot be understood apart from an assessment of their material aspects. But the connection between freedom and the body is also, so to speak, dependent and practical. Finite freedom, while retaining its spontaneity, exists in a body and thus depends on and requires sensible objects in order to act.[60] Moreover, as embodied, freedom from the start finds itself in a context of given internal and external conditions that both limit and make possible its exercise. These conditions limit freedom in the sense that they impose constraints on what freedom can accomplish. The individualistic, Promethean fantasy of freedom bursting all boundaries is just that—a fantasy. In turn, these conditions make possible freedom's exercise in the sense that they evoke desires and aversions about which freedom, in its spontaneity, must decide in light of reason and the good. Walter Kasper calls such conditions the "theonomy of the order of creation" and says that they constitute the "given relations" constitutive of human existence that "[make] freedom possible."[61] Among these incarnate conditions that accompany embodiment are internal characteristics like

---

59. Rahner, *Foundations of Christian Faith*, 108–9.

60. Rahner, "The Theology of Power," 396. Rahner also says: "Thus with the same metaphysical necessity with which a finite freedom (a spiritual power, that is to say!) must be given its object if it is to become active, there precedes the free operation a spontaneous (and spiritually spontaneous too!) act of the appetitive power; and this act ultimately is no other than the innate dynamic orientation of man to his goods." See Rahner, "The Theological Concept of Concupiscentia," 365.

61. Kasper, *Theology and Church*, 52–53.

spirit, rationality, emotion, desire, hunger, and thirst as well as external traits such as family, friends, neighborhood, history, culture, and political and social structures.[62] Rahner notes the delicate balance—freedom is always both spontaneous and dependent; constrained and enabled; transcendent and in the flux of history. In one of his few comments specifically on the topic, he argues that the equality of freedom should be considered in light of the many different spheres or conditions of freedom—some, for instance, economic, others political, and others cultural. Such varied spheres present distinct limits and opportunities for freedom. Moreover, the conditions constitutive of such spheres are both permanent and changing. All of this means, he argues, that the equality of rights or freedom should be affirmed as a fundamental norm of social ethics. In turn, it is essential to pay close attention to internal and external conditions as an indispensable component of the meaning of such equal rights. Freedom, Rahner says, belongs to the "absolute dignity" of persons. Insofar as freedom depends for its exercise on such internal and external conditions, attention to such conditions is normatively demanded by the dignity of the person. At the same time, though, Rahner also argues that it is a mistake to insist too strongly on fixed magnitudes of such conditions—as if the measure of equality could be determined once and for all in the face of historical change.[63]

It is important to emphasize that for however positive the correlation is between freedom and the body, it is not positive without qualification. Freedom's embodied nature involves more than just irenic dependence; it also involves the suffering of constriction to the point of great consequence. As Rahner puts it: "Man as a bodily being . . . is open to being seized by a creaturely influence which is independent of him. . . . There is no 'zone' of the person which is absolutely inaccessible to such influences from without. Every 'external' event can be significant and menacing for the ultimate salvation of the person."[64] How the person is "seized" by such influences can be seen more clearly by considering freedom in light of the concepts of power (which I will here understand as physical force) and necessity. Several theological theses by Rahner on the nature of power as physical force are especially useful here. According to one of these theses, power is a good thing of creation and as such a participation in God's power in the world. This thesis also states that, in common with all created things, power is ambivalent and able to be used for good or ill.[65] With this thesis in mind, it is possible

---

62. Rahner, "Dignity and Freedom of Man," 239–40.
63. Rahner, "Dignity and Freedom of Man," 248.
64. Rahner, "Dignity and Freedom of Man," 242.
65. Rahner, "Theology of Power," 395. I am focusing in this discussion on two of the

to see more clearly the given quality of constriction and vulnerability that marks created human freedom. Such freedom exists amid force, sickness, and death that derive from the created, bodily nature of the person.[66] In fact, it is never possible in the concrete person to separate out entirely these regions of necessity and freedom.[67] Moreover, it simply follows from the fact of freedom's created, embodied character that all acts of freedom are always physical acts that intrude on a space common to others and as such are always acts implicated to some degree in the exercise of force and violence. It is because of this given, created sphere of material force amid which freedom must exercise itself that Rahner says power exists as the condition of the possibility of freedom.[68] He adds that freedom and power are distinct concepts—with freedom having a higher normative nature—but that they are nevertheless "mutually and dialectically independent."[69] There are no individual acts of freedom utterly detached from the constraints of such a common sphere.

But a second theological thesis about power as physical force fills out this picture of created freedom. This thesis holds that power ought never to have existed, that it stems from sin, and that it is one of the forms in which guilt manifests itself.[70] Rahner says of this view of power: "The fact of being threatened from without is . . . a consequence of man's perversion from within."[71] Thus this thesis holds that persons should be in a state of integrity and free from what Rahner calls the theological concept of "concupiscence" or the claim that a person is never able to integrate oneself fully in any decision of freedom but is always affected by forces outside the self that make her suffer.[72] The role of sin gives Rahner's language darker tones

---

three theses on power that Rahner articulates in this essay—one thesis about power as a created reflection of God, the other thesis, as we shall see, about power as a consequence of sin. Rahner's third thesis on power in the essay holds that in the actual order of things the exercise of power is a process of either salvation or perdition. This thesis is pertinent to my discussion here but not as relevant as the other two; hence, I will not focus on it here. For Rahner's discussion of the third thesis, see Rahner, "Theology of Power," 402–7.

66. Rahner, "Theology of Power," 395.
67. Rahner, *Foundations of Christian Faith*, 97.
68. Rahner, "Theology of Power," 396.
69. Rahner, "Theology of Power," 399.
70. Rahner, "Theology of Power," 393.
71. Rahner, "Dignity and Freedom of Man," 242.
72. Rahner, "Theology of Power," 393. See also Rahner, "Theological Concept of Concupiscentia," 360–69. Rahner also speaks of concupiscence in a non-theological fashion as the appetitive act for determinate goods proper to natural human dynamism. In this more philosophical sense, concupiscence can be said to be a "presupposition" for the acts of a finite freedom: Without the natural appetite for already given goods,

when describing the constriction of freedom. Thus it is not enough that freedom must first of all accept the necessity that comes with a world of material force and other persons. Rather, freedom must accept this larger sphere with "courage" in the face of this sphere's "danger."[73] Indeed, Rahner says, the Paschal Mystery is meant to liberate human freedom from its sinful, confined participation in "the prison of the world."[74]

Thus far this discussion of the material aspect of created freedom has focused on two material characteristics of freedom—its mediated and embodied nature. On the basis of these two characteristics, Rahner articulates a range of qualities that evoke the created nature of freedom: the contingency and frailty that mark the body; powerlessness in the face of death;[75] the limits imposed by sensible objects as such; the dialectical interdependence of freedom and power; the inevitable conflict with others in the sphere of freedom or, in another way of putting it, the co-determination of freedom by the free history and guilt of others.[76] It is this last category—that of "others"—that now must be considered more closely. For while the qualities of "mediation" and "embodiment" are crucial aspects of Rahner's concept of freedom, it is essential here to note that the fundamental category by which to understand the material aspect of created freedom is that of personhood. As Rahner puts it: The "environment of persons is the world through which man finds himself and fulfills himself. . . . From a personal and moral point of view, the world of things is of significance only as a factor for man and for his neighbor."[77] That freedom is mediated and embodied is consistent with traditional conceptions of creation; each person, in these conceptions, is created to be at home in the natural world. But that created freedom is understood fundamentally in terms of personhood signals Rahner's more historical understanding of createdness. It also signals the radically personal nature of freedom. On the basis of freedom's mediated and embodied nature, Rahner can affirm that freedom is realized in the "common sphere of the unity of historical subjects."[78]

In fact, Rahner puts this issue in more explicitly personalist terms when he says that freedom has both its origin and fulfillment in the love of

---

finite freedom would not have a world of goods amid which to act. It is on this basis that Rahner says that finite freedom must be given its object in order to become active.

73. Rahner, "On the Origins of Freedom," 126.
74. Rahner, "Theology of Freedom," 196.
75. Rahner, *Foundations of Christian Faith*, 104.
76. Rahner, *Foundations of Christian Faith*, 107.
77. Rahner, "Reflections on the Unity of Love," 240.
78. Rahner, "On the Origins of Freedom," 122.

others as such. Thus he says, for example, of the origin of freedom that the person is "given to himself in freedom by entering in love into the world around him, and by personal encounter and communication with the Thou of intramundane experience."[79] And he adds of the highest achievement of freedom: "The free self-disposal, when morally right and perfect, is precisely the loving communication with the human *Thou* as such (not as mere negation of nor as something different from the 'ego' which wants merely to find *itself*, even though in the other)."[80] Moreover, for Rahner the original relationship to God is through love of neighbor.[81] Thus the deepest meaning of freedom understood as self-transcendence is ultimately "that total believing and hoping surrender of man to God which we call love and which alone justifies men."[82] Thus the dependence of created freedom is manifest in the constraints and conditions of human life. But this dependence is manifest most of all in the "uncontrollable and unplanned" demands and possibilities of human love best understood as the doorway to the divine.

Rahner, then, offers a persuasive account of created freedom that is embodied, finite, and sinful. He affirms freedom's spontaneity even as he affirms a world of constraints and conditions amid which freedom exercises itself—or, tragically, is unable to exercise itself. Thus he rejects the abstract freedom of the present day; freedom is always embodied, never the pure, rational product of a technocratic notion of human capital nor of any other image of a detached libertarianism. And he rejects the atomist vision of solitary, disconnected individuals who have no inherent relation to each other. Instead freedom is oriented toward and fulfilled in the love of other persons, from those close at hand in one's family to persons in broader society to any person as such. Indeed, the fulfillment of freedom in the love of other persons is also the fundamental place of encounter with divine love. But one more aspect of created freedom remains to be examined: created freedom and Christ.

Created Freedom and Christ

We have thus far identified two primary ways in which freedom manifests its createdness. The first is that freedom is "borne and empowered" by its transcendental horizon; the second is that freedom is always mediated by an environment and by intersubjectivity. Here I would like to turn to the

79. Rahner, "Reflections on the Unity of Love," 245.
80. Rahner, "Reflections on the Unity of Love," 241.
81. Rahner, "Theology of Freedom," 189.
82. Rahner, "Reflections on the Unity of Love," 236.

Christological dimension of what Rahner calls the "absolute nearness" toward which created freedom is oriented. This nearness is one other manifestation of freedom's created nature and as such links the transcendental and mediated aspects of createdness. The divine presence is transcendent and immanent; high above and closer to me than I am to myself. Rahner refers to the notion of nearness in two ways, one more philosophical and one more theological. Using the general terminology of createdness, he refers to the "absolute nearness of God." As he puts it, freedom reveals its created character insofar as freedom experiences its empowerment by the transcendental horizon toward the absoluteness of being as a movement toward the "absolute *nearness* to this goal."[83] By emphasizing nearness, Rahner deploys a metaphor that roots the origin and goal of freedom more firmly in human personhood and in the concrete conditions of the world—without, however, identifying the reality of divine being either with human beings or with the world.

But that is a more philosophical way of putting things. Rahner also says that this experience of empowerment or grace to the nearness of divine being is "made clearly objective" only through an interpretation by faith in light of Christian revelation.[84] Thus, for Rahner, human freedom is created by God as the presupposition for the possibility of receiving God's love in Christ.[85] As Walter Kasper puts it, the nature presupposed by grace is freedom.[86] In terms of the incarnation, this means that created freedom never exists in a merely natural world but always is taken up by the supernatural dynamism of our spiritual being that tends toward the absolute nearness of God in Christ. (This is the dynamism signaled by the presence in persons of what Rahner calls the "supernatural existential.")[87] In terms of redemption, this means that created freedom immersed in finitude and sin is ultimately empowered by Christ toward a concrete liberation in Christ in which the "horizon and object of this love liberated for itself are identical."[88] The drive

---

83. Rahner, "Theology of Freedom," 193. It is important here to note that Rahner affirms both that createdness is experienced fundamentally in the process of the transcendence and that createdness "is expressed completely only in and through the whole of the Christian message." See Rahner, *Foundations of Christian Faith*, 75–77.

84. Rahner, "Theology of Freedom," 193.

85. Rahner, "On the Origins of Freedom," 120.

86. Kasper, *Theology and Church*, 50–52.

87. Rahner, "Theology of Freedom," 182–83.

88. Rahner, "Theology of Freedom," 196. Rahner notes that God in Christ gives God's self as absolute nearness to the injured freedom of men and women and that God in Christ also gives God's self as the ground of the free acceptance of this absolute nearness. See Rahner, "Theology of Freedom," 195.

of redeeming love is toward the nearness—the here and now—of concrete human life. Kasper offers a helpful interpretation consistent with this book's theme of "freedom under the sign of the Cross." He says that the path of redeeming love will always involve the struggle of the self-emptying love of the cross seeking the value of others as such.[89] Kasper also says that the "theonomy of the order of salvation" reminds human beings that freedom is always greater than any possible fulfillment and thus that there are no fixed and final achievements or ideologies.[90]

CONCLUSION

Rahner's theology of created freedom provides a compelling account of freedom that is embodied; immersed in history; oriented to relationship; oriented to the good and to God; and consistent with the right to religious freedom at the heart of a liberal political order. In concluding this chapter, I would like briefly to consider such Rahnerian ideas as they apply to the notion of an equality—a norm of great controversy in the Age of Fracture. In doing so, I have been influenced by philosopher Bernard Williams's argument in his classic article, "The Idea of Equality," that the norm of equality can in part be understood as requiring the effort to identify with another human being from the "human point of view." This means, Williams says, that each person as such is owed respect and thus the effort to see the world from his or her point of view and in light of the internal and external conditions that affect the choices he or she has made or will make. I wish to extend what constitutes the "human point of view" to a wider range of concrete conditions; I also wish to complement this wider meaning of the "human" with an explicit appeal to love that includes but goes beyond what is suggested by Williams's use of the requirement of "respect."[91]

To understand what Williams calls the "human point of view," it is helpful to see how theologian Don S. Browning makes a specific connection between the affirmation of equality and the experience of embodied, finite existence. "We meet something in the other," he says, "any human other, be it woman, slave, or person from another race—that tells us that the person thinks, feels, and listens like we do, and has talents like ours and therefore must be a *person* in many respects like us."[92] In fact, Browning argues, without the experience of the latter it is not possible to affirm the former. Too

---

89. Kasper, *Theology and the Church*, 69–70.
90. Kasper, *Theology and the Church*, 53.
91. Williams, "Idea of Equality," 112–18.
92. Browning, *Fundamental Practical Theology*, 179.

many narrative philosophies and technical economic theories, he says, offer no firm ground for equality because they abstract from a "level of bodily interaction with the environment that is below our higher-level linguistic construals."[93] This level of bodily interaction, Browning says, is the scene of the "thickness, resistance, and intractability of experience" that provide the data that permit practical reason to make the reversible and universalizable judgments that support human equality and are integral to the law of love.[94] Browning does not spell out specifically how this is so but closely connects the experience itself of the "thickness and resistance" of reality and of others with the affirmation of shared personhood and equality. Or, as Browning puts it: "Our ongoing direct experience of the agency, initiative, and resistance of other persons may convince us that they are indeed persons and need to be treated according to the principle of equal regard."[95]

Rahner does not speak as specifically as does Browning to a precise experience or logic of equal regard. For instance, in his extended discussion of the law of love, Rahner does not specifically engage the subject of reversibility as a key component of a notion of equality. Nevertheless, Rahner provides ample grounds—and more clear metaphysical ones than does Browning—for arriving at similar conclusions about the integral relationship between the apprehension of the transcendental, equal worth of the other and the experience of intersubjective, limited historical existence. Our experience of the latter is the doorway to the former. For instance, Rahner points to this logic of equality when he identifies the acceptance of historical existence not just with freedom but, even more, with love. As ontological fact, the formal object of love is identical with the a priori horizon of the will: Rahner understands this formal object as God.[96] As concrete task, love is oriented to the value of the person as such and, accordingly, requires the acceptance of the whole of the person for her own sake and of her life in the world. Thus Rahner frequently links love to such phrases as "the totality of the acceptance of one's own nature, i.e., love"[97] and "the complete self-realization of the one person in its very unity."[98] Here, then, Rahner adds the imperative of Christian love to the egalitarian respect that Williams sees as necessary for understanding the "human point of view." And here Rahner confirms Browning's insight: We come to value the equality of others not

---

93. Browning, *Fundamental Practical Theology*, 180–81.
94. Browning, *Fundamental Practical Theology*, 179.
95. Browning, *Fundamental Practical Theology*, 181.
96. Rahner, "'Commandment' of Love," 446.
97. Rahner, "'Commandment' of Love," 442.
98. Rahner, "'Commandment' of Love," 443.

through things like abstract neoliberal accounts of freedom but through the visceral, loving encounter with an embodied, intersubjective world. In this chapter, Rahner has provided a fundamental theological logic for a renewed theology of freedom. In the next chapter, I will turn to a constructive public theological account of "created freedom under the sign of the Cross" for the United States.

CHAPTER FIVE

A Catholic Public Theology of Freedom for the United States

IN AN APT ILLUSTRATION of the American age of neoliberalism, Mark Janus was willing to freeload to get the benefits of his union-negotiated job. Janus worked as a child support specialist at the Illinois Department of Healthcare and Family Services. As an employee of state government, he was required by law to be represented by the American Federation of State, County, and Municipal Employees. But he was opposed to the union's public policy positions. To resolve this contradiction, Janus did not seek a non-union job at another institution. Nor did he accept the then-existing precedent of the United States Supreme Court that prohibited unions from using dues paid by members to support public policy advocacy by unions. (The precedent required union-represented employees to pay dues to support the union in contract negotiations but permitted all union-represented employees *not* to pay additional dues to support union policy advocacy.)[1] Instead, Janus sought to retain the pay and benefits of his union job (in all likelihood, higher pay and benefits than he would get in a comparable position at a non-union shop). And he also sued to pay no dues whatsoever—neither for contract negotiation nor for policy advocacy—to the union legally required to represent him. Janus couched his position as a constitutional claim of free speech. By having to pay union dues of any kind, he argued, his freedom of speech was compelled to be in support of any public policy positions a union might take. In a 2018 decision, the US Supreme Court sided with Janus on

---

1. Abood v. Detroit Board of Education, 431 US 209 (1977).

free speech grounds and allowed him to opt out of paying any union dues at all, whether for contract negotiations or for policy advocacy. In doing so, the court sidestepped the argument that Janus was a freeloader who received the contractual benefits of the union without paying to support the union that negotiated those benefits. The court also as a matter of law saw little difference between union contract negotiations and union public policy advocacy; the longstanding precedent distinguishing these actions was thrown out. In effect, for the Supreme Court majority, the payment of dues for contract negotiation became indistinguishable from the payment of dues for explicit political activity. To be sure, the *Janus* case came before the US Supreme Court as a right-to-work stalking horse for a long-desired neoliberal aim: to decimate the political power of public employee unions by denying them the dues by which they are enabled to represent workers and to advocate in the public square. With the conservative majority's tendentious opinion, this neoliberal aim was accomplished.[2]

In the *Janus* case, we can see the world described by Daniel Rodgers in *Age of Fracture*. It is not simply that freedom has normative and constitutional primacy; to a greater or lesser degree, that has been the case throughout American history. Instead, as Rodgers puts it, since the late 1970s in the United States an abstract and reductionist understanding of freedom has obtained such primacy under the influence of a formalized, microeconomic thought. Rodgers describes this freedom in a way that captures the notion of freedom holding sway in the *Janus* case: It is freedom "individualized and privatized, released of its larger burdens . . . cut loose from the burdens and responsibilities that had once so closely accompanied it."[3] Rodgers also speaks of a turn in the last decades not simply away from a sense of community or society but, more specifically, away from the integration of freedom into a sense of community or society. In words that again capture the letter and spirit of the anti-union *Janus* case, Rodgers says of the Age of Fracture: "Strong metaphors of society were supplanted by weaker ones. Imagined collectivities shrank; notions of structure and power thinned out."[4] Amartya Sen's critique of libertarian freedom also clarifies the problematic, reductionist nature of freedom in the *Janus* case. For Sen, libertarianism mistakenly identifies freedom only with what a person can control—in the *Janus* case, with the payment of union dues for contract negotiation.[5] But this narrow identification of freedom with personal control means that one

2. See also Chicago Tribune Staff, "5 Things to Know."
3. Rodgers, *Age of Fracture*, 40.
4. Rodgers, *Age of Fracture*, 3.
5. Sen, "Liberty as Control," 207–8, 215–18.

is free only to the extent that one personally exercises levers of power and that one is *not* free in the event that anyone or any institution exercises such levers of power, even if on one's behalf and for the sake of one's freedom and in cooperation with oneself. Finally, the historical sociology of Evelyn Nakano Glenn should give us pause before the *Janus* case's preeminent claim of freedom-as-independence. In American history, she argues, such claims of independence have usually come at the racialized and gendered expense of others—others whose hidden, dependent work makes such independent freedom possible, or others to whom an inherent, dependent nature has been attributed (for instance, African Americans and women) over against the independent nature of the free, white, and male.[6]

The *Janus* case is representative of the Age of Fracture and thus a helpful place to begin this final chapter. The work of Rodgers, Sen, and Glenn all help to identify the flaws in the *Janus* version of freedom (the Catholic bishops of the United States criticized the freedom at issue in the case as "too absolute and extreme").[7] In this chapter, I will complement such criticisms by making a constructive case for a Catholic public theology of freedom. I will proceed by using Rahner's theology of created freedom as a framework. At a minimum, Rahner sets out what ought to be the content of such a theology: the "constitutive polarity" of the transcendental and concrete dimensions of freedom.[8] In particular, I will focus on these dimensions in terms of the categories of freedom and the body; freedom and history; freedom and relationship; and liberal freedom, the good, and God. I will appeal to three American writers to address these categories. First, I will turn to the theology of Shawn Copeland to address freedom and the body and freedom in history. Next I will draw on the work of philosopher Elizabeth Anderson to discuss freedom and relationship. And last I will examine the work of Jesuit theologian David Hollenbach to establish the basis of liberal freedom in the context of the common good and of the possibility of belief in God. Rahner's "constitutive polarity" lays down the necessary ingredients for a theology of freedom. The work of Copeland, Anderson, and Hollenbach provide specifically American responses to key aspects of Rahner's thought. A synthesis of their views yields a powerful and plausible Catholic public theology of freedom for the United States.

---

6. Glenn, *Unequal Freedom*, 20–24.

7. Brief for the United States Conference of Catholic Bishops as Amicus Curiae, *Janus v. American Federation of State, County, and Municipal Employees*, 585 US___ (2018).

8. I am borrowing the term "constitutive polarity" from Maureen Junker-Kenny. See Junker-Kenny, *Approaches to Theological Ethics*, 210.

FREEDOM, EMBODIMENT, HISTORY

Drawing on the concept of createdness, Rahner argues that freedom must be understood in terms of embodiment and history. Human freedom, he says, is "bodily freedom" and as such freedom becomes itself in part by accepting the dependence associated with embodiment. Moreover, he notes, freedom can only be known in history; there is no vantage point from which to understand freedom apart from the push and pull of forces like conflict and class. In turning in the second chapter to the work of Evelyn Nakano Glenn and Orlando Patterson, I sought to explore sociological implications of these aspects of Rahner's theology of freedom. I noted above how Glenn shows that issues of race and gender derived specifically from attributes of embodiment like skin color and sex have played decisive roles in the interpretation of freedom in much of American history. Patterson's work shows how the most elemental bodily freedom—to have the chains of slavery removed—stands at the cultural source of the entire Western history of freedom. He also shows how throughout this history the meaning of freedom has become a battleground with constant efforts by the wealthy and powerful to define freedom in rarefied categories far removed from the elemental concerns of embodiment present to the enslaved and oppressed.

The force of Rahner's claims and the findings of the work of Glenn and Patterson point toward the need for a Catholic public theology of freedom that provides sufficient attention to embodiment and history. The powerful work of African American theologian Shawn Copeland responds to this need. What should the starting point be for a Catholic public theology of freedom for the American context? In the usual run of things, that starting point has been something like the freedom invoked by Mark Janus in his US Supreme Court case: individualistic, male, with European roots, more or less libertarian. But Copeland's theology points toward a different place to begin: freedom as it is experienced by poor women of color. After all, we have to start somewhere. Freedom is only known in history and, standing in the tradition of thinkers like Glenn and Patterson, Copeland appeals to the insights into freedom by arguably the most oppressed population in the world—poor women of color. In making such a claim, she is not arguing in terms of identity politics. Throughout she presumes a universal notion of personhood and its accompanying capacity for self-transcendence. (Notions about identity in her argument are both indispensable and subordinate to presumptions about personhood.) Thus the insights into freedom of poor women of color are not meant to displace insights into freedom on the part of all others. Nor are such insights by poor women of color meant to be a sectarian body of knowledge inaccessible to all who are not poor women of color. Instead, Copeland argues that we change our lens: When we think about freedom, what can we learn about the meaning of freedom to everyone by beginning our reflection with the meaning of freedom to the most oppressed? In what follows in this section of the chapter, I will consider the ways that Copeland draws on the body and history to make her case.

Freedom and the Body

At the heart of her argument are two symbiotic historical developments: the fifteenth-century European imperial drive to conquer indigenous lands and enslave millions, and the later emergence of Enlightenment thought. "From the middle of the fifteenth century forward," she says, "a totalizing dynamic of domination, already obvious in antisemitism and misogyny, made itself felt in the so-called 'new worlds' through colonialism and genocide, cultural imperialism and racism."[9] This was domination fueled by the creation of "demonized difference"; the identification of embodied traits of Blackness and brownness that rendered whole populations less than human subjects and thus worthy of oppression.[10] The insidious abstractness of Enlightenment thought rationalized and reified this turn. Rationality was prized over the body—a philosophical move propelled by a racist logic. "The enervating dimensions and underside of Enlightenment evaluations that correlated white skin with reason, intelligence, civilization, goodness, and creativity also correlated non-white skin, black skin with unreason, ignorance, savagery, depravity, and mimicry," Copeland says.[11] But the fault did not lie only in philosophy. Christian theology, too, was caught up in the unholy trinity of empire, domination, and difference. "At times willingly, ambivalently, actively, silently, Christianity partnered in that domination," she argues. "This complicity, no matter how fleeting or how superficial, compromised Christian theology's reverence, regard, and defense of the human."[12] Copeland's theology of freedom should be read as a response to this catastrophic history of contempt for the body.

But how to redeem this history of contempt for the body in a contemporary theology of freedom? Copeland does so by making the body a central focus of her work. Moreover, it is not the body as a philosophical abstraction but the body in time, space, history.[13] The notion of "subject"

---

9. Copeland, "Turning Theology," 768.
10. Copeland, *Enfleshing Freedom*, 2.
11. Copeland, *Enfleshing Freedom*, 10.
12. Copeland, "Turning Theology," 768.
13. Copeland, *Enfleshing Freedom*, ix–x.

favored by the Enlightenment, she argues, is "abstract, bloodless, disembodied, deracinated, and distant."[14] By contrast, the notion of "person" to which theology should instead turn is "tangible and solid, flesh and blood, material and embodied; rooted in space and time, in culture and relationships."[15] The opaqueness of such embodied, historical experience may resist theological efforts to refine and specify its meaning.[16] But such challenges do not diminish the obligation of theology to grapple with the meaning of the body in history. For Copeland, human freedom is oriented toward a "transcendental end or purpose for which human beings are divinely created."[17] The great sin of the enslavement of African American women (I note them here because they play a central role in Copeland's argument) was its violation of this end. But to leave the matter of violation there is to miss the agonizing, embodied point of it all; the violation cried to heaven precisely because it was against the bodies of these women. If we abstract from the embodiment, we miss the sin. If we fail to contemplate the embodied agonies of enslaved women, we miss the reality that cries out for redemption. Thus Copeland evokes the "constitutive polarity" manifest in the unity-in-distinction of the transcendental and concrete dimensions of freedom. Rahner emphasized the transcendental dimension while including the concrete. Copeland emphasizes the concrete—and especially the body as a manifestation of the concrete—while including the transcendental.

In what follows, I engage Copeland's argument for the role of the body in a theology of freedom in four ways: the body and freedom in the doctrines of creation and incarnation; the body, freedom, and the cross; the primacy of poor women of color in a theology of freedom; and the body, freedom, and history. For Copeland, the creaturely status of persons is made manifest by the body's immersion in space and time and by the body's orientation to others.[18] But this creaturely status is infused with spirit. For Copeland, the incarnation works especially as a theological principle that signals the presence of spirit in matter, of divinity in humanity. Thus she speaks of the body as "the medium through which human spirit incarnates and exercises freedom in time and space."[19] She also says "the body is an essential quality of the soul," and that the body is sacramental and as such "constitutes a site

14. Copeland, "Turning Theology," 768.
15. Copeland, "Turning Theology," 768.
16. Copeland, *Enfleshing Freedom*, 7.
17. Copeland, *Enfleshing Freedom*, 48.
18. Copeland, *Enfleshing Freedom*, 2–5, 92.
19. Copeland, *Enfleshing Freedom*, 39.

of divine revelation."[20] Still another way she approaches the image of the human being as a spirit-infused creature is through the language of "essential freedom." For Copeland, what is "essential" about freedom refers to a reality and a possibility. The "essential" character of freedom appears to be the inalienable aspect of a person that with resounding clarity or with an inarticulate cry signals a refusal to be considered an object. "Not even the most unlettered women and men could be convinced," Copeland argues, "that they ought to be objects or property, bought and sold at whim—that they ought to relinquish a claim on humanity. This was true, even when necessity or self-preservation forced them to dissemble and to deny a love of liberty."[21] But that inalienable, transcendent reality of essential freedom is paired with Copeland's concrete sense that freedom is also a possibility meant to be worked out in the dynamism of embodied human life. "In and through embodiment, we human persons grasp and realize our essential freedom through engagement and communion with other embodied selves," she says.[22]

Thus freedom is not a matter of intellect alone; nor of conformity with abstract truth; nor of escape from the constraints of embodiment; nor of consistency with so-called natural laws of biology conceived in ahistorical fashion. Instead, freedom is always expressed or "enfleshed"—to borrow language from the title of Copeland's book—for good or for ill in the historicity of embodied human life. In saying this, Copeland makes both a descriptive and normative statement: It is the nature of human freedom to be expressed in the body; it is also the fulfillment of freedom to be expressed in the body in ways consistent with our created ordering toward love, friendship, family, justice, and more. The conceptual problem to which she responds is a modern-day Gnosticism that writes any realistic engagement with the body out of a theology of freedom or that remains oblivious to the symbolic role of the body in shaping communal possibilities for freedom. Indeed, for Copeland, human freedom cannot be understood in abstraction from complexities of society and history. In particular, in the West at least, human freedom cannot be understood apart from the post-fifteenth-century era of empire, colonialism, and enslavement that found its fuel for rule in the perverse energies generated by the "demonized difference" of racialized and gendered bodies. Thus Copeland situates human freedom amid a vast field of forces. On the one hand, in what Copeland calls the "social body" or society, there is the power of cultural valuations of white, Black, brown,

20. Copeland, *Enfleshing Freedom*, 8.
21. Copeland, *Enfleshing Freedom*, 41–42.
22. Copeland, *Enfleshing Freedom*, 8.

gendered, and sexualized bodies. Moreover, this cultural power interacts with vast practices and systems of politics, economics, and technology. The modern era may have produced the freedom at the heart of liberalism. But it did so on the backs of millions trapped in the domination fostered by vast systems of oppression. Copeland does not want us to think about the meaning of human freedom at the expense of situating persons amid such oppressive realities that existed in the past and remain unredeemed in the present.

Copeland, then, reimagines the relationship between the body and freedom for her theological anthropology. The body and freedom are placed in history; freedom is and ought to be "enfleshed" in time and space. By insisting on this, Copeland strips away the possibility that freedom can rightly be identified with the abstract, rational configurations common to the Enlightenment's European white male subject and manifest in the irruption of libertarian thought in our Age of Fracture. But a crucial aspect of her argument is her connection of theological anthropology and Christology; the concept of the body plays a mediating role in this connection. When Copeland says that the body mediates God's presence in history, she is speaking in the key of both the incarnation and the cross. In the former sense, the body manifests transcendent spirit to the world. In the latter sense, the redemptive power of the crucified and risen body of Jesus Christ gathers in and lifts up the brutalized bodies of history. Indeed, for Copeland, theological anthropology earns its credibility to the extent that it conceives of the body and freedom in a way that allows for the placement of "black broken bodies beside [Jesus Christ's] crucified broken body."[23]

In turn, Copeland makes the connection between Christology and the broken Black and brown bodies of history in several steps. The first is that she takes seriously Christ's assumption of a human body as prone as any other to the racialized, oppressive forces of history.[24] Moreover, she establishes Jesus Christ as the "paradigm" of enfleshed freedom, as out of love he sacrificed his body on the cross for the sake of the kingdom of God. Thus the life of Jesus Christ stands as the ideal for what it means to be free and as such both confirms that freedom is fulfilled in service to the kingdom and judges that freedom detached from such a purpose falls far short of the ideal.[25] Copeland also draws on the analogies of history: Jesus Christ was killed by the forces of imperial Rome and so, too, were millions of Black and brown persons crushed by the enslavement and colonization of European imperial

---

23. Copeland, *Enfleshing Freedom*, 130.
24. Copeland, *Enfleshing Freedom*, 81.
25. Copeland, *Enfleshing Freedom*, 53.

powers.[26] But beyond these appeals to exemplar and analogy, Copeland makes clear the salvific connection between a Christological focus on the crucified and risen body of Christ and a theological anthropological focus on the broken bodies of history. Chiefly, this connection works "proleptically": Christ's death and resurrection transcends time and anticipates and encompasses all death, including the abject and fatal misery of the racialized and gendered victims of modernity.[27] In this process, Christ evokes the anguished memory of the lost.[28] He neither empties nor obscures the identity of the persons who have died. Rather, his death and resurrection "interrupts" their abjection in history and points toward a final horizon of hope.[29] Moreover, the salvific power of the self-giving of the cross makes possible the practice of solidarity with the dispossessed for the sake of the Kingdom.[30] Finally, in the Eucharist the joining of the broken lack and brown bodies of history (and of all bodies) to the Mystical Body of Christ is made tangible to the church.[31] Christology and theological anthropology are joined in the sacramentality of the Eucharist.

Freedom and History

In *Age of Fracture*, Rodgers argued that the United States since the 1970s has developed a pronounced libertarian emphasis on freedom oriented to an immediate present at the self-deceptive expense of a complex past. For Rodgers, the price of this largely market-based logic of immediacy and manifold choice has been the loss of a sense of history as a slow, agonizing process rife with racial injustice.[32] The Catholic theologian Margaret Farley notes the feminist criticism of such an abstract freedom, whether in its libertarian version of the last years or in longer-standing versions of the solitary male subject: "Feminists know that freedom turns up empty when abstracted from social histories and concrete, specific bonds."[33] Farley also argues that what should oblige our respect for persons is their freedom in the context of our histories of desires and loves all of which are shaped by our embodied,

---

26. Copeland, *Enfleshing Freedom*, 55–61.
27. Copeland, *Enfleshing Freedom*, 5.
28. Copeland, *Enfleshing Freedom*, 53.
29. Copeland, *Enfleshing Freedom*, 5.
30. Copeland, *Enfleshing Freedom*, 99.
31. Copeland, *Enfleshing Freedom*, 5.
32. Rodgers, *Age of Fracture*, 112, 188–91, 254.
33. Farley, "Feminist Version," 184.

relational selves.[34] I note the work of Rodgers and Farley because Copeland stands in their stream of thought and deepens and widens the current.

Copeland makes three key claims about the body, freedom, and history: that the meaning of freedom is only attainable by engagement with the history of American slavery; that the narratives of freed African American women slaves can tell us about the meaning of freedom; and that the freedom of poor women of color should become the measure by which we think about the freedom of all human persons. First, then, about the turn back to slavery to understand freedom. In the second chapter, I appealed to the sociology of Orlando Patterson to show how in the Western world freedom has always drawn its deepest meaning from the structure and culture of slavery. Copeland focuses the logic of Patterson's argument on the enslavement that followed the onset of fifteenth-century colonialism. For these centuries, she argues, a toxic mix of raw domination, blind racism, and technological distraction conspired to hide this oppressive history.[35] But the inalienable connection of Christology and theological anthropology provides the rationale for the defiance of such forgetfulness. "There is one who does not forget—Jesus of Nazareth, who is the Christ of God. He does not forget poor, dark, and despised bodies. For these, for all, for us, he gave his body in fidelity to the . . . reign of God, which opposes the reign of sin."[36] Those crushed by enslavement still have a story to tell about freedom. And theology may not forget such stories. "From the perspective of a contextual theology of social transformation, the full meaning of human freedom . . . can be clarified only in grappling strenuously with the 'dangerous memory' of slavery."[37]

To be sure, there are many such stories. But we have to start somewhere. Copeland starts with the stories told by African American women after their emancipation in the nineteenth century. If we want to know the meaning of freedom, why not pay special attention to the experience and reflection of those who became free after prolonged enslavement? Several things stand out in Copeland's retelling of these stories. One is that freedom exists within a transcendent, given framework. The freed women testified to refusals, compromises, and challenges as they navigated the brute slaveowner force that sought to compel the violation of their transcendent end.[38] The liberation from such compelling force meant the recovery of their divinely ordained birthright: freedom. Indeed, Copeland notes that freed women

---

34. Farley, "Feminist Version," 196–98.
35. Copeland, *Enfleshing Freedom*, 2–3.
36. Copeland, *Enfleshing Freedom*, 53.
37. Copeland, *Enfleshing Freedom*, 3.
38. Copeland, *Enfleshing Freedom*, 48.

understood that God was the source of their freedom and meant for them to be free.[39] Moreover, biblical values provided a framework for understanding what freedom was for—a framework that contrasted with the scope of what had been taken from them in slavery.[40] Thus Copeland notes that freed women understood that freedom was for marriage, family, and community—all things torn from them in slavery.[41] Moreover, Copeland takes special note of the degree of intrusive coercion done to women's bodies, including but going beyond their compelled labor. Here we think of children taken from their mothers, sold, and never to be seen by their mothers again; the prohibition on marriage to someone they love; and the rape, sexual assault, and concubinage regularly imposed on women by slavemasters and their families.[42] In the face of such violations of bodily freedom, freed women savored the connection between freedom and self-possession and self-love. As Copeland tells it, freedom for them meant not allowing their sexual and reproductive being to be used for another's purposes; and it also meant they could delight—even with abandon—in these aspects of their selves, too. To be sure, the existence of freedom within such a transcendent, realist framework did not mean that autonomy was unimportant. Copeland notes its essential significance: "The abolition of slavery was a necessary condition if [freed women] were to enjoy autonomy, the exercise of choice, free will, and action. But escape, abolition, and emancipation, in and of themselves, were insufficient. Freedom required resources, chief among these the skills of reading and writing, tools critical for formal education."[43] Negative freedom alone was not enough. To be freed was to be free for something. Such positive freedom required conditions to be fulfilled—like the provision of schooling—to enable its exercise.

Orlando Patterson has argued that the sociological origins of the value of freedom in Western consciousness can be traced to women's terror of enslavement in ancient Greece.[44] Copeland invites an analogous object of attention: to understand the meaning of freedom today in the United States, it is imperative to turn to the testimony of African American women who in the nineteenth century were freed from slavery. By hearing such stories from the past, we validate each such person in her own right. And we also learn to train our ear to hear what freed women said of freedom and to

39. Copeland, *Enfleshing Freedom*, 42, 48.
40. Copeland, *Enfleshing Freedom*, 42.
41. Copeland, *Enfleshing Freedom*, 48–49.
42. Copeland, *Enfleshing Freedom*, 50.
43. Copeland, *Enfleshing Freedom*, 40.
44. Patterson, *Freedom*, 78.

consider how their insights can help us assess the vast experience of constraint of poor women of color today. "What might it mean," Copeland asks, "for poor women of color to grasp themselves as human subjects, to grapple with the meaning of liberation and freedom?"[45] For Copeland, this priority of the freedom of poor women of color—whom she says should be the "new anthropological subject of Christian theological reflection"—is demanded by the untold anguish of history and by the evident oppression of the present.[46] But it is also an imperative that follows from her understanding of the role of the body in theological anthropology and Christology. Our attention to suffering bodies in history should lead us to the suffering body on the Cross. And on the Cross we find in the death of Jesus Christ the manifestation of a divine, redemptive love in solidarity with all, but especially with the most oppressed—a category that surely in today's world includes poor women of color.[47]

It's important to recognize the specific character of Copeland's claim. She is not invoking identity politics or political correctness. She is saying, "Look! Look at those we've missed because we've been looking in so many other places for the meaning of freedom!" She rejects what since the Enlightenment has been the long-assumed identification of the meaning of freedom with the experience of white males of European origin. But she is not rejecting white males of European origin; she is inviting them to consider anew the meaning of freedom in light of the experience of poor women of color. She is rejecting old standby theories of gender that obscured the depth and breadth of the experience of freedom of poor women of color: for instance, the assumption that all experience can be subsumed by male experience or the assumption of women's essential nature in theories of complementarity.[48] But she rejects these evasive universalisms for the sake of the universalism of the freedom of the created spirit of the human person. The experience of freedom of poor women of color is one instance of this universalism. The consideration of such particular experience should be undertaken for the sake of all persons.

I have argued that a Catholic public theology of freedom for an American context should include in prominent fashion the concepts of the body and history. Copeland's theology of freedom draws precisely on such concepts and, in doing so, connects the suffering bodies of the past and present to the suffering body of Christ. As a consequence, the freedom of poor

---

45. Copeland, *Enfleshing Freedom*, 88.
46. Copeland, *Enfleshing Freedom*, 90.
47. Copeland, *Enfleshing Freedom*, 89.
48. Copeland, *Enfleshing Freedom*, 90–91.

women of color becomes a starting point for theological reflection or, to use Copeland's phrasing, a new anthropological subject for the consideration of freedom. The false universal derived from the experience of the white male of European origins recedes into the background. The pervasive and long-neglected experience of poor women of color comes into view. By making such an argument, Copeland powerfully expands the scope of the political community. But I would like to call attention to two ways in which her account could be developed. One way pertains to the connection between freedom and relationality. To be sure, she certainly establishes this connection at the heart of her theology of freedom: the created body inherently conveys relationality. But in her overall account, the concept of relationality remains underdeveloped relative to the notion of the body. Another lacuna in her account stems from its silence on the issue of political authority. Her work on freedom stands in the tradition of prophetic political theology demanding the inclusion of all in the political community. But it engages the political more as a matter of critique, not construction: as a matter of who has been left out of the political community but not as much as a matter of who has authority within the political community. Accordingly, in the next sections of the chapter, I will consider more specifically freedom and relationality and freedom and political authority. First, I will examine the implications for Catholic public theology of relationality in the theory of freedom of American philosopher Elizabeth Anderson. In the final section of the chapter, I will consider Catholic theologian David Hollenbach's arguments on behalf of freedom, political authority, and liberalism.

ELIZABETH ANDERSON AND THE "SOCIAL CONDITIONS" OF FREEDOM

The concrete and transcendent dimensions of the constitutive polarity of freedom provide a guiding light to the argument for a Catholic public theology of freedom for the American context. Shawn Copeland's work provides a compelling account of freedom in relation to the body and to history, two of the concrete and crucial aspects of this constitutive polarity. I will next turn to the work of American philosopher Elizabeth Anderson for a similarly compelling account of another concrete, crucial aspect of this polarity: relationship. Of course, the social and relational nature of the person is a central theme of Catholic thought. Not infrequently, the encyclical tradition of Catholic social teaching has invoked such concepts as solidarity and the common good as antidotes for a runaway freedom in liberal societies. But I think we are at a new moment of Catholic engagement with such ideas. One challenge facing Catholic social thought is the survival of liberal political societies at all in the face of the global rise of autocratic ethnic nationalism. Another challenge is the integration into Catholic thought of the sophistication of feminist reflection on the nature of relationality. Catholic thought often appeals to relationality in a more benign fashion to point to possibilities for community in a relentlessly self-interested world. Feminist thought includes such possibilities but also points to the brazen and subtle ways in which relationality is distorted into a tool of oppression. On both counts—for her commitments to liberalism and to a complex view of relationality—Anderson is a promising partner for Catholic thought on freedom in the present day.

From Libertarianism to the Social Conditions of Freedom

Anderson sets her understanding of freedom sharply against the libertarianism of the Age of Fracture, and her integration of the concepts of freedom and relationship is at the root of this contrast. Where libertarians, for instance, celebrate the solitary entrepreneurial "job creator," Anderson rejects what she calls a "Robinson Crusoe" vision of the economy. Instead, she argues for an understanding of economic freedom that underscores the dependence of any entrepreneur on a complex world of relationships that includes laborers, education systems, care workers, and more.[49] In more theoretical terms, Anderson rejects the libertarian position that the legal right to do what one wants without having to ask permission and without interference from others is definitive of freedom. What can it mean to affirm such a notion of freedom, she asks, if one has little internal capacity or external means actually to act? Here we can think, for instance, of persons who are chronic targets of racial discrimination or chronically unemployed. Such social conditions surely wear down internal capacities and wash away external means of assistance. Moreover, Anderson asks, what can it mean to identify freedom with non-interference alone if in fact actual free action almost always requires participation in relationships that involve communication, organization, and more? Here we can think of those pushed to the margins of society who may not face legal interference but who may be excluded from the relationships and institutions that would facilitate their action. In Anderson's account, libertarianism's excessive individualism abstracts people from the world of relationships that is definitive of freedom.[50]

Anderson, then, rejects libertarianism as an acceptable basis for a free society. But she does so as a liberal committed to the dignity of the

49. Anderson, "What Is the Point of Equality?," 321–24.
50. Anderson, "What Is the Point of Equality?," 315.

individual, if not to libertarian individualism. Thus she draws on Kant to argue that persons have a worth or dignity that requires respect regardless of anyone's preferences or desires.[51] She associates that worth or dignity with freedom, which she defines at minimum to mean that persons "govern their lives by their own wills."[52] On the basis of such dignity and freedom, she asserts that persons are equally moral agents with powers for moral responsibility; for cooperation according to the principles of justice; and for shaping a conception of the good.[53] On this Kantian substructure, Anderson teases out and emphasizes an inalienable dimension of personal relationality. On the one hand, the reality of relationship provides the context for the fundamental moral tension of social life. Our inherently equal worth and its association with freedom establishes the obligation for each citizen to respect and provide the social conditions of this worth and freedom for any other citizen. The aim is not to provide precisely equal amounts of goods understood as social conditions to all persons. Rather, the obligation is to secure the particular social conditions that each citizen requires to have equal standing over a whole life.[54] The equal worth of citizens requires such equal standing—a standing that fundamentally reflects a citizen's freedom in the context of relationship. Anderson calls the demand of equal worth understood in such fashion "democratic equality" and defines it to mean that "the social condition of living a free life is that one stand in relations of equality with others."[55] However, this may be what equal worth demands but such a demand—and even the valuation of worth itself—is in constant tension with the destructive allure of unequal relations. Anderson imbues such unequal relations with malevolent moral power. They arise from and result in superior and inferior attributions of moral worth. Those on top of a hierarchy tend toward the assumption that their greater worth justifies their power—perhaps to the point of violence—over those of lesser worth.[56]

Thus the moral demand for democratic equality is fraught with possibilities for failure. But this is a merit of Anderson's proposal, not a defect. In her argument, democratic politics become an inescapable dimension of the possibility of democratic equality; apart from democratic politics, the structures of unequal relations cannot change.[57] This emphasis on politics

---

51. Anderson, "What Is the Point of Equality?," 319.
52. Anderson, "What Is the Point of Equality?," 315.
53. Anderson, "What Is the Point of Equality?," 312.
54. Anderson, "What Is the Point of Equality?," 318.
55. Anderson, "What Is the Point of Equality?," 315.
56. Anderson, "What Is the Point of Equality?," 312.
57. Anderson, "What Is the Point of Equality?," 288–89.

is a welcome addition to Catholic social thought, which tends to downplay conflict and the challenge of politics. This emphasis also points to an especially helpful aspect of Anderson's account of freedom and relationship: that freedom is at stake at both a structural and distributive level (or, in terms of Catholic social thought, as both a matter of social justice and distributive justice). Indeed, her argument for democratic equality is an effort to move away from a misplaced emphasis on what she calls "equality of fortune," which is the standard theory in the United States by which we engage the normative value of social equality. This is a "starting-gate theory" in which each person is assumed to begin with an equal measure of freedom. Moreover, the theory of the equality of fortune assumes "*atomistic egoism and self-sufficiency as the norm for human beings.*"[58] In turn, assumptions about personal responsibility and individual talents play an outsized role in normative judgements of distributive justice about who ought to get what from both the market economy and from schemes of social welfare. For Anderson, there are numerous problems with such a distributive scheme—its atomistic egoism chief among them. But its great failing is how it has come to operate independently from a more encompassing structural analysis; distributions are far more a matter of socially constructed relationships than of inherent personal qualities. Indeed, it would be more correct to say that structural relations profoundly affect distributive opportunities. Or, in another way of putting it, unequal structural relations that constitute oppression and constrain freedom lead to unequal distributions of freedoms for essential social goods. Or, in Anderson's phrasing, "democratic egalitarians are fundamentally concerned with the relationships within which goods are distributed, not only with the distribution of good themselves."[59] For these reasons, Anderson insists—and Catholic social thought should too—that democratic equality should "integrate the demands of equal recognition with those of equal distribution."[60]

The Social Conditions of Freedom: Negative and Positive Aspects

In the theory of democratic equality, then, citizens are obliged to secure for each other the social conditions of freedom. These conditions encompass both structural and distributive matters; they also have a negative ("freedom from") and positive ("freedom for") character. Anderson's account of the negative conditions—which she calls "oppression"—is especially salient. She rejects the singular, neo-Marxist mode of oppression that often afflicts

---

58. Anderson, "What Is the Point of Equality?," 311.
59. Anderson, "What Is the Point of Equality?," 314.
60. Anderson, "What Is the Point of Equality?," 314.

postmodern thought. She also offers a bracing analysis of the mutual dependence of freedom and equality that dovetails with longstanding concerns in Catholic social thought about the different kinds of oppression to which persons are vulnerable. In a powerful telling of the different, insidious ways in which oppression manifests itself, Anderson says of arbitrary coercion; of being pushed to the edges or outside society; of domination; of exploitation; and of cultural imperialism:

> Equals are not subject to arbitrary violence or physical coercion by others. Choice unconstrained by arbitrary physical coercion is one of the fundamental conditions of freedom. Equals are not marginalized by others. They are therefore free to participate in politics and the major institutions of civil society. Equals are not dominated by others; they do not live at the mercy of others' wills. This means that they govern their lives by their own wills, which is freedom. Equals are not exploited by others. This means they are free to secure the fair value of their labor. Equals are not subject to cultural imperialism: they are free to practice their own culture, subject to the constraint of respecting everyone else.[61]

Anderson affirms a view in which the right is prior to the good. But she also argues that the theory of democratic equality is biased toward certain conceptions of the good (and, I believe, Catholic social thought is one such conception).[62] We can see the implications of this balancing act between right and good in her rejection of the assumption that freedom is only negative—merely a freedom from without any orientation toward what freedom is for. Thus, she says of the obligations to remove the social conditions of oppression: "To live in an egalitarian community, then, is to be free from oppression to participate in and enjoy the goods of society, and to participate in democratic self-government."[63] Anderson enumerates the morally necessary threefold aspect of such participation. First, one should be free to participate in society as a "human being" in the sense of "having effective access to the means" of being able to sustain "biological existence—food, shelter, clothing, medical care—and access to the basic conditions of human agency—knowledge of one's circumstances and options, the ability to deliberate about means and ends, the psychological conditions of autonomy, including the self-confidence to think and judge for oneself, and freedom of thought and movement."[64] Second, one should have effective access to the means of participation in a system of cooperative production, including

---

61. Anderson, "What Is the Point of Equality?," 315.
62. Anderson, "What Is the Point of Equality?," 329–30.
63. Anderson, "What Is the Point of Equality?," 315.
64. Anderson, "What Is the Point of Equality?," 317–18.

access to education, the right to make contracts and to receive fair value for one's labor, and freedom of occupational choice.[65] Finally, as a citizen one should have effective access to the rights of political participation like "freedom of speech and franchise, and also effective access to the goods and relationships of civil society."[66] Anderson likens the conditions of freedom to the capabilities central to the work of Amartya Sen (in other words, if each person has sufficient capabilities, each person can be understood to have sufficient social conditions of freedom). The contextual nature of Sen's theory allows for the flexible approach favored by Anderson. Contrary to a starting gate theory of equal freedom, Sen's capability approach presumes from the start a widely diverse range of constraints and opportunities facing differently situated persons. Sen's capabilities approach—in which a capability is a set of functionings that a person may choose—also underscores the liberal ground of the theory of democratic equality. What citizens owe each other is freedom understood as effective access over a whole life to the rejection of oppression and to participation in democratic society.[67] Anderson says of such obligatory freedom: "Most of the freedoms that democratic equality guarantees are prerequisites to exercising responsible agency" (for instance, access to the education to deliberate on means; or access to the means of subsistence that prevent a fall into criminality; or access to a vote that figures in political change to remove oppression).[68] Finally, this is a liberalism with an obligatory bite. A perverse refusal to take advantage oneself of such freedoms does not negate the obligation to provide them to others.

In a 2014 tweet, Pope Francis said, "Inequality is the root of social evil."[69] Coming during the liberty-loving Age of Fracture in which equality at all has been called into question,[70] the tweet evoked predictable neoliberal outrage.[71] But the criticisms both assumed the pope was speaking specifically about economic inequality and failed to engage the meaning of a decisive word in the tweet—"social." To be sure, Pope Francis has criticized an unhinged market economy and the destructive effects of excessive and enduring economic inequality.[72] But his tweet can better be understood by

---

65. Anderson, "What Is the Point of Equality?," 318.
66. Anderson, "What Is the Point of Equality?," 318.
67. Anderson, "What Is the Point of Equality?," 318–19.
68. Anderson, "What Is the Point of Equality?," 328.
69. Francis, "Inequality Is the Root . . ."
70. Rodgers, *Age of Fracture*, 190.
71. Gibson, "Analysis."
72. Francis, *Evangelii Gaudium*, §§53–60, 202–8. For an illuminating study of Pope Francis on economic inequality, see Weithman, "Piketty and the Pope."

considering it in light of Anderson's theory of democratic equality and her connection of the equal moral worth of each person to relationship as an interpersonal and structural reality. The temptation toward unequal relationships is always knocking at the door; this is the evil of social life in which such inequalities of relationships both shape and are shaped by accompanying assumptions of superior and inferior worth. By contrast, the antidote to such evil is the obligation to secure the social conditions of freedom for each person, which means that "one stand[s] in relations of equality with others."[73] In Anderson's work, I think, is an account of the dignity of the human person that accords with the fundamental assumptions of the social ethic of Pope Francis. In any case, I will next turn to the theology of Jesuit David Hollenbach for the final piece of the puzzle of the constitutive polarity of a public theology of freedom for the American context: freedom in light of the good and God. In effect, on what grounds can a Catholic public theology of freedom that integrates the body, history, relationality, and a Catholic conception of the good also be liberal?

DAVID HOLLENBACH, CATHOLICISM, AND LIBERAL FREEDOM

Drawing on Rahner's concept of created freedom, I have thus far in this chapter emphasized freedom's dependent, concrete character. Freedom is properly understood when it is integrated with embodiment, history, and relationality. I will now turn to freedom's complementary dimension—its transcendental aspect as it relates to the good and to God, and to the possibility of a liberal democratic political order from within the perspective of faith. In turning to the social ethics of David Hollenbach, we can see this polarity of the concrete and transcendental at work in crucial ways that justify a Catholic public theology of freedom in an American context. First, I will discuss Hollenbach's connection of freedom to the body, history, and relationship. Then I will focus on his arguments on behalf of liberal freedom.

Body, History, Relationship

In his writing on what he calls a "community of freedom," Hollenbach connects freedom to notions of the body and history. For instance, he is keenly attentive to universal normative claims of bodily well-being that are

---

73. Anderson, "What Is the Point of Equality?," 315.

an indispensable aspect of a Catholic vision of the common good.[74] He also evokes the constraints imposed on the racialized body in his evocation of the impaired agency of the Black poor in American cities as a consequence of zoning laws, education policy, and restrictive residential covenants.[75] And he is attuned to the way that our concepts of freedom emerge out of particular histories, whether we recognize those histories or not. Thus he calls "historical and contingent" what often is presented as an absolute norm of liberal political culture: the assumption that any effort to identify a common good necessarily violates respect for the equal liberty of each person to decide for themselves their particular vision of the good.[76] Thus, he also notes that what is often absolutized as the self-sufficiency of libertarian freedom was only made possible in the early modern era by institutions and practices that engendered a sense of being an agent in society at all.[77] But for all of his integration of the body and history into his work, still Hollenbach does not include as visceral a sense of the crushed, racialized body that characterizes Copeland's writing, and that surely should inform a public theology of freedom in the American context.

In one way of putting it, Hollenbach's concept of a community of freedom arises from his extensive efforts to connect freedom and relation. I will note three primary ways in which he does so—and note how Anderson's work on freedom and relation offers a complement to his. Drawing on Catholic theology and natural law philosophy, Hollenbach argues that human dignity can only be fulfilled in relationship.[78] In turn, there are instrumental, intrinsic, and epistemological implications to this moral fact. Without recognizing the essential nature of relationality, it is neither possible to see the dependence at the roots of human vulnerability nor the indispensable role of such interdependent webs of relation in meeting basic human needs.[79] Such instrumental relations constitute the conditions of the common good—for example, systems of justice or education—without which persons' individual good cannot develop. But Hollenbach also insists on the intrinsic importance of relationship to the fulfillment of dignity. On one hand, he says that the incorporation of mutual respect into the norms and designs of the institutions of society is itself an aspect of the common

---

74. Hollenbach, *Common Good*, 152.
75. Hollenbach, *Common Good*, 184.
76. Hollenbach, *Common Good*, 10.
77. Hollenbach, *Common Good*, 71–72.
78. Hollenbach, *Common Good*, 160.
79. Hollenbach, *Common Good*, 8–9, 81.

good.[80] Even more, Christian imperatives push the intrinsic nature of relationships in a direction that includes but goes beyond the significance of respect. Here Hollenbach notes the appeal of love: that a people or a community that lives as one this side of the eschaton is a good in itself.[81] Finally, Hollenbach appeals to the epistemological significance of the moral fact of relationality. Here he sets himself against an atomistic liberalism premised on the assumption that a common good cannot be known because of the irreconcilable plurality of individual visions of the good. By contrast, Hollenbach argues, the assumption from the start of the essential nature of human relationality points toward possibilities for a common vision of a life together that cannot be imagined in an atomistic world. "We can know a good in common that we cannot know alone," said moral philosopher Michael Sandel.[82]

It is important to situate Hollenbach's claims in light of the two important purposes that Anderson's account of freedom and relation provides to my argument. First, she finds freedom and relation in feminist thought, the work of Amartya Sen, and in the borderlands of Kant, and thus offers an analogue to arguments that Hollenbach makes largely in terms of Catholic philosophical and theological thought. Her notions of the "social conditions" of freedom and of "democratic equality" can be likened to Hollenbach's idea of a community of freedom. Second, Anderson's account of the scope and dynamics by which relations can oppress—as exploitation, marginalization, exclusion, and more—intensifies similar categories in Hollenbach's work. For instance, he describes "unequal interdependence" as the imposition of structural constraints in a way that renders the capacity of the agency of the poor as far less equal to the capacity of the agency of those living in the suburbs.[83] Anderson echoes such an account but amplifies it by turning to a number of revelatory conceptual tools: the evocation of a broader range of kinds of oppression; the analysis of the insidious energy of domination fueled by perceptions of superiority and inferiority; and the critique of the deceptive simplicity of "starting-gate" theories of equality detached from such structural concerns. In the end, I think the work of Copeland and Anderson points powerfully toward what Anderson calls the freedoms that are the prerequisite to responsible agency, and that are exercised amid the various forms of oppression that constrain the poor, racialized, and gendered.[84]

80. Hollenbach, *Common Good*, 70.
81. Hollenbach, *Common Good*, 81, 124–26, 136.
82. Sandel, *Liberalism*, 183, quoted in Hollenbach, *Common Good*, 18.
83. Hollenbach, *Common Good*, 184.
84. Anderson, "What Is the Point of Equality?," 328.

Hollenbach is deeply sympathetic to this elemental aspect of freedom even if its evocation is more attenuated in much of his work.

Catholicism and Liberal Freedom Reimagined

It is important now to turn to those aspects of Hollenbach's thought to which I am especially appealing in my argument: the justification of liberal freedom amid his commitments to relationality and to a Catholic vision of the good. Hollenbach's work in this regard is especially timely because it responds both to the pervasive libertarianism of the Age of Fracture and to the rise of a renewed Catholic sympathy for authoritarian populism. Thus he argues that the biggest obstacles to recognizing the moral interdependence between American cities and suburbs are the paired libertarian assumptions that the successful in the suburbs earned all they have through their own good efforts and that the poor in the cities are entirely responsible for their impoverished fate.[85] What informs his criticism is not whether there is freedom and responsibility. His concern is for the prevalence in the United States of a gnostic-like assumption that persons are beings for whom material and social conditions are irrelevant or minimally relevant to the exercise of freedom and responsibility in pursuit of the good.[86] Such libertarianism represents one challenge to a Catholic understanding of freedom. But another challenge comes from within the Catholic world in the form of a Catholic affection for authoritarian populism—evident in a renewed movement of Catholic "integralism"—that represents a return to an era before the Second Vatican Council and an understanding of freedom as a function of a highly specified notion of truth. Hollenbach identifies two general problems with such an integralism, whether in its pre- or post-conciliar versions. First, such integralism moves without mediation from the assumption of God's sovereignty over the world to the assumption of the Catholic Church's privileged role in a political community. Second, such integralism reduces the rightful autonomy of spheres of knowledge and practice—for example, science, economics, culture—to a select and largely unfiltered set of directives drawn from Catholic magisterial theology.[87]

Catholicism was a latecomer to democracy. Hollenbach is keenly aware of the fragility of this commitment in a modern arc of history that includes an intense rejection of democracy in much of nineteenth-century

---

85. Hollenbach, *Common Good*, 208.
86. Hollenbach, *Common Good*, 27.
87. Hollenbach, *Common Good*, 115. For an example of contemporary Catholic integralism, see Vermeule, "Beyond Originalism."

papal writing; widespread Catholic compliance with mid-twentieth-century fascist governments; the affirmation of the right to religious freedom at the Second Vatican Council; a wave of democratization in the 1980s and 90s in predominantly Catholic countries;[88] and a retrenchment in the 2010s in places like Eastern Europe where a pre-conciliar Catholicism has joined forces with "authoritarian democracies" founded on populist power.[89] Hollenbach anchors the Catholic commitment to constitutional democracy in arguments made on behalf of the human right to religious freedom at the Second Vatican Council. He has noted that the Council grounded religious freedom on the "fact that the act of faith must itself be free if it is to be a genuine act of faith."[90] And he has added: "Because of this essential connection between authentic faith and freedom, the civil protection of personal religious freedom is closely associated with the advancement of freedom more generally understood. Securing religious freedom is thus closely linked with the institutions of democracy that protect freedom more broadly conceived."[91]

Hollenbach makes two distinct moves that allow more readily for the integration of the Catholic understanding of the right to religious freedom with contemporary democracy. First, he insists on the mutuality and reciprocity between truth and freedom. So, for instance, he affirms the Catholic conviction that by nature persons are oriented to truth and therefore are obliged to seek and adhere to it.[92] But he pairs that affirmation with an equal emphasis on freedom. Thus he argues that truth can only be sought and adhered to in freedom. Such freedom includes the notion of freedom of choice, but goes beyond it. Here Hollenbach grounds his claim in the concept of human dignity, which is reflected in a person's responsibility for herself and for the world and which "comes to expression in human freedom."[93] Or, as he says, "the religious freedom that is a deep expression of human dignity is the freedom of the person to decide who she is and what she will become."[94] By putting things this way, he reorients the understanding of the truth that ought to guide government and civil society in the manner

88. Hollenbach, "Freedom and Truth," 124–34.

89. Tomasky, "Do Republicans Even Believe?"

90. Hollenbach, "Religious Freedom," 254; Second Vatican Council, *Dignitatis humanae*, §10.

91. Hollenbach, "Religious Freedom," 254.

92. Hollenbach, "Religious Freedom," 253–54; Second Vatican Council, *Dignitatis humanae*, §2.

93. Hollenbach, "Religious Freedom," 255.

94. Hollenbach, "Religious Freedom," 254; Second Vatican Council, *Dignitatis humanae*, §2.

of religious freedom. First, there *is* a truth at stake: We are not in a relativist world in which it is assumed to be impossible to find any common normative vision of the human person. Second, the truth at issue is not a sectarian set of religious teachings but the truth that each person is responsible before God for the risk of one's whole existence.[95] Thus Hollenbach's emphasis on the mutuality and reciprocity of truth and freedom brings into vivid focus each *person* who is as such the subject of the right to religious freedom. As he puts it, the right is oriented to the "innermost identity of persons."[96] Moreover, this mutuality and reciprocity means that "religious truth claims should not be excluded from public discourse"[97] and that such truth claims "must be subject to the same criteria of the free exchange of ideas as are all other proposals about laws and policies in a democratic society."[98]

Hollenbach's second key step in the integration of the right of religious freedom into contemporary democracy involves his emphasis on the connection of freedom and relation. For him, dignity is an inalienable attribute of an individual but is only able to be fulfilled through free interactions within a community (as he puts it, dignity is both inherent and relational and is realized through the "free, socially embodied quest for meaning").[99] Thus the equality of each person or religious community is affirmed by the right to religious freedom understood as a negative immunity; each person or community is to be free from the coercive power of the state in the pursuit of their vision of the good. But equality is also affirmed by the right to religious freedom understood as an empowerment connected to relation; each person or religious community achieves their due equality by participating freely in society in the determination of the common good of the whole political community.[100] By putting things this way, Hollenbach is better able to forestall the limits of a cramped liberalism and the creep of religious triumphalism. Against a liberalism that would limit religions to private life, Hollenbach's understanding of religious freedom allows them a robust public space. Against religious triumphalism, his emphasis on the personal and social dimensions of dignity leads coherently to a recognition of the personal and social dimensions of religious freedom. Religious freedom is never simply the purview of already existing religious institutions within a society and not also of individual members of such institutions.

95. Hollenbach, "Freedom and Truth," 137, 141.
96. Hollenbach, "Religious Freedom," 252.
97. Hollenbach, "Freedom and Truth," 143.
98. Hollenbach, "Freedom and Truth," 143.
99. Hollenbach, "Freedom and Truth," 137–38, 141.
100. Hollenbach, *Common Good*, 32; Hollenbach, "Freedom and Truth," 142.

Moreover, the freedom of such religious communities does not have a normative priority over the freedom of other communities. All such rights are founded on the common grounds of human dignity and its relational dimension. In Hollenbach's rendering, religious freedom is a right whose fate is connected to other rights in democratic society.

Finally, it is important to consider more specifically how Hollenbach construes religious freedom and constitutional democracy in light of a Catholic vision of the good. On one hand, he appeals to the insistence of the biblical and Christian tradition that the spiritual has primacy over the material, and that one's ultimate obedience is to God, not a political ruler. He also notes how such ideas were embodied in a notion like the "freedom of the Church" from the Middle Ages.[101] Indeed, such notions set out a general Catholic framework that puts a clear limit on the state's reach into the realm of the spirit and of the Church. But Hollenbach specifies this framework by his consideration of the Church in the pluralist context of modern constitutional democracy. Here in particular, he articulates how and why Catholicism can at the same time collaboratively seek the common good of a pluralist society; pursue the Church's ultimate vision of the heavenly city; and reject any alliance with the power of the state. Hollenbach relies especially on the role of speech in constitutional democracy. Thus he writes of Catholic engagement in conversation about the common good in terms of the virtue of "intellectual solidarity," which is a disposition and set of practices animated by Christian love and a readiness to speak and listen in a context in which difference is not a sectarian conversation stopper but an opportunity to understand.[102] And thus he also speaks of pursuing such a conversation in a Catholic spirit of "dialogic universalism." First, there is the universalism consistent with Catholic commitments to a created, normative order. In the face of relativism, this commitment holds that there are universal norms that constitute the basic sense of the common good. These norms require, for instance, that basic bodily needs are met; that provision is made for education; that freedom of conscience is respected in matters pertaining to the meaning of life; and that participation in social life is supported for all. But this universalist commitment is a general set of norms, not a more concrete plan for how such norms are to be respected in the common good of a particular society. And here dialogue enters the scene. Indeed, Hollenbach argues, the universalist assumptions of Catholicism must be paired with dialogue in order for the common good to move from the aspirational

---

101. Hollenbach, "Religious Freedom," 265.
102. Hollenbach, *Common Good*, 137.

to the specified or, in other words, for the universal to be made concrete in a specific time and place.[103]

It is important to understand dialogic universalism as a set of convictions and practices that reflect the compatibility of Catholicism and liberalism. On the one hand, a public theological commitment to dialogic universalism is animated by love and directed by faith: by the inalienable dignity of each person; by a vision of a reconciled community; by universalist convictions about truth and normativity; by an option for the poor; and more. But such universalist convictions come with a humility compatible with liberalism. Thus this effort understands that the final hope for the common good is beyond history. What can be accomplished now in any liberal society is at best only a distant analogue of the heavenly, reconciled city.[104] This realization tempers the drive for the use of state power to enforce a specifically Catholic version of the good. In the end, a mutuality and reciprocity are assumed consistent with freedom in a world of relations and in a liberal society; the truths of faith direct engagement while the freedom of dialogue specifies the shape of the good.

Hollenbach offers a theology of freedom in which convictions about human dignity, relationship, and the common good resist both a reductive liberalism and a triumphalist Catholicism. In his work, truth and freedom; faith and reason; the individual and the community are all paired and kept in complementary tension. No category can be isolated without departing from the dependent, historical, created order we are fated to inhabit and in which freedom must find its way.

CONCLUSION

There are many versions of the American tendency to detach human agency from the body, history, relationships, and the good—and to call such detached agency "freedom." This chapter began with one such example: the claim in the *Janus* case decided by the US Supreme Court that it was an unjust violation of freedom to require a state employee to pay dues to support the capacity of a union to negotiate the wages and benefits the state employee enjoyed in his union job. If that seems hard to follow, it is because it is hard to follow. And the confusion arises in large measure because what is defined as "freedom" in the case is so detached from its due context that basic assumptions about plausibility and justice are upended. The *Janus* case is a textbook instance of what Rodgers has called the Age of Fracture,

---

103. Hollenbach, *Common Good*, 152.
104. Hollenbach, *Common Good*, 124–26.

in which freedom is formalized in largely economic terms and reductively shorn of its connections to institutions and power. In this chapter, the work of Shawn Copeland points toward the long historical roots behind the particular reductionism of the Age of Fracture. So, for instance, there has long been the prized American valuation of freedom as independence, when in fact such independence was often only made possible by the dependent labor of women or enslaved African Americans. Elizabeth Anderson specifies the philosophical problems behind such reductionist definitions of freedom. What can it mean, she asks, to say that freedom is defined by non-interference when surely our capacity to act freely at all is in part a function of internal conditions and of the assistance that comes from external relations? Similarly, she criticizes a staple of the Age of Fracture: the distributive notion of "equality of fortune" that assumes as companion articles of faith both an equal capacity for freedom and an atomistic, self-sufficient human nature. Such distributive concerns about freedom, Anderson argues, must always be considered within the context of larger structural relations. David Hollenbach joins in this trajectory of critique when he says that the greatest single obstacle to addressing poverty in the central cities of the United States is the assumption that freedom is largely unaffected by structure and culture. Thus, no matter their advantage, too often the rich think they've earned everything by themselves and, no matter their disadvantage, too often the poor are held entirely responsible for their fate.

In all of these criticisms of the reflexive American turn to a detached freedom, the observation of sociologist Orlando Patterson is proven right: the rich and powerful always seek to define freedom in refined ways set against the concrete experiences of constraint shared by the poor.[105] Patterson also notes that our definitions of freedom are far more socially constructed than the rich and powerful would have us believe. We get the definitions of freedom that we value for good or ill out of a complex mix of communal consent, common practice, and social struggle.[106] A Catholic public theology of freedom for the United States must not fall into the trap of detached abstraction. Moreover, such a theology must seek in the contested space of American society a valuation of freedom in connection to the vulnerable body; to the unredeemed past; to the role of relationship in oppression and in liberation; and to a Catholic liberal vision of the good founded on the dignity of freedom and on the divine distance between the justice we can accomplish now and the final victory of the City of God. Drawing on the work of Karl Rahner, I believe such a theology

105. Patterson, *Freedom*, 2.
106. Patterson, *Freedom*, 41.

must integrate freedom with the living body, history, relationship, and the Catholic vision of the good and God. And I believe that in combination the work of Shawn Copeland, Elizabeth Anderson, and David Hollenbach points toward a way of doing so. Copeland powerfully evokes freedom in relation to the body and to history. She returns to the past experience of the enslavement and liberation of African American women to reflect on the imperative of "enfleshing freedom": of recognizing and responding to the radical constraints experienced by the gendered, racialized female body and to the changes needed to foster embodied freedom. For Copeland, it is long past time to retire the cultural icon of the free, independent, self-reliant American man not because freedom, independence, or self-reliance are moral evils in themselves but because the myth of such a man has almost always obscured how dependent he is on the labor of many others. In place of that myth, Copeland recommends instead that Catholic public theology seek the meaning of freedom in the embodied experience of poor women of color. Anderson also powerfully evokes the challenges to what she calls the basic freedoms that are the prelude to personal responsibility. She does this in particular by moving the conversation from the natural—what each person is given—to the relational—how each person's life is structured by social and political choices. In democratic society, she argues, what we owe each other is equality in the social conditions of freedom—an equality that does not signal equal outcomes and that treats citizens similarly across a wide range of difference. To such connections of freedom to the body, history, and relationship, Hollenbach especially adds a robust sense of freedom in a reimagined engagement of Catholicism and liberalism. At the heart of his argument is a social and historical understanding of human dignity: each person expresses such dignity in their freedom. On the one hand, such freedom involves the risk of one's life before God. The religious freedom of the liberal state protects the possibility of such risk. On the other hand, even such a deeply personal freedom is never risked entirely alone. Consider the freedom of a poor woman of color in such a reimagined liberalism: The possibility of her self-transcendent freedom immersed in an embodied existence marked by the constraints of gender and race handed down over time; her freedom to seek the good empowered or inhibited by the relationships in her world; her awareness of a transcendent destiny not floating above but inseparable from such dignified and vulnerable freedom.

    I will call this "created freedom under the sign of the cross." In doing so, I am drawing on Rahner's concept of "created freedom." I am also heeding Hollenbach's call for a "social ethics under the sign of the Cross."[107] He

---

107. Hollenbach, "Social Ethics."

proposed such an ethic on behalf of Catholic Christian engagement with a Western, democratic pluralism that had lost its confidence in shared norms for life together. In his analysis, he argued that we are stuck in a normative wilderness between liberal irony, exclusively market-based solutions, and an encroaching atavism in which social life becomes—and, in ways, already is—a pure power game. One path of response for Catholic theology should be ruled out: the affirmation of an essentialist, ahistorical view of the freedom of the created human person that floats above such challenges and is coopted easily by idealized notions befitting the rich and powerful.[108] Another theological path of response is more promising: the affirmation of a humanism grounded in createdness, marked by vulnerability, and oriented toward compassionate solidarity and the transforming power of the cross.[109] By putting things this way, Hollenbach opens the door to a way of thinking about freedom consistent with what I have emphasized in this book: a freedom that is embodied, historical, relational, and both liberal and oriented toward the good and God. Freedom under the sign of the cross is really freedom. Even in the face of agony, it signals the possibility of choice. Freedom under the sign of the cross connects our created dependence with redemptive hope. Such a freedom emerges from the radical, dependent vulnerability that marks embodied, relational existence. Such a freedom is also oriented toward the disinterested love that is the basis of solidarity with all men and women on account of their inherent worth. Finally, such a freedom finds its fulfillment in the risk of one's life in a compassionate solidarity animated by faith in the transforming power of the cross now and forever.

108. Hollenbach, "Social Ethics," 11.
109. Hollenbach, "Social Ethics," 12.

Conclusion

As a work of public theology, the general aim of this book has been to affirm a public role for Catholic theology in the pluralist context of the United States. More specifically, the aim has been to draw on the great Christian themes of creation and the Cross to illuminate the many moral questions arising from the interpretation of freedom in American civil society and to offer a constructive idea of freedom for this society.[1] As a public theologian, I am working in the key of David Hollenbach's idea of "dialogic universalism" (which I discussed in the last chapter). As such, this work stands squarely in the Catholic tradition's affirmation that there are universal values toward which freedom is oriented—even if such values require specification in a particular context. Animated by Christian love of neighbor, this work assumes that such specification for the sake of the common good can occur through candid dialogue with the pluralist partners of American society. Accordingly, I believe that Catholic public theology is appropriately considered a dialogical process in which the theological content emerges from ecclesial tradition and enters into conversation with an inclusive understanding of reasoned reflection on human experience and of the grace that accompanies creation itself.[2] The dialogue can be contrarian. By turning to creation and the cross, I have shown the sharp contradiction between a Catholic understanding of freedom and the abstract neoliberal models of freedom common in our Age of Fracture. But the dialogue can also be one of correspondence. Thus Rahner's integration of freedom with the dependence of createdness—a dependence manifest in embodiment, historicity, and relationship—finds affinities, complements, and analogues in the secular work of Glenn, Patterson, Sen, and Anderson. In turn, the notion

---

1. My account of public theology is indebted to Graham, *Between a Rock and a Hard Place*, 70.

2. Graham, *Between a Rock and a Hard Place*, xxi.

of "freedom under the sign of the cross" provides a theme that collects and orients such assumptions about createdness. Here the freedom in question takes as its point of departure the identification of the radical constraint of Christ on the cross with the oppression of the exploited and marginalized and excluded of this country. Moreover, the disinterested love that drove Christ to take up the cross for the sake of all animates the duty of solidarity with the oppressed. Faith in the salvific power of such participation in the love of the cross offers hope for contemporary struggles for justice and, even in the face of failure, the assurance of a final eschatological victory.

I also undertake this work of public theology in a time that I think is best described as the "post-secular." By this I mean to move away from more familiar patterns like the assumption of secularization in which religion gradually fades away[3] or the assumption of the inherent irrationality of religious belief and hence its appropriately restricted entry into the public square.[4] Drawing on Elaine Graham's work, I consider the post-secular as a complex, changing mix of the religious and the secular.[5] On the one hand, religious institutional affiliation is declining and the world of the "spiritual-but-not-religious" has taken root. Moreover, as Charles Taylor has argued, we live in a time when religious belief is one option among many; cultural expectations to believe have faded away.[6] But religions are nevertheless resurgent. They are making powerful plays in the public square, often in an identitarian key and often by bemoaning the collapse of morality in secular society. On the other hand, secularism has often intensified its skepticism of religious claims while retaining an alert wariness to the legitimacy of such claims in public life. Moreover, secularism has had to grapple with postmodern claims about race and gender and the contextual nature of knowing. At the same time, even from within secularist worldviews more questions have been raised about the adequacy of secular values alone to provide sufficient accounts of human dignity and of community life to sustain liberal civil societies in the face of neoliberalism, an enfeebled state, and the relentless relativism and sectarianism fostered by social media.[7] Into such an age, Catholic public theology must walk with humility and generosity and courage. The identitarian option must be ruled out. It has been co-opted by populist politics and in any case rejects too readily the moral and theological significance of the common reason and common grace binding people

---

3. Graham, *Between a Rock and a Hard Place*, 32.
4. Graham, *Between a Rock and a Hard Place*, 45.
5. Graham, *Between a Rock and a Hard Place*. See, for instance, pp. ix–xxvii.
6. Taylor, *Secular Age*, 1–14.
7. Graham, *Between a Rock and a Hard Place*, 49–51, 89.

together beyond claims of identity. Taylor points toward a more helpful path when he says that our time is marked by a back-and-forth dialectic between religious faith and secular wisdom.[8] I have sought to follow Taylor's direction here. I have turned to Catholic theological convictions about freedom in light of creation and the cross. I have put such convictions into conversation with secular wisdom. The result is a Catholic public theology of freedom that emphasizes embodiment, history, relationship, the good, and the risk of one's life before God in a manner consistent with the right to religious freedom at the basis of liberal societies like the United States. I offer this public theology as a response to the reckless freedom and communal breakdown that characterize our Age of Fracture.

---

8. Taylor, *A Secular Age*, 2–3; Graham, *Between a Rock and a Hard Place*, 40–41.

Bibliography

Alexander, Michelle. *The New Jim Crow: Mass Incarceration in the Age of Colorblindness.* New York: New Press, 2012.

Allen, Danielle. "Charlottesville Is Not the Continuation of an Old Fight. It Is Something New." *The Washington Post*, August 13, 2017. https://www.washingtonpost.com/opinions/charlottesville-is-not-the-continuation-of-an-old-fight-it-is-something-new/2017/08/13/971812f6-8029-11e7-b359-15a3617c767b_story.html?utm_term=.e1cf400ob4.

Anderson, Elizabeth S. "The Great Reversal." *Institute for Public Policy Research Progressive Review* 25.2 (2018) 202–13.

———. "What Is the Point of Equality?" *Ethics* 109.2 (1999) 287–337.

Arendt, Hannah. *The Human Condition.* Chicago: University of Chicago Press, 1958.

Badhwar, Neera K., and Roderick T. Long. "Ayn Rand." In *The Stanford Encyclopedia of Philosophy*, edited by Edward N. Zalta. https://plato.stanford.edu/archives/fall2020/entries/ayn-rand/.

Balthasar, Hans Urs von. *The Moment of Christian Witness.* Translated by Richard Beckley. San Francisco: Ignatius, 1969.

Beckley, Harlan. "Capability as Opportunity: How Amartya Sen Revises Equal Opportunity." *Journal of Religious Ethics* 30.1 (2002) 107–35.

Bell, Daniel. *The Coming of Post-Industrial Society.* New York: Basic, 1976.

Bellah, Robert N., et al. *Habits of the Heart: Individualism and Commitment in American Life.* Berkeley: University of California Press, 1996.

Brooks, Arthur C. "Confessions of a Catholic Convert to Capitalism." *America: The Jesuit Review*, February 6, 2017. https://www.americamagazine.org/politics-society/2017/02/06/confessions-catholic-convert-capitalism.

Browning, Don S. *A Fundamental Practical Theology.* Minneapolis: Fortress, 1991.

Buckley, Michael. "Within the Holy Mystery." In *A World of Grace: An Introduction to the Themes and Foundations of Karl Rahner's Theology*, edited by Leo J. O'Donovan, 31–49. Washington, DC: Georgetown University Press, 1995.

Carr, Anne E. "Starting with the Human." In *A World of Grace: An Introduction to the Themes and Foundations of Karl Rahner's Theology*, edited by Leo J. O'Donovan, 17–30. Washington, DC: Georgetown University Press, 1995.

Case, Anne, and Angus Deaton. "Mortality and Morbidity in the 21st Century." *Brookings Papers on Economic Activity* (2017) 397–476.

———. "Rising Morbidity and Mortality in Midlife among White Non-Hispanic Americans in the 21st Century." *Proceedings of the National Academy of the Sciences* 112.49 (2015) 15078–83.

Chicago Tribune Staff. "5 Things to Know about Illinois State Government Employee Mark Janus—and His Supreme Court Victory." *Chicago Tribune*, June 27, 2018. https://www.chicagotribune.com/news/breaking/ct-met-who-is-mark-janus-20180627-story.html.

Christiansen, Drew. "On Relative Equality: Catholic Egalitarianism after Vatican II." *Theological Studies* 45 (1984) 651–75.

Clark, Megan J. *The Vision of Catholic Social Thought: The Virtue of Solidarity and the Praxis of Human Rights*. Minneapolis: Fortress, 2014.

CNN. "4 Wild Things Kanye Said This Week." *CNN*, May 4, 2018. https://www.cnn.com/videos/entertainment/2018/05/02/kanye-tmz-charlamagne-interview-orig-zw-llr.cnn.

Coates, Ta-Nehisi. "I'm Not Black, I'm Kanye." *The Atlantic*, May 7, 2018. https://www.theatlantic.com/entertainment/archive/2018/05/im-not-black-im-kanye/559763/.

Cohen, Patricia. "On Health and Welfare, Moral Arguments Can Outweigh Economics." *The New York Times*, May 7, 2017. https://www.nytimes.com/2017/05/07/business/economy/congress-benefits-fairness.html.

Coleman, John A. "Every Theology Implies a Sociology and Vice Versa." In *Theology and the Social Sciences: College Theology Society Annual 46*, edited by Michael Horace Barnes, 12–33. Maryknoll, NY: Orbis, 2001.

Copeland, M. Shawn. *Enfleshing Freedom: Body, Race, and Being*. Minneapolis: Fortress, 2010.

———. "Functioning and Capability: The Foundations of Sen's and Nussbaum's Development Ethic: Part 2." In *Women, Culture, and Development: A Study of Human Capabilities*, edited by Martha Nussbaum and Jonathan Glover, 153–98. Oxford: Clarendon, 1995.

———. "Turning Theology: A Proposal." *Theological Studies* 80.4 (2019) 753–73.

Crocker, David. "Functioning and Capability: The Foundation of Sen's and Nussbaum's Development Ethic." *Political Theory* 20.1 (1992) 584–612.

Cunningham, Paige Winfield. "The Health 202: Cruz Picks Government Health Care Subsidies as Lesser of Two Evils." *The Washington Post*, July 10, 2017. https://www.washingtonpost.com/news/powerpost/paloma/the-health-202/2017/07/10/the-health-202-cruz-picks-government-health-care-subsidies-as-lesser-of-two-evils/59611958e9b69b7071abcae4/.

Cupich, Blasé. "Response to Presentation by Cardinal Oscar Rodriguez Maradiaga." Presented at the "Erroneous Autonomy: The Catholic Case Against Libertarianism" conference, Catholic University of America, June 3, 2014.

Daniels, Norman. "Equal Liberty and Unequal Worth of Liberty." In *Reading Rawls: Critical Studies on Rawls' A Theory of Justice*, edited by Norman Daniels, 253–81. Stanford: Stanford University Press, 1989.

DeCosse, David E. Review of *Development as Freedom*, by Amartya Sen. *Theological Studies* 62.1 (2001) 190–91.

Deneen, Patrick J. *Why Liberalism Failed*. New Haven: Yale University Place, 2018.

Dun, Frank van. "Freedom, Liberty, Autonomy." Paper Presented at the Seminar on Freedom and Economy, University of Padua, May 24, 2010. https://biblio.ugent.be/publication/1216510/file/6728046.pdf.

Dworkin, Gerald. "Autonomy." In *A Companion to Contemporary Political Philosophy*, edited by Robert E. Goodin et al., 443–51. Oxford: Blackwell, 2007.

Dych, William V. "Theology in a New Key." In *A World of Grace: An Introduction to the Themes and Foundations of Karl Rahner's Theology*, edited by Leo J. O'Donovan, 1–16. Washington, DC: Georgetown University Press, 1995.

Eggemeier, Matthew T., and Peter Joseph Fritz. *Send Lazarus: Catholicism and the Crises of Neoliberalism*. New York: Fordham University Press, 2020.

Everett, William W., and T. J. Bachmeyer. *Disciplines in Transformation: A Guide to Theology and the Behavioral Sciences*. Washington, DC: University Press of America, 1979.

Farley, Margaret. "A Feminist Version of Respect for Persons." *Journal of Feminist Studies in Religion* 9 (1993) 183–98.

Feder, J. Lester. "This Is How Steve Bannon Sees the Entire World." *Buzzfeed News*, November 16, 2016. https://www.buzzfeednews.com/article/lesterfeder/this-is-how-steve-bannon-sees-the-entire-world.

Finn, Daniel. *The Moral Ecology of Markets: Assessing Claims about Markets and Justice*. Cambridge: Cambridge University Press, 2006.

Foner, Eric. "The Meaning of Freedom." In *Reconstruction: America's Unfinished Revolution, 1863–1877*, 77–123. New York: Harper Perennial, 2014.

Ford, Lewis S. "Can Freedom Be Created?" *Horizons* 4.2 (1977) 183–88.

Francis, Pope. *Evangelii Gaudium*. http://www.vatican.va/content/francesco/en/apost_exhortations/documents/papa-francesco_esortazione-ap_20131124_evangelii-gaudium.html.

———. "Inequality Is the Root . . ." *Twitter*, April 28, 2014. https://twitter.com/pontifex/status/460697074585980928?lang=en.

Gallagher, Kevin. "The Eclipse of Catholic Humanism." *American Affairs*, August 20, 2018. https://americanaffairsjournal.org/2018/08/the-eclipse-of-catholic-fusionism/.

George, Robert P. *Conscience and Its Enemies: Confronting the Dogmas of Liberal Secularism*. Wilmington, DE: ISI, 2013.

Gibson, David. "Analysis: Conservatives Squawk over Pope's Tweet on Inequality." *The Washington Post*, April 29, 2014. https://www.washingtonpost.com/national/religion/analysis-conservatives-squawk-over-popes-tweet-on-inequality/2014/04/29/5e4ec3e6-cfd0-11e3-a714-be7e7f142085_story.html.

Glasser, Susan B., and Glenn Thrush. "What's Going on with America's White People?" *Politico Magazine*, October 2016. https://www.politico.com/magazine/story/2016/09/problems-white-people-america-society-class-race-214227.

Glenn, Evelyn Nakano. *Unequal Freedom: How Race and Gender Shaped American Citizenship and Labor*. Cambridge: Harvard University Press, 2002.

Graham, Elaine. *Between a Rock and a Hard Place: Public Theology in a Post-Secular Age*. London: SCM, 2013.

Gutierrez, Gustavo. "Liberation and Salvation." In *A Theology of Liberation*, translated by Caridad Inda and John Eagleson, 83–105. Maryknoll, NY: Orbis, 1990.

Hare, R. M. *Freedom and Reason*. Oxford: Clarendon, 1963.

———. *The Language of Morals*. Oxford: Clarendon, 1952.

Hart, H. L. A. "Rawls and Liberty and Its Priority." In *Reading Rawls: Critical Studies on Rawls' A Theory of Justice*, edited by Norm Daniels, 230–52. Stanford: Stanford University Press, 1989.

Hazony, Yoram. "Nationalism and the Future of Western Freedom." *Mosaic: Advancing Jewish Thought*, September 6, 2016. https://mosaicmagazine.com/essay/history-ideas/2016/09/nationalism-and-the-future-of-western-freedom/.

Hennenberger, Melinda. "Can You Be Catholic and Libertarian?" *The Washington Post*, June 6, 2014. https://www.washingtonpost.com/politics/can-you-be-catholic-and-libertarian/2014/06/06/92e602d4-ed00-11e3-9f5c-9075d5508f0a_story.html?utm_term=.13fe0a34584a.

Himes, Michael J., and Kenneth R. Himes. *Fullness of Faith: The Public Significance of Theology*. Mahwah, NJ: Paulist, 1993.

Hinze, Christine Firer. "Dirt and Economic Inequality: A Christian-Ethical Peek under the Rug." *Annual of the Society of Christian Ethics* 21 (2001) 45–62.

———. *Glass Ceilings and Dirt Floors: Women, Work, and the Global Economy*. Mahwah, NJ: Paulist, 2015.

Hobgood, Mary. "White Economic and Erotic Disempowerment: A Theological Exploration of the Struggle against Racism." In *Interrupting White Privilege: Catholic Theologians Break the Silence*, edited by Laurie M. Cassidy and Alex Mikulich, 40–55. Maryknoll, NY: Orbis, 2007.

Hollenbach, David. *The Common Good and Christian Ethics*. Cambridge: Cambridge University Press, 2002.

———. "Freedom and Truth." In *The Global Face of Public Faith: Politics, Human Rights, and Christian Ethics*, 124–46. Washington, DC: Georgetown University Press, 2003.

———. "Religious Freedom in Global Context Today: Some Contributions by Vatican II and John Courtney Murray." In *The Legacy of Vatican II*, edited by Massimo Faggioli and Andrea Vicini, 248–72. Mahwah, NJ: Paulist, 2015.

———. "Social Ethics under the Sign of the Cross." *Annual of the Society of Christian Ethics* 16 (1996) 3–18.

Hurd, Robert L. "The Concept of Freedom in Rahner." *Listening* 17 (1982) 138–53.

Hutter, Reinhard. "(Re-)Forming Freedom: Reflections 'After Veritatis Splendor' on Freedom's Fate in Modernity and Protestantism's Antinomian Captivity." *Modern Theology* 17.2 (2001) 117–61.

John Paul II, Pope. *Centesimus annus*. http://www.vatican.va/content/john-paul-ii/en/encyclicals/documents/hf_jp-ii_enc_01051991_centesimus-annus.html.

———. *Evangelium vitae*. http://www.vatican.va/content/john-paul-ii/en/encyclicals.index.html#encyclicals.

Junker-Kenny, Maureen. *Approaches to Theological Ethics: Sources, Traditions, Visions*. London: T. & T. Clark, 2019.

Kasper, Walter. *Jesus the Christ*. Translated by V. Green. Mahwah, NJ: Paulist, 1976.

———. *Theology and Church*. London: SCM, 1989.

Lambert, Craig. "The Caribbean Zola: Orlando Patterson May Be the Last of Harvard Sociology's Big Thinkers." *Harvard Magazine*, December 2014, 43–49.

Lay Commission on Catholic Social Teaching and the US Economy. *Toward the Future: Catholic Social Thought and the US Economy: A Lay Letter*. New York: American Catholic Committee, 1984.

Long, Heather, et al. "The COVID-19 Recession Is the Most Unequal in Modern U.S. History." *The Washington Post*, September 30, 2020. https://www.washingtonpost.com/graphics/2020/business/coronavirus-recession-equality/.

Lovin, Robin W. "Christian Realism: A Legacy and Its Future." *Annual of the Society of Christian Ethics* 20 (2000) 3–18.

———. *Reinhold Niebuhr and Christian Realism*. Cambridge: Cambridge University Press, 1995.
Maritain, Jacques. *The Person and the Common Good*. Notre Dame: University of Notre Dame Press, 1966.
———. *Three Reformers: Luther, Descartes, Rousseau*. London: Sheed and Ward, 1928.
Marmion, Declan. "Rahner and His Critics: Revisiting the Dialogue." *Australian eJournal of Theology* 4 (2005) 1–20.
Marx, Reinhard. "Roger W. Heyns Lecture: The Contribution of Christian Values to the Common Good." Stanford University, January 15, 2014. https://www.youtube.com/watch?v=Y790gvRr_uo.
McGreevy, John. *Catholicism and American Freedom: A History*. New York: Norton, 2004.
Metcalf, Stephen. "Robert Nozick, Father of Libertarianism: Even He Gave Up on the Movement He Inspired." *Slate*, June 20, 2011. http://www.slate.com/articles/arts/the_dilettante/2011/06/the_liberty_scam.html
Metz, Johann Baptist. *Faith in History and Society: Toward a Practical Fundamental Theology*. Translated by David Smith. New York: Seabury, 1980.
Miller, Vincent J. "What Does Catholic Social Teaching Say about the Economy? It's More Complicated Than You Think." *America: The Jesuit Review*, March 22, 2019. http://www.americamagazine.org/faith/2019/03/22/what-does-catholic-social-teaching-say-about-economy-its-more-complicated-you.
Monbiot, George. "Neoliberalism—The Ideology at the Root of All of Our Problems." *The Guardian*, April 15, 2016. https://www.theguardian.com/books/2016/apr/15/neoliberalism-ideology-problem-george-monbiot.
Morrison, Toni. *Playing in the Dark: Whiteness and the Literary Imagination*. New York: Vintage, 1992.
Murray, John Courtney. "Arguments for the Human Right to Religious Freedom." https://www.library.georgetown.edu/woodstock/murray/1968.
Neuhaus, John Richard. *The Catholic Moment: The Paradox of the Church in the Postmodern World*. San Francisco: Harper & Row, 1987.
Noonan, John T., Jr. *A Church That Can and Cannot Change: The Development of Catholic Moral Teaching*. Notre Dame: University of Notre Dame Press, 2004.
Novak, Michael. *The Catholic Ethic and the Spirit of Capitalism*. New York: Free, 1993.
———. "Creation Theology." In *Co-Creation and Capitalism: John Paul II's Laborem Exercens*, edited by Oliver F. Williams and John W. Houck, 17–41. Washington, DC: University Press of America, 1983.
———. *Free Persons and the Common Good*. Lanham, MD: Madison, 1989.
———. *The Spirit of Democratic Capitalism*. New York: Lanham, 1991.
Nozick, Robert. *Anarchy, State, Utopia*. Cambridge: Harvard University Press, 1974.
———. *The Examined Life*. New York: Simon & Schuster, 1989.
Nussbaum, Martha. "Human Functioning and Social Justice: In Defense of Aristotelian Essentialism." *Political Theory* 20.1 (1992) 202–46.
———. "Nature, Function, and Capability: Aristotle on Political Distribution." In *Oxford Studies in Ancient Philosophy*, edited by Julia Annas and Robert H. Grimm, 145–84. Oxford: Clarendon, 1988.
———. "Non-Relative Virtues: An Aristotelian Approach." In *Quality of Life*, edited by Martha Nussbaum and Amartya Sen, 242–69. Oxford: Oxford University Press, 1993.
———. *Women and Human Development: The Capabilities Approach*. Cambridge: Cambridge University Press, 2000.

O'Connor, Timothy, and Christopher Franklin. "Free Will." In *The Stanford Encyclopedia of Philosophy*, edited by Edward N. Zalta. https://plato.stanford.edu/archives/spr2021/entries/freewill/.

Patterson, Orlando. "Freedom, Slavery, and the Modern Construction of Rights." In *Historical Change and Human Rights: The Oxford Amnesty Lectures 1994*, edited by Olwen Hufton, 131–78. New York: Basic, 1995.

———. *Freedom: Volume I: Freedom in the Making of Western Culture*. New York: Basic, 1991.

———. "Making Sense of Culture." *Annual Review of Sociology* 40 (2014) 1–30.

———. *The Ordeal of Integration: Progress and Resentment in America's "Racial" Crisis*. Washington, DC: Counterpoint, 1997.

———. *Slavery and Social Death: A Comparative Study*. Cambridge: Harvard University Press, 1982.

———. "Slavery: The Underside of Freedom." *Slavery and Abolition* 5.2 (1984) 87–104.

———. "The Unholy Trinity: Freedom, Slavery, and the American Constitution." *Social Research* 54.3 (1987) 543–77.

"Paul Ryan and Ayn Rand's Ideas: In the Hot Seat Again." *The Atlas Society*, April 30, 2012. https://www.atlassociety.org/post/paul-ryan-and-ayn-rands-ideas-in-the-hot-seat-again.

"Paul Ryan Rejects Ayn Rand in the New York Times." *The Atlas Society*, September 15, 2014. https://www.atlassociety.org/post/paul-ryan-rejects-ayn-rand-in-the-new-york-times.

Piketty, Thomas. *Capital in the Twenty-First Century*. Translated by Arthur Goldhammer. Cambridge: Harvard University Press, 2014.

Pradhan, Rachana. "Conservative Health Care Experiment Leads to Thousands Losing Coverage." *Politico*, December 30, 2018. https://www.politico.com/story/2018/12/30/conservative-health-care-experiment-leads-to-thousands-losing-coverage-1076876.

Putnam, Robert. *Our Kids: The American Dream in Crisis*. New York: Simon & Schuster, 2015.

Qizilbash, Mozaffar. "Capabilities, Well-Being, and Human Development: A Survey." *The Journal of Development Studies* 33.2 (1996) 143–62.

Rahner, Karl. "The 'Commandment' of Love in Relation to the Other Commandments." In *Theological Investigations*, translated by Karl H. Kruger, 5:439–59. London: Darton, Longman & Todd, 1966.

———. "The Dignity and Freedom of Man." In *Theological Investigations*, translated by Karl H. Kruger, 2:253–63. London: Darton, Longman & Todd, 1963.

———. *Foundations of Christian Faith: An Introduction to the Idea of Christianity*. Translated by William V. Dych. New York: Seabury, 1978.

———. "On the Origins of Freedom." In *Karl Rahner: Theologian of the Graced Search for Meaning*, edited by Geoffrey B. Kelly, 117–27. Minneapolis: Augsburg Fortress, 1992.

———. "Reflections on the Unity of Love of Neighbor and the Love of God." In *Theological Investigations*, translated by Boniface Kruger and Karl H. Kruger, 6:231–49. London: Darton, Longman, and Todd, 1969.

———. "The Theological Concept of Concupiscentia." In *Theological Investigations*, translated by Cornelius Ernst, 1:347–82. Baltimore: Helicon, 1966.

———. "Theology and Anthropology." In *Theological Investigations*, translated by Karl H. Kruger, 5:28–45. Baltimore: Helicon, 1966.

———. "Theology of Freedom." In *Theological Investigations*, translated by Karl H. Kruger and Boniface Kruger, 6:178–96. New York: Crossroads, 1982.
———. "The Theology of Power." In *Theological Investigations*, translated by Kevin Smyth, 4:391–409. Baltimore: Helicon, 1966.
Rahner, Karl, et al., eds. "Freedom." In *Sacramentum Mundi: An Encyclopedia of Theology*, 2:361–62. New York: Herder & Herder, 1968.
———. "Person." In *Sacramentum Mundi: An Encyclopedia of Theology*, 4:415–19. New York: Herder & Herder, 1968.
Rand, Ayn. *Atlas Shrugged*. New York: Penguin, 1992.
Rawls, John. *Political Liberalism*. New York: Columbia University Press, 1993.
———. *A Theory of Justice*. Cambridge: Harvard University Press, 1971.
Rodgers, Daniel. *Age of Fracture*. Cambridge: Harvard University Press, 2014.
Rosen, Michael. *Dignity: Its History and Meaning*. Cambridge: Harvard University Press, 2012.
Rothbard, Murray N. *For a New Liberty: The Libertarian Manifesto*. New York: Collier, 1978.
Rutenberg, Jim. "Paul Ryan: 'I Call This Getting Wienermobiled.'" *The New York Times Magazine*, September 12, 2014. https://www.nytimes.com/2014/09/14/magazine/paul-ryan-wienermobiled.html.
Sandel, Michael. *Liberalism and the Limits of Justice*. Cambridge: Cambridge University Press, 1982.
Schwartz, Stuart B. "An Attempt at Universal Definition, Review of *Slavery and Social Death: A Comparative Study* by Orlando Patterson." *Contemporary Sociology: A Journal of Reviews* 15.3 (1986) 358.
Second Vatican Council. *Dignitatis humanae*. https://www.vatican.va/archive/hist_councils/ii_vatican_council/documents/vat-ii_decl_19651207_dignitatis-humanae_en.html.
Sen, Amartya. *Commodities and Capabilities*. Oxford: Oxford University Press, 1987.
———. *Development as Freedom*. New York: Knopf, 1999.
———. "Equality of What?" In *The Tanner Lectures on Human Values, 1980*, edited by Sterling M. McMurrin, 197–220. Salt Lake City: University of Utah Press, 1980.
———. "Freedom of Choice: Concept and Content." *European Economic Review* 32 (1988) 269–94.
———. "Human Rights and Asian Values." *The New Republic*, July 14, 1997, 33–40.
———. *The Idea of Justice*. Cambridge: Harvard University Press, 2009.
———. "Individual Freedom as a Social Commitment." *The New York Review of Books*, June 14, 1990. https://www.nybooks.com/articles/1990/06/14/individual-freedom-as-a-social-commitment/.
———. *Inequality Reexamined*. Cambridge: Harvard University Press, 1992.
———. "Justice: Means versus Freedoms." *Philosophy and Public Affairs* 19.2 (1990) 111–21.
———. "Liberty and Social Choice." *The Journal of Philosophy* 80.1 (1983) 207–21.
———. "Liberty as Control: An Appraisal." In *Midwest Studies in Philosophy*, edited by Peter A. French et al., 7:207–21. Minneapolis: University of Minnesota Press, 1982.
———. "The Moral Standing of the Market." *Social Philosophy and Policy* 2.2 (1985) 1–9.
———. *Poverty and Famines: An Essay on Entitlement and Deprivation*. Oxford: Clarendon, 1981.
———. "Rights and Agency." *Philosophy and Public Affairs* 2.1 (1981) 3–39.

———. "Well-Being, Agency, and Freedom: The Dewey Lectures 1984." *Journal of Philosophy* 82.4 (1985) 185–90.
Sen, Amartya, et al. "Liberty as Control: An Appraisal." In *Midwest Studies in Philosophy, Vol. VII: Social and Political Philosophy*, 207–22. Minneapolis: University of Minnesota Press, 1982.
Sirico, Robert. *Defending the Free Market: The Moral Case for a Free Economy.* Washington, DC: Regnery, 2012.
Slade, Stephanie. "A Libertarian Case for the Common Good." *America: The Jesuit Review*, August 6, 2018. https://www.americamagazine.org/politics-society/2018/08/06/libertarian-case-common-good.
Somin, Ilya. "Is Libertarian Skepticism about Democracy a Major Cause of Our Current Ills—or Part of the Cure?" *The Washington Post*, November 5, 2017. https://www.washingtonpost.com/news/volokh-conspiracy/wp/2017/11/05/will-wilkinson-on-libertarian-democracy-skepticism/.
Stewart, Matthew. "The 9.9 Percent Is the New American Aristocracy." *The Atlantic*, June 2018. https://www.theatlantic.com/magazine/archive/2018/06/the-birth-of-a-new-american-aristocracy/559130/.
Stoker, Elizabeth. "An Adviser to Pope Francis Says Catholicism Is Incompatible with Libertarianism. He's Right." *The Week*, June 12, 2014. https://theweek.com/articles/446214/adviser-pope-francis-says-catholicism-incompatible-libertarianism-hes-right.
Taylor, Charles. "The Nature and Scope of Distributive Justice." In *Philosophy and the Human Sciences: Philosophical Papers 2*, 289–317. Cambridge: Cambridge University Press, 1985.
———. *A Secular Age.* Cambridge: Harvard University Press, 2007.
Tilly, Charles. *Durable Inequality.* Berkeley: University of California Press, 1998.
Tomasky, Michael. "Do Republicans Even Believe in Democracy Anymore?" *The New York Times*, July 1, 2019. https://www.nytimes.com/2019/07/01/opinion/republicans-trump-democracy.html.
van der Vossen, Bas. "Libertarianism." In *The Stanford Encyclopedia of Philosophy*, edited by Edward N. Zalta. https://plato.stanford.edu/archives/spr2019/entries/libertarianism/.
Vermeule, Adrian. "Beyond Originalism." *The Atlantic*, March 31, 2020. https://www.theatlantic.com/ideas/archive/2020/03/common-good-constitutionalism/609037/.
Weigel, George. "Two Ideas of Freedom: The Inaugural William E. Simon Lecture." Ethics and Public Policy Center, December 5, 2001. https://eppc.org/publications/two-ideas-of-freedom/.
Weithman, Paul. "Piketty and the Pope: A Dialogue Begun." *Theological Studies* 76.3 (2015) 572–95.
Wilkinson, Will. "How Libertarian Democracy Skepticism Infected the American Right." *Defending the Open Society* (blog), November 3, 2017. https://niskanencenter.org/blog/libertarian-democracy-skepticism-infected-american-right/.
Williams, Bernard A. O. "The Idea of Equality." In *Philosophy, Politics, and Society, 2nd Series*, edited by Peter Laslett and W. G. Runciman, 110–31. Oxford: Basil Blackwell, 1972.
Williamson, Kevin. "Catholics against Capitalism." *National Review Online*, June 10, 2014. https://www.nationalreview.com/2014/06/catholics-against-capitalism-kevin-d-williamson/.

Author Index

Alexander, Michelle, 36–38, 37nn76–81, 38nn82–84, 45
Allen, Danielle, 3, 3n10
Anderson, Carol, 32, 32n61
Anderson, Elizabeth, 2, 2n4, 5n17, 8, 14, 101, 101n97, 104, 131, 141–47, 142nn49–50, 143nn51–57, 144nn58–60, 145nn61–64, 146nn65–68, 147n73, 149, 149n84, 155–56, 158
Arendt, Hannah, 27, 27n40, 28n41, 29
Aristotle, 93–94n64

Bachmeyer, T. J., 50nn12–13
Badhwar, Neera K., 23nn20–21, 25n30
Balthasar, Hans Urs von, 106, 106n3
Bannon, Steve, 12–13, 31
Beckley, Harlan, 102–3, 102nn99–100, 103n104
Bell, Daniel, 16–19, 17nn1–2, 18n3, 41, 44
Bellah, Robert N., 50n12
Brooks, Arthur C., 2, 2n3, 25n32
Brooks, Mo, 73
Browning, Don S., 105n1, 126–27, 126n92, 127nn93–95
Buckley, Michael, 109n14, 114, 114n36, 116, 116n43

Calvin, John, 102
Carr, Anne E., 108n11
Case, Anne, 31–33, 32nn57–61, 45, 79, 79n23

Christiansen, Drew, 8n29
Clark, Meghan J., 7
Coates, Ta-Nehisi, 47n2, 48–49
Cohen, Patricia, 73n2
Coleman, John, 50, 50n14, 50nn12–13
Copeland, Shawn, 8, 14, 69–72, 69n71, 71nn72–74, 72n75, 104, 131, 133–141, 133nn9–13, 134nn14–19, 135nn20–22, 136nn23–25, 137nn26–31, 138nn35–38, 139nn39–43, 140nn45–48, 149, 155–56
Crocker, David, 81n28, 90n54, 100n91
Cunningham, Paige Winfield., 73n1
Cupich, Blasé, 22, 22n17

Daniels, Norman, 86–87, 86n42, 87n45
Deaton, Agnus, 31–33, 32nn57–61, 45, 79, 79n23
DeCosse, David E., 76n12
Deneen, Patrick, J., 4, 4nn14–16, 5nn18–19
Douglass, Frederick, 62
Dun, Frank van, 9nn34–35
Dworkin, Gerald, 9n36
Dych, William V., 108n11, 113n33

Eggemeier, Matthew T., 7
Everett, William, 50, 50n12

Farley, Margaret, 40–41, 40n93, 41n94, 137–38, 137n33, 138n34
Feder, J. Lester, 31nn54–55

Author Index

Finn, Daniel, 21n14, 33, 33nn63–64, 34nn65–66, 45
Ford, Lewis S., 108n10
Francis, Pope, 146–47, 146n69, 146n72
Franklin, Christopher, 8n33
Friedman, Milton, 21n14
Fritz, Peter Joseph, 7, 8

Gallagher, Kevin, 30–31, 30n49, 30nn51–53
Galt, John, 23n19
George, Robert P., 25n32, 26, 26nn34–35
Gibson, David, 146n71
Glasser, Susan B., 32n61
Glenn, Evelyn Nakano, 12–14, 50–55, 51nn15–17, 52nn18–21, 53nn22–27, 54nn28–31, 68, 105, 131–32, 131n6, 158
Graham, Elaine, 10, 10nn40–41, 158nn1–2, 159, 159n7, 159nn3–5, 160n8
Gutierrez, Gustavo, 69n71

Hare, R. M., 76n9
Hart, H.L.A., 84n36
Hazony, Yoram, 31, 31n54
Hennenberger, Melinda, 22n17
Himes, Kenneth R., 9n38, 11n44
Himes, Michael J., 9n38, 11n44
Hinze, Christine Firer, 7
Hinze, Firer, 38–41, 39nn85–89, 40nn90–92, 45
Hobgood, Mary, 69n71
Hollenbach, David, 8, 14, 14n47, 104, 131, 141, 147–58, 148nn74–79, 149n83, 149nn80–81, 150nn85–87, 151n88, 151nn90–94, 152nn95–100, 153nn101–2, 154nn103–4, 156n107, 157nn108–9
Hurd, Robert L., 114n34, 115, 115nn38–39, 116n42
Hutchinson, Asa, 100
Hutter, Reinhard, 10n42, 108, 108n12

Janus, Mark, 129
Jefferson, Thomas, 67

John Paul II, Pope, 8n30, 10, 29, 29n48, 108
Junker-Kenny, Maureen, 13, 13n46, 105–8, 105n2, 106n5, 107nn6–8, 108n13, 109n15, 131n8

Kant, Immanuel, 143, 149
Kasper, Walter, 8, 106, 106n3, 109n16, 117, 117n51, 120, 120n61, 125, 125n86, 126, 126nn89–90

Lambert, Craig, 55nn32–33, 59n41
Leo XXX, Pope, 8
Long, Heather, 3n11
Long, Roderick T., 23nn20–21
Lovin, Robin, 105, 105n1

Malthus, Thomas, 101
Maritain, Jacques, 28, 28nn43–45
Marmion, Declan, 11n43, 106n4
Marx, Reinhard, 8, 8n32
McGreevy, John, 16–17, 45–46, 45nn102–103, 46nn105–6
Metcalf, Stephen, 35n72
Metz, Johann Baptist, 106, 106n3
Miller, Vincent, 33n63
Monbiot, George, 3, 3n12
Morrison, Toni, 48–49, 48nn4–7
Murray, John Courtney, 5, 5n20

Neuhaus, John Richard, 30n50
Noonan, John T. Jr., 69n71
Novak, Michael, 11, 20, 25–30, 25n32, 26n33, 26n35, 27nn36–39, 28nn42–45, 29n46
Nozick, Robert, 87n46
Nussbaum, Martha, 94n64, 94n73

O'Connor, Timothy, 8n33

Patterson, Orlando, 8, 12–14, 50, 55–72, 56n34, 57nn35–36, 58nn37–39, 59nn41–43, 60nn44–45, 61n47, 62nn49–53, 63nn54–57, 64nn58–61, 65n62, 66nn63–68, 67nn69–70, 72n76, 103n105, 105, 132,

138, 139–40, 139n44, 155, 155nn105–6, 158
Piketty, Thomas, 2, 2n6, 3n7, 35–36, 35nn67–71, 36nn73–75, 45
Pradhan, Rachana, 100n96
Putnam, Robert, 2, 2nn1–2, 18, 18n4, 19nn5–6

Qizilbash, Mozaffar, 95n73, 97n81

Rahner, Karl, 1, 9–13, 9n37, 11n43, 47n3, 49–50, 54, 69, 93, 103–28, 107n9, 108nn10–11, 109n14, 110nn17–20, 111nn21–25, 112nn26–27, 113nn28–32, 114n35, 114n37, 115nn40–41, 116nn44–47, 117nn48–50, 118nn52–54, 119nn55–58, 120nn59–60, 121nn62–65, 122nn66–72, 123nn73–78, 124nn79–82, 125nn83–85, 125nn87–88, 127nn96–98, 131–32, 134, 155–56
Rand, Ayn, 11, 20, 23–25, 24n22, 24nn25–29, 25n31, 31
Rawls, John, 83–87, 83n33, 84nn34–36, 86nn43–44, 87n45
Rodgers, Daniel, 5, 5n21, 6n21, 6nn22–25, 7nn26–27, 16, 19, 31–32, 33n62, 44, 49, 49nn8–11, 74, 74n3, 75, 75n4, 78, 81, 93, 104, 130–31, 130nn3–4, 137–41, 137n32, 146n70, 154–55
Rodriguez Maradiaga, Oscar, 22n17
Rosen, Michael, 8n28
Rothbard, Murray, 20–22, 21n15, 21nn10–13
Rutenberg, Jim, 24n24
Ryan, Paul, 24, 24n24

Sandel, Michael, 149, 149n82
Schwartz, Stuart B., 59n40
Sen, Amartya, 8, 11, 11n45, 13–14, 74–93, 75nn5–6, 76nn7–12, 77nn13–16, 78n17, 79nn20–22, 80nn24–25, 81nn26–28, 82nn29–31, 83nn32–33, 84n36, 85nn37–40, 86n41, 87n47, 88nn48–51, 89nn52–53, 90nn54–58, 91nn59–63, 93–94n64, 94nn65–68, 95nn69–74, 96nn75–76, 97nn77–80, 97nn82–83, 98nn84–85, 99nn86–89, 100n90, 100nn92–95, 101n98, 103n105, 103nn101–3, 105, 130n5, 131, 146, 149, 158
Slade, Stephanie, 21–25, 22n16, 23n18
Somin, Ilya, 20n8
Stewart, Matthew, 2, 2n5, 3nn8–9
Stoker, Elizabeth, 22n17

Taylor, Charles, 10n39, 12, 16, 41–45, 41n95, 42nn96–98, 43nn99–101, 159–60, 159n6, 160n8
Thomas of Aquinas, 30
Thrush, Glenn, 32n61
Tilly, Charles, 3, 4, 4n13
Tomasky, Michael, 151n89
Trump, Donald, 30

van der Vossen, Bas, 20n7
Vermeule, Adrian, 150n87

Weigel, George, 25n32
Weithman, Paul, 146n72
Wilkinson, Will, 20, 20nn8–9, 126n91
Williams, Bernard, 126–27
Williamson, Kevin, 22n17

Young, Iris Marion, 38

Subject Index

Abood v. Detroit Board of Education (1977), 129, 129n1
abortion, 23, 31, 46
absolute nearness, 125–26, 125n83, 125n88
African American population
    hierarchy of race, 48
    incarceration rate, 36–37
    mortality rates, 32, 79
    public theology and, 45–46
    race from 1870–1930 in U. S., 51–55
    slavery (*See* slavery)
    See also Copeland, Shawn
Age of Fracture, as a concept, 13, 31, 49, 106–9, 154–55
Age of Fracture (Rodgers), 5–7, 32–33, 74, 104–5, 130, 137
agency freedom, 97–99
Alexander, Michelle, 36–38, 45
Allen, Danielle, 3
America (newsweekly), 21
American inequality, 2
Anderson, Carol, 32
Anderson, Elizabeth
    mentioned, 8, 104, 158
    neoliberal ideology, 5n17
    reductionist definitions of freedom, 155–56
    relationships, 2, 14, 131, 149
    responsible agency, 149–50
    social conditions, 141–47
    welfare reform, 101
    work requirements, 101
Arendt, Hannah, 27–28
Aristotle, 93–94n64
Asian cultures, 103n105
atomism
    atomist freedom, 16
    libertarianism and, 20–21
    term usage, 41–44
autonomy, term usage, 9

Bannon, Steve, 12, 31
base, term usage, 77–78n16
Beckley, Harlan, 102–3
Bell, Daniel
    The Coming of Post-Industrial Society, 17
    human capital, value of, 35
    market-based freedom, 44
    problematics of freedom, 17–19, 41
    Rodgers analysis and, 16, 17
biblical values, 139
bodily freedom, 119, 121, 147–150
Brooks, Arthur C., 2
Brooks, Mo, 73
Browning, Don S., 105n1, 126–28
Buckley, Michael, 109n14, 114, 116

Calhoun, John C., 47
Calvin, John, 102
capability, 99–101
Capital in the Twenty-First Century (Piketty), 35
care workers, inequality and, 38–41

Subject Index

caritas, virtue of, 27
Case, Anne, 31–32, 45, 79
categorical freedom, 111–12n25
Catholic public theology
    Anderson's social conditions, 141–47
    embodiment and, 133–37
    future focus for, 159–60
    history and, 137–41
    overview, 129–33, 154–57
    Patterson's sociology of freedom and, 67–72
    preferential option for the poor, 14
    problematics of freedom, 16–17
Catholicism
    cultural capitalists, 25–29
    freedom, concept of, 8–10, 30–34, 45
    "fusionists," 30
    integralism and, 150–51
    liberal freedom reimagined, 150–54
    libertarianism, 20–25
    natural law and, 25
    Rand, Ayn, 23–25
    Second Vatican Council, 8, 150–51
    social teaching, 22–25
Catholicism and American Freedom (McGreevy), 45
Centesimus Annus (John Paul II), 29
change, indeterminacy of, 18
Christian realism, 105
Christological dimension, of created freedom, 124–26
citizenship, 51–55
Clark, Meghan, J., 7
Coates, Ta-Nehisi, 47–49
Coleman, John, 55–72
collectivist totalitarian state, 24
The Coming of Post-Industrial Society (Bell), 17
concupiscence, 122–23n72
consequentialism, 81
constitutive polarity, 13, 106, 131, 131n8, 134, 141, 147
Consumer Freedom Amendment (proposed 2017), 2, 73–74
contribution principle, 43–44

Copeland, Shawn
    Enfleshing Freedom, 70, 70n71
    enslaved African American women, 14
    on freedom, 156
    mentioned, 8, 104
    poor women of color, 70–72, 132–41
    reductionism of the Age of Fracture, 155
    responsible agency, 149–50
created freedom concept
    Catholic theology and, 10–11
    Christological dimension, 124–26
    human person as autonomous, 112–13
    material world concerns, 118–124
    overview, 112–13, 126–28
    term usage, 1
    transcendental aspect of, 113–17
creation, doctrine of, 108
cultural capitalists, 25–29, 68
culture
    meaning of, 59n41
    values and, 67–72
Cupich, Blasé, 22

Daniels, Norman, 86–87
"deaths by despair," 32, 34, 79
Deaton, Angus, 31–32, 45, 79
Declaration of Independence, U. S., 67
democratic egalitarians, 144–45
democratic politics, 143–44
demonized difference, 133
Deneen, Patrick J., 4–5
desires, 83
dialogic universalism, 153–54, 158
dignity of persons, 22–23, 62–64, 121, 143, 152
disembedded markets, 33–34
distributive theories of equality, 78
diversity, equality and, 77, 80, 85
Divine Mystery, 117
Douglass, Frederick, 62

economic inequality, 35–36
economic "zeroes," 24, 25
effective freedom, 89n53, 90–93

Eggemeier. Matthew T., 7
elementary form of freedom, 62–63
enfleshed freedom, 14
Enfleshing Freedom (Copeland), 70, 70n71
equal opportunity, 17–19, 102–3
equality
    commodities approach to, 79n18
    distributive theories of, 78
    of fortune, 144
    income as basis of, 79–81
    libertarian, 87–89
    normative conception of equality, 75n6, 76
    of primary goods, 81–83
    utilitarian equality criticism, 81–83
    of what, 75–78
equitable index of primary goods, 85n38
"Erroneous Autonomy: The Catholic Case Against Libertarianism" 2014 conference, 22
Everett, William, 50

fair value, 87n45
Farley, Margaret, 40–41, 137–38
feminist and feminism, 137, 142
Finn, Daniel, 33, 45
focal variable, term usage, 77–78n16
Francis, Pope, 146–47
freedom
    abstract concept of, 1, 45, 55
    agency, 97–99
    atomist, 16
    as bodily freedom, 119, 121, 147–150
    categorical, 111–12n25
    chord of, 57, 64–67, 69
    civic, 57, 66, 69–70
    community of, 147–49
    concept of, 8–10, 30–34, 45
    culture and history, 110
    effective, 89n53, 91–93
    elementary form, 62–63
    as fact and task, 110–12
    framework of, 93–101
    fundamental option, 111–12n25
    market-based, 44
    negative, 90–91, 144–47
    neoliberal, term usage, 34, 158
    overview, 102–3
    personal, 57, 66–67, 69
    plural idea of, 75
    political, 90–91, 104n105, 141
    populist turn, 30–34
    positive, 71, 88, 90, 100, 102, 139, 144–47
    realization-based theory, 75
    from slavery (*See* slavery)
    social conditions of, 141–47
    sovereignal, 57, 67, 70
    term usage, 1–2, 8–9
    thin, 48
    well-being, 91–97
freedom, problematic of
    equal opportunity, 17–19
    human capital, 17–19
    neoliberalism and, 19–34, 41–44
    overview, 16–17
Fritz, Peter Joseph, 7, 8
functionings, or person's being, 94–99, 94n73, 102, 146
fundamental option, 111–12n25
fusionists, 30

Gallagher, Kevin, 30–31
gender, inequality and
    in ancient Greece, 66, 139
    Copeland on, 70–71, 132–141
    Glenn on, 51–55
    Hinze on, 38–41
    Patterson on, 66
genuine freedom, concept of, 10
George, Robert, 26
Glass Ceilings and Dirt Floors (Hinze), 7
Glenn, Evelyn Nakano
    focus of her work, 12–14, 132–33
    freedom-as-independence, 131
    on gender inequality, 51–55
    mentioned, 158
    on slavery, 51–55, 105
    Unequal Freedom, 50
globalization, 19, 30, 33
Gnosticism, 135
governments, libertarianism's view of, 21–22

Graham, Elaine, 10, 159
"Great Reversal" (Anderson), 5n17
Greece, women's enslavement, 66, 139

Hans Urs von Balthasar, 106
Hare, R. M., 76
Hart, H.L.A., 84n36
Hazony, Yoram, 31
health care, 100–101
Hinze, Christine Firer, 7, 38–41, 45
Hollenbach, David, 8, 14, 104, 131, 147–54, 155–57
hourly earnings, educational level and, 19
human capital, 17–19
The Human Condition (Arendt), 27
human dignity, 22, 62–64, 121
human diversity, equality and, 77, 80, 85
human point of view, 126
Hurd, Robert L., 114
Hutchinson, Asa, 100
Hutter, Reinhard, 10, 108

"The Idea of Equality" (Williams), 126
incarceration rate, 36–37
income
    as basis of equality, 78–81
    inequality, 2–3
    term usage, 79n18
indeterminacy of change, 18
inequality
    economic, 35–36
    meritocratic income, 3, 36
    opportunity, 2
    perspectives on, 2–4
    political, 3
injustice, 62, 95n74
insurance premiums, 73–74
integralism, 150–51
interdependence, 88–89, 92–93
intrinsic values, 22–23

Janus, Mark, 129–130, 132
Janus case (*Janus v. AFSCME* (2018)), 130–31, 154–55
Jefferson, Thomas, 67
John Paul II, Pope

Centesimus Annus, 29
Veritatis Splendor, 10, 108
Junker-Kenny, Maureen, 13, 105, 106–7, 131n8
justice
    equality and, 75–77, 76n12, 83n33, 84n35
    libertarian, 87–89

Kant, Immanuel, 143, 149
Kasper, Walter, 8, 106, 117, 120, 125–26

labor, 51–55
labor unions, 129–30
Leo XIII, Pope, 8
liberal freedom, 109–12
liberal freedom reimagined, 150–54
liberalism, 4–5
"Libertarian Democracy Skepticism" (Wilkinson), 20n8
libertarian equality, 87–89
libertarianism, 20–25, 43–44
liberty
    as control, 89–93
    negative, 86, 87–89
    priority of, 83n33, 84–87, 84n36
    term usage, 9, 42–43
Lovin, Robin, 105

Malthus, Thomas, 101
marginal productivity theory, 35
Maritain, Jacques, 28
market-based freedom, 44
Marmion, Declan, 11n43
Marx, Reinhard, 8
Marxism, 28, 29
material mediation, 118, 120
McGreevy, John, 16–17, 45–46
mediation, 118, 120
Medicaid, 100, 101
meritocracy, 17
meritocratic income inequality, 3, 36
Metz, Johann Baptist, 106
Miller, Vincent, 33n63
Monbiot, George, 3
Morrison, Toni, 48–49
mortality rates, race and, 32, 79

multilateral interdependences, 88
Murray, John Courtney, 5

natal alienation, 60
natal injustice, 62
natural law, Catholic social teaching, 25
naturalistic movement, 105n1
nearness, absolute, 125–26, 125n83, 125n88
negative freedom, 90–91, 144–47
negative liberty, 86, 87–89
neoliberalism, 19–34, 41–44
The New Jim Crow (Alexander), 36
normative conception of equality, 75n6, 76
normatively human, 105
Novak, Michael, 11, 20, 25–30
Nozick, Robert, 87n46
Nussbaum, Martha, 94n64, 95n73

opportunity
    gap, 18–19
    term usage, 103n102
    types, 78
oppression, 144–45
original sin, 24, 119n56
Our Kids: The American Dream in Crisis (Putnam), 18–19
outcome types, 78

pandemic
    inequalities and, 3
    liberty and, 91–92
    sovereignal freedom and, 70
Paschal Mystery, 123
patent injustice, 95n74
Patterson, Orlando
    on culture, 59n41
    focus of his work, 132, 138
    on freedom, 103n105, 155
    mentioned, 8, 50, 158
    on slavery, 12–14, 55–72, 105
    sovereignal freedom, 67
    women in Greece, 139
personal responsibility, 24, 26, 144, 156
personhood, 28–29, 116, 118, 123–24, 133–37
physical condition neglect, 82

Piketty, Thomas, 2–3, 35, 45
Political Liberalism (Rawls), 86n44
poor, preferential option for the, 14
poor women of color, 70–72, 132–41
post-secular, term usage, 159
preferential option for the poor, 14
primary goods, equality of, 81–83
procedural priority, of negative income, 90–91
producers, of goods and services, 23–25
property rights, 20n8, 21–22
public theology
    African American history and, 45–46
    term usage, 9, 14–15
    See also Catholic public theology
Putnam, Robert
    "our kids," 2
    Our Kids: The American Dream in Crisis (Putnam), 18–19

race
    from 1870–1930 in U. S., 51–55
    hierarchy of, 48
    incarceration rate, 36–37
    mortality rates, 32, 79
Rahner, Karl
    on Age of Fracture concept, 106–9
    created freedom, concept of, 10–13
    on createdness, 108–9, 108n10
    on freedom, 109–12, 155–57, 158
    freedom, in abstract terms, 47
    fundamental option, 111–12
    grace of God and freedom, 9, 108–9, 108n11
    liberal freedom, 109–12
    mentioned, 50, 93
    Original sin, 24, 119n56
    overview, 104–6
    public theology and, 9
    real freedom of choice, 110
    "Theological Concept of Concupiscentia," 122–23n72
    "Theology of Freedom," 113, 113n28, 118
    "Theology of Power," 120n60
    transcendent and the historical, 11n43

Rand, Ayn, 11, 23–25, 31
Rawls, John
  Political Liberalism, 86n44
  primary goods, 83–87
  A Theory of Justice, 83n33, 86
real freedom of choice, 110
real income theory, 80
realization-based theory of freedom, 75
religious institutional affiliation, 159
"Robinson Crusoe" vision of the economy, 142
Rodgers, Daniel
  Age of Fracture, 5–7, 32–33, 74, 104–5, 130, 137
  Bell on, 16, 17
  mentioned, 31, 44, 75, 78, 81, 93, 154
Rothbard, Murray, 20–21
Ryan, Paul, 24, 24n24

Sandel, Michael, 149
Second Vatican Council, 8, 150–51
secularism, 9–10, 159
self-transcendence, 38
Sen, Amartya
  created freedom and, 73–74
  distributive theories of equality, 78
  effective freedom, 90–93
  equality of what, 75–78
  income as basis of equality, 78–81
  libertarian equality, 87–89, 146
  libertarian freedom, 130
  liberty, as control, 89–93
  mentioned, 8, 11, 13, 14, 105, 149, 158
  negative freedom, 90–91
  normative conception of equality, 75n6, 76
  procedural priority, 90–91
  Rawlsian equality of primary goods, 83–87
  utilitarian equality criticism, 81–83
  "Well-Being, Agency, and Freedom," 82
Send Lazarus (Eggemeier & Fritz), 7
Slade, Stephanie, 21–22, 23
slavery
  abstract definition of freedom, 55

crucial inferences, 57–58
dignity of persons, 62–64
emergence of freedom, 64–65-n61
equality and, 65–67
Glenn, Evelyn Nakano, 51–55, 105
meaning of, 56–57
nature and definition of, 59–62, 61n47
overview, 47–50
Patterson, Orlando, 55–72
poor women of color and, 138
social death, 60–62
social policies, individual responsibility and, 100–101
space, term usage, 77–78n16
The Spirit of Democratic Capitalism (Novak), 25–26, 30
Stewart, Matthew, 2
suffering, liberty and, 1n61
sum-ranking, 81
supermanager, 35–36
supernatural existential, 125

Taylor, Charles, 12, 16, 41–44, 45, 159–160
technocracy, 18
"Theology of Freedom" (Rahner), 113, 113n28, 118
"The Theology of Power" (Rahner), 122–23n72
"Theology of Power" (Rahner), 120n60
A Theory of Justice (Rawls), 83n33, 86
Thomas, of Aquinas, 30
Tilly, Charles, 3–4
transcendental aspect of created freedom, 113–17
Trump, Donald, 30
truth, 152
Tubman, Harriet, 47

Unequal Freedom (Glenn), 50
United States
  Declaration of Independence, 67
  Supreme Court, on freedom issue, 130–31, 154–55
universalism, 153–54
utilitarian equality, 81–83

value, term usage, 77–78n16
values
    biblical, 139
    culture and, 67–72
    human capital and, 35
    intrinsic, 22–23
Veritatis Splendor (John Paul II), 10, 108
Virginian slavery, 66
The Vision of Catholic Social Thought (Clark), 7
voluntariness, 36–38

War on Drugs, 37

welfarism, 81
well-being, 91–97
"Well-Being, Agency, and Freedom" (Sen), 82
West, Kanye, 47–48
white Americans, outcome declines, 32
Why Liberalism Failed (Deneen), 4
Wilkinson, Will, 20
Williams, Bernard, 126, 127
women. *See* gender, inequality and
worth, term usage, 86

Young, Iris Marion, 38

www.ingramcontent.com/pod-product-compliance
Lightning Source LLC
Chambersburg PA
CBHW062046220426
43662CB00010B/1680